Praise for *West Asia After Washington*

"*West Asia After Washington* is critical to understanding why a better future for West Asia depends on Iran, a relatively small country in the region in terms of GDP or weapons reserves and why it is often misunderstood by many parties due to Western media propaganda. Iran has a very strategic geopolitical position, so the alliance between Iran and China and Russia will produce a multipolar power capable of fighting U.S. hegemony. Anderson tells the story in detail, enabling readers to see the big map of all the conflicts and that all are intertwined."

Dr. DINA SULAEMAN, Indonesian Centre for Middle East Studies, author, *Snow in Aleppo*

"A fascinating research on how the U.S. regime-change invasions and proxy wars ... [have] sparked acceleration of geopolitical changes ... building a resistance joint front and the dismantling of Israel while paving the way for ... alternative international and regional organizations."

Dr. AMAL WAHDAN, founder and editor, *Arab Gazette*

"A great analysis of how the western colonial empire led itself towards demise on west Asia, after decades of looting natural resources, instigating wars, funding terrorism, murdering millions and eventually pushing the birth of a regional resistance that pinned the last nail in the coffin of U.S. hegemony and domination in our region. The unipolar world is no more, reading Professor Tim's book explains how and why it started from west Asia."

Dr. MARWA OSMAN, academic and TV presenter, Lebanon

WEST ASIA
AFTER WASHINGTON
Dismantling the Colonized Middle East

Tim Anderson

Clarity Press, Inc.

ISBN: 978-1-949762-83-9
EBOOK ISBN: 978-1-949762-84-6

In-house editor: Diana G. Collier
Book design: Becky Luening

Library of Congress Control Number: 2023934023

Clarity Press, Inc.
2625 Piedmont Rd. NE, Ste. 56
Atlanta, GA 30324, USA
https://www.claritypress.com

Table of Contents

1. West Asian Resistance in the Changing Global Order

As Washington's multiple wars for a 'New Middle East' (NME) fail, the global order is shifting against the North American giant. Not only is China displacing the USA as the productive and economic centre of the world, new global organisations are competing with those created by the Anglo-Americans. This book argues that it is in that global context that we must understand the trajectory of the Arabic and Islamic countries of the 'Middle East,' now often called 'West Asia.'

Sustained resistance to the NME interventions forced a partial retreat by Washington. In 2019 the Trump administration withdrew part of the U.S. occupation of North Syria, while its failing war on Yemen led to a search for peace talks. Despite moves by Trump to cement Israeli dominance over the Palestinian territories, multiple reports emerged branding the Israeli regime as an apartheid state which had to be dismantled (CCHS 2022). That in turn incited conflict between the liberal Zionists and the openly fascist faction which now runs Tel Aviv. Frustrated at apparent gains by the Iran-led bloc, in January 2020 Trump murdered the top Iranian and Iraqi national heroes, Qassem Soleimani and Abu Mahdi al Muhandis, imagining he could thus decapitate the regional resistance. Instead, what emerged were widespread calls for the removal of the U.S. military presence from the entire region. Iraqi factions came together for the first time to demand the withdrawal of the U.S. occupation, while Palestinian resistance factions openly acknowledged their debt to both Soleimani and Iran. In 2021 the Biden administration carried out a chaotic and humiliating withdrawal from the 20-year occupation of Afghanistan, sending shock waves through all other U.S. collaborators in the region, from Kurdish separatists to the Israelis.

At the same time, global disillusion with U.S.-led Western institutions had been growing, leading to the creation of eastern and southern counterparts. In Latin America the ALBA, UNASUR and the CELAC filled a regional gap left by popular rejection of Washington's Free Trade Area of the Americas (FTAA) project. China joined the World Trade Organization (WTO) in 2001 but, dissatisfied with the governance of both the WTO and the IMF, went on to form the Shanghai Cooperation Organization (SCO) and to join with Russia and others in the increasingly popular BRICS group (Devonshire-Ellis 2022). The expansion of U.S. proxy wars and unilateral coercive measures ("sanctions") finally reached Russia and China. The USA, in economic decline, imagined it could act against its perceived rivals with impunity. That only added impetus to the counterweight in global restructuring and to the search for alternatives to the dollar. All this has important implications for the independent states and peoples of West Asia.

However, in Western circles, the world is more often seen in terms of American 'exceptionalism.' Much writing on international relations, and on the 'Middle East' in particular, imply that the principles of 'sovereignty' and 'non-intervention' in the UN Charter are subordinate to the need for a great hegemonic power to 'stabilise' and, they suggest, bring a necessary order to the world. That great power, either represented or led by the United States of America, cannot be subject to the same rules as others. Such ideas are reinforced by centuries of Anglo-American privilege.

This book takes a distinct approach, using as a starting point the right of peoples to self-determination and the consequent need for post-colonial states to build strong and independent social systems in the face of relentless hegemonic power. Strong independent states are necessary to build and then defend distinct policies, such as national resource control and public services. History has shown that weak independent states are easily destabilised and destroyed. The ones that survive are branded 'dictatorships' for standing up to imperial dictates. To study such resistance a counter-hegemonic approach is necessary, where the voices, experiences and alliances of independent peoples matter.

This is my third research work on the West Asian region. *The Dirty War on Syria* (Anderson 2016) set out to expose the massive proxy war against the small but resilient Syrian nation-state, the most secular and pluralist regime of the region. After that, *Axis of Resistance: Towards an Independent Middle East* (Anderson 2019) argued that the multiple wars against the people of Palestine, Lebanon, Syria, Iraq, Iran and Yemen could only be understood as a single regional war. In this volume, *West Asia After Washington: Dismantling the Colonized Middle East,* I argue that important aspects of the future of the region, in the shifting global context, can be reasonably assessed by the evidence of current trends, without much recourse to speculation.

This book takes as given—since it has been argued and well documented in the previous two—that at the turn of the century Washington launched a series of invasions and proxy wars against all the independent peoples and states of the region in the name of creating a 'New Middle East.' That offensive involved a massive propaganda onslaught and the use of large proxy terrorist armies, especially sectarian Islamist groups armed and financed by Washington and its regional allies Saudi Arabia, Qatar, Turkey and Israel Resistance to that regional war led to the formation of a loose regional bloc led by Iran, which is now forming more substantial relations with the wider counter-hegemonic blocs led by China and Russia, in particular the BRICS and the Shanghai Cooperation Organization (SCO).

Among other things, this alliance is making real what North American intelligence has long feared and termed an 'Iranian land-bridge,' extending to the Mediterranean in the west and as far as China in the east (Stratfor 2011). That link between East Asia and Europe centres on Iran, the largest independent state of the so-called 'Middle East.' From a Zionist perspective this 'land bridge' is thought to represent "the most serious long term existential threat to Israel" (Milburn 2017: 35) because it forms a united resistance front in support of the colonised Palestinian people.

The other side of this matter is that land integration from the Mediterranean to China represents a great hope for the independent peoples of the region—and especially the peoples of Palestine, Lebanon, Syria, Yemen, Iraq and Iran, who have been divided by invasions, proxy wars, occupations and economic siege for decades. The road, rail, energy, and communications links which other nations pursue have been denied to the peoples of West Asia under a relentless U.S.-led strategy of 'divide and rule.' Agencies such as NATO, the

European Union, the IMF-World Bank and the SWIFT system have been used against them. That helps explain why there is such enthusiasm in West Asia about the global restructuring represented by the BRICS and the SCO.

Naturally, there are substantial differences and asymmetries in ideology and history among the West Asian peoples and states. Iran represents the most religious of all the independent nations and Syria the least, but that has not prevented high levels of cooperation. Similarly, the Syrian and Iranian states resisted the Western onslaught while the Iraqi and Afghan states were smashed, the democracy movement in Bahrain was crushed, the Lebanese state remains crippled from birth and a unique revolution emerged in Yemen. It is certainly the case that successful resistance generates longer term political will, while historical defeats crush it. Nevertheless, all these nations share some common history, culture and principles of co-existence, cooperation and autonomous development.

The political economic developments and regional alliances of West Asia, as elsewhere, have everything to do with unique histories and little to do with outside idealism. That simple fact is missed by many western polemics, which childishly speak of "good guys versus bad guys" and confuse support for independence and self-determination with adulation of a particular resistant culture. This writer has had to clarify and highlight, for example, support for the leading role of Iran in West Asia in strategic terms (see box below, "Why Support Iran?"). In other words, one need not be a Muslim nor a fan of religious states to appreciate the important counterweight role played by Revolutionary Iran.

Resistance matters, and West Asian resistance has been regionalising and globalising in response to the hegemonic interventions. I maintain that the particular histories of this resistance are important and should be considered alongside the changing global order. With that logic this book is divided into two parts, a first which charts developments in the political history of the regional conflict and a second which looks into the future.

Why Support Iran?

This person is a strategic supporter of the Islamic Republic of Iran because:

- The Iranian revolution kicked out a foreign power which had crippled the country and prevented independent development;
- The leadership of this revolution was and remains Islamic;
- Iran has invested in its people, making massive advances in the health and education of girls and boys (UNDP);
- Iran directly supports the resistance of the independent peoples of the region—Palestine, Syria, Iraq, Yemen and Lebanon—for the most part without sectarian consideration;
- Iran leads a West Asian Alliance with the best chance of liberating the region from U.S.-Israeli-Saudi terrorism and zionism.

In Part One: The Legacy of Failed Ambition, "Wars of Hegemonic Decline" links U.S. economic decline with the greater breadth of its warfare (especially proxy and economic warfare) in the world, noting some revised imperial doctrines of intervention. In view of the frequent Western recourse to 'human rights' pretexts for intervention, "The Roots of Western Fascism" traces the history of the worst abusive regimes from European colonialism through fascism and the fascist collaboration of the 20th century to the multiple wars of the 21st century. "Zionist Cancel Culture" examines the global campaign of accusing as 'racist' all critics of the Israeli colony; this is an extraordinary inversion as deepest racism springs precisely from colonialism. "The Kurdish Card" in Syria charts the use of Kurdish separatism as an additional tool of intervention and fragmentation, using false claims of self-determination which parallel those of the Israeli colonists. Kurds are one of a number of minorities in NE Syria, with the separatist faction directed by Turkish Kurds. The chapter "Purging Christians from the 'New Middle East'" deals with a phenomenon often mentioned but poorly understood. It explains how the Western interventions have displaced the ancient Christian communities of the Arab and Muslim world. Inside Syrian Idlib offers a glimpse of the partial liberation of that NW Syrian province from NATO sponsored, al Qaeda affiliated armed groups—a process prolonged by NATO's threats of escalation. Finally "The Betrayal of Yemen" charts the one real revolution to emerge from the so-called Arab Spring, but one which has been betrayed by most of the international community. Whereas the economic siege on Syria, Lebanon, Iraq and Iran employ unilateral coercive measures, in breach of international law, the sanctions on the revolutionary government and the majority of the people of Yemen have been fully endorsed by the UN Security Council.

Part Two: Recreating the Future begins with a brief overview of "Washington's Strategic Retreat" from the West Asian region, followed by a chapter on the legacy of the murdered Iranian Commander Qassem Soleimani, since Soleimani's Ghost still haunts the foreign occupation. Based on evidence and trajectories, the chapter "Dismantling Apartheid Israel" considers the logic driving the demise of the Israeli colony, suggesting that its dissolution will come sooner than expected but with participation from disaffected liberal Zionists. Yet even equal rights for Palestinians in their own land will not automatically resolve the questions of war crimes, land theft and refugees. "Syria, Siege and Recovery" explains the vicious economic blockade on Syria which has spread to much of the region, and the prospects of recovery in the short and medium term. "An Iranian Landbridge to China" studies what is on the one hand the great fear of the colonists and imperialists, yet on the other the great promise for the peoples of the region: an extensive reintegration of the region into the eastern and southern world. "Iran's Resistance Economy and Regional Integration" studies Iran's efforts to make a virtue of the economic blockade it faces, using U.S. siege measures to strengthen domestic industry, while linking that 'resistance economy' to growth of a counter hegemonic regional bloc. "The Challenge of Multipolarity" takes a step back to review the concept of 'multipolarity,' increasingly seen as a counter to Washington's dream of maintaining a unipolar order. *West Asia After Washington* brings together the key threads of the book, together with some thoughts on the long standing idea of a Levantine Federation.

References

Anderson, Tim. *The Dirty War on Syria.* Montreal: Global Research, 2016.

———. *Axis of Resistance: Towards a New Middle East.* Atlanta: Clarity Press, 2019.

CCHS. "SIX (6) important reports on Israeli Apartheid." Center for Counter Hegemonic Studies. February 24, 2022. https://counter-hegemonic-studies.site/israeli-apartheid-6/

Devonshire-Ellis, Chris. "The New Candidate Countries for BRICS Expansion." Silk Road Briefing. November 9, 2022. https://www.silkroadbriefing.com/news/2022/11/09/the-new-candidate-countries-for-brics-expansion/

Milburn, Franc. "Iran´s Land Bridge to the Mediterranean: Possible Routes and Ensuing Challenges." *Strategic Assessment* 20, no. 3 (October 2017). INSS. https://www.inss.org.il/publication/irans-land-bridge-mediterranean-possible-routes-ensuing-challenges/

Stratfor. "The Geopolitics of Iran: Holding the Center of a Mountain Fortress." *WorldView.* RANE. December 16, 2011. https://worldview.stratfor.com/article/geopolitics-iran-holding-center-mountain-fortress

2. Learning from the Enemy: Method Failures in Western War Analysis

"There is no greater danger than underestimating your enemy."
—Lao Tzu

Even Wikipedia "recognises that Wikipedia is not a reliable source." Students must read widely.

Washington's role in at least eight Middle East wars of the 21st century (against the peoples of Palestine, Afghanistan, Iraq, Lebanon, Libya, Syria, Iran and Yemen) has been hotly debated between two broad camps: those (including this writer) who regard them all as illegal wars of aggression, and those who either imagine they are not connected or defend them as the necessary policing measures of a global hegemon.

However, this debate is plagued by poor method, and in particular by a strategic bias which adopts obligatory 'loyalty' elements, failing to study what are seen as 'enemy' facts and perspectives. That cripples even the most articulate and apparently critical discussions.

Yet failing to read and understand one's enemy is dangerous, as Lao Tzu said many centuries ago, leading to the creation of an ignorant 'yes man' culture of self-deception. The refusal to read and learn from a substantial enemy is simply childish or ignorant cynicism.

Let me illustrate this problem with a few articles from the 'New Middle East' wars, a piece on Yemen by Bruce Riedel (Brookings, 2017), an article on Iran by Hassan Hassan (Politico, 2020) and a discussion on terrorism by Paul Pillar (Responsible Statecraft, 2021). These are far from the worst of western war analyses, but all share similar problems in method.

The obligatory but misleading element: Strategic loyalty

Many years into these various wars, in order to 'qualify' as publishable war discussion, contributors to Western journals purvey some initial expression of loyalty to the overall Western project, if not to all its tactics. In the most obvious version of this phenomenon, the analyst directly identifies with a state party at war, and speaks in the first person plural ("we").

So Riedel speaks of "our de facto enemies," asking "why are we at war" with "the Houthis" (i.e. the Ansarallah-led Yemeni government), while Pillar refers to "our allies" and Hassan to "our adversaries." This is an immediate sign of biased orientation, but also of a desire to please and so qualify for the support of likely patrons.

Loyalty is also expressed by an early denunciation of the enemy. Most of the permissible Western media criticisms of Israel, for example, begin with a denunciation of the Palestinian resistance, or of Iranian support for the resistance. At the least, loyalty to the dominant power must be demonstrated by suggesting some kind of moral equivalence between that power and the dominated Others.

The targets of terrorism should also be relatively privileged groups. In the case of Pillar's criticism of Israeli terrorism, itself a departure from the normal western defence of the Zionist state, he chooses the earlier British victims of Israeli terrorism—rather than the many thousands of contemporary Palestinian victims—and makes a moral equivalence with Palestinian resistance in order to legitimize the latter—which is then typically reduced to "Hamas" and their alleged "poorly guided rockets." All this is necessary in order for the writer's article to qualify for Western publication and consumption.

Terminology also plays an important part in demonstrating loyalty, with the enemy described as a "regime" (implicitly illegitimate) and the intervening Western power cloaked in an assumed stabilising or conflict resolution role.

With this in mind Hassan speaks of Iranian influence as "a problem for the United States," the Syrian government as a "regime." Middle Eastern nations are said to be riven by sectarian conflicts (e.g. Sunni v. Shi'ite) and other "complexities." On the other hand Washington faces problems as a "stabilising ally." Pillar speaks of the Saudi backed idea for repartition (and weakening) of Yemen as a "federal solution."

Allowable criticism, within permissible space

Taking the problem-solving and stabilising role of Washington as a given, criticism is allowed mainly as regards tactics. Accepting the benevolence of hegemonic prerogatives is a general principle for qualification. It is unimportant that this has little to do with post-colonial international law.

So Riedel writes of the U.S. supposedly looking for a "political solution" in Yemen, while Hassan speaks of Washington seeking to "stabilize" the region in face of the allegedly opportunistic agendas of Iran and the Saudis.

Riedel also spoke of Yemen as a "complex problem" for U.S. President Obama, while Pillar comfortingly agreed that it is necessary for Washington to "conduct business" with both Israel and Saudi Arabia, despite their terrorism. No real question is raised concerning what business the USA has initiating war after war in the Middle East region.

Indeed, any serious questioning of the overall aims or strategy of western interventions would most likely invalidate or disqualify the article. It would not be published. Yet criticism of the tactical and chronic failure of interventionist wars to achieve their goals is allowed.

What can be learned from the enemy?

State integrated media (which includes most corporate media, as they are typically key associates of Western states) typically steer mass audiences away from enemy media, particularly at times of war. Many analysts also either accommodate or fall prey to that prohibition.

In recent decades we have seen many exhortations to stay away from the 'regime media' of China, Russia, Cuba, Venezuela, Iran, Syria and so on. Enemy 'regime' media is often labelled as such in the western social media. Not so the BBC, Voice of America, etc. In fact the U.S. government has been busy taking down dozens of Iranian websites (DOJ 2021) and banning or blocking Russian (AFP 2021), Venezuelan, Chinese, Cuban and other social media accounts linked to these various 'enemy' nations.

The problem for Western war analysts, having been forced to adopt this *dictat,* is that their analyses are necessarily constrained, with important lessons left unaddressed and/or missed. In general, it is short-sighted to ignore 'enemy' sources because they might be seen as "biased" or "unreliable." Any source with detailed information (as opposed to just spin and slogans) can be informative, properly read, in at least the following ways.

Concessions and admissions: Biased or enemy sources, when they contain detailed information, can provide significant information on particular matters. While concessions can help avoid pointless and endless debate—for example, senior U.S. officials admitted in 2014 that U.S. allies were funding and arming virtually all the Middle Eastern terrorist groups including ISIS, in support of U.S. efforts to remove the Syrian Government (HOS 2020)—Syrian and Iranian sources had said this for some years. U.S. admissions helped expose the charade.

Alerts to information and argument: Hostile or 'unreliable' sources may alert us to notable information or arguments, including independent factual information as well as enabling the discovery of vulnerabilities in enemy arguments. Any serious researcher or observer must remain open to the possibility that information from hostile sources might be correct and valuable, at least on some particular matters, in order to provide more accurate analyses. The Israeli media, for example, understands this well. It has made the statements of Hezbollah leader Hassan Nasrallah virtually mandatory reading, while the man is effectively banned in much other Western media, including social media (Anderson 2019).

The lesson for analysts—and indeed both for the publications that constrain them and for policymakers who draw on same for their own understanding and policy formation—should be how to intelligently read 'enemy' sources, rather than avoid them. This must be done with regard to principle, using traditional forensic tools while recognising self-interest. Such skills require developing an ability to distinguish between self-serving statements and admissions against interest, a common distinction in law.

Learning in this regard has more to do with observing the detail of argument and particular evidence, and less about the adoption and recitation of conclusions.

References

AFP. "Russia Demands Explanation From Facebook Over Blocked Accounts." *The Moscow Tines.* March 4, 2021. https://www.themoscowtimes.com/2021/03/04/russia-demands-explanation-from-facebook-over-blocked-accounts-a73152

Anderson, Tim. "Nasrallah: Banned in the West but Mandatory Viewing in Israel." Tajammo3. July 22, 2019. https://www.tajammo3.org/24388/nasrallah-banned-in-the-west-but-mandatory-viewing-in-israel.html

Hassan, Hassan. "The Middle Eastern Problem Soleimani Figured Out." *Politico.* December 1, 2020. https://www.politico.com/news/magazine/2020/01/12/iran-middle-eastern-problem-soleimani-figured-out-097350

Pillar, Paul R. "How we conveniently ignore the 'terrorists' among our allies." Responsible Statecraft. June 15, 2021. https://responsiblestatecraft.org/2021/06/15/lazy-use-of-the-terrorist-label-makes-for-bad-foreign-policy/

Riedel, Bruce. "Who are the Houthis and why are we at war with them?" December 18, 2017. https://www.brookings.edu/blog/markaz/2017/12/18/who-are-the-houthis-and-why-are-we-at-war-with-them/

HOS. "Syria by admissions—revisited." Hands Off Syria. November 13, 2020. Video, 5:33. https://www.youtube.com/watch?v=fjtdJX2gVmI

DOJ. "United States Seizes Websites Used by the Iranian Islamic Radio and Television Union and Kata'ib Hizballah." United States Department of Justice. June 22, 2021. https://www.justice.gov/opa/pr/united-states-seizes-websites-used-iranian-islamic-radio-and-television-union-and-kata-ib

PART 1

The Legacy of Failed Ambition

3. Wars of Hegemonic Decline

The USA, in economic decline for several decades, faces decline in its global influence. Source: CGTN

Washington's failing New Middle East Wars are best understood in context of the wider rise in global conflict, provoked mainly by the U.S. anxiety at losing its supposed dominant place in the world. The struggles and realignments in West Asia are best seen as part of a broader series of 21st century hybrid wars, including economic wars, linked to this failing North American hegemonic project.

There have been several recent reports on the escalation of U.S.-driven violence (Turse and Speri 2022; TUFTS 2022; Kushi and Toft 2022), mainly through proxy wars. One recent study notes the USA "militarily intervening over 200 times after World War II" and 100 times "during the post-Cold War era." Contrary to many of its stated aims, the U.S. has tended to intervene "in countries with higher levels of democracy" (Kushi and Toft 2022).

While subverting the independent Latin American states, Washington backed coups and invasions in North Africa, drove multiple wars in West Asia in the name of a 'New Middle East' (NME) and remained obsessed with blocking links between Europe and Asia. With dozens of countries subject to unilateral 'sanctions' and with ominous threats against third party states refusing to comply with the latest siege war, the old neoliberal order is losing its liberal gloss.

Where are these wars leading? Will there be a war between the USA and China, as suggested by proponents of the 'Thucydides trap" (Allison 2017)? The globalisation of conflict may mean that might not happen, but there are already dozens of U.S. proxy wars (Turse and Speri 2022; TUFTS 2022). This chapter argues that most of these are driven by the declining hegemon's fear of losing its dominant place in the world (Cooley and Nexon 2020). The multiple attempts to weaken, destabilise and divide rivals and independent states revolve around that concern.

The Trump and Biden administrations represent tactical variations of this same strategy, to save U.S. 'exceptional' rule. Republicans have tended to stress their rivalry with China while Democrats maintained greater focus on Russia. Yet the overall motivation remains the same. Iran is seen as a common target (Porter 2015) as it leads the coalition of independent West Asian states and peoples—Palestine, Syria, Yemen and the resistance forces in Lebanon and Iraq. Venezuela plays a similar role to Iran, by supporting independent states in the Americas. Other states which threaten disobedience or normalise with independent 'poles' of power have been targeted. In South Asia, for example, India and Pakistan have both been pressured (Pasricha 2022; Gul 2022) for their reluctance to engage in the latest hybrid war against Russia.

What connects U.S. economic decline with this greater breadth of warfare in the world? Let's take it step by step: U.S. decline, growth in conflict and links between the two. Then there are some revised doctrines of intervention.

U.S. in decline, more war

It is widely accepted that the U.S. economy is in relative decline, as against other rising economies, principally China. From his historical study Kennedy (1987: 438-439) argued that the strength of great powers is always relative to their potential competitors, and linked to resources and economic productivity. Most such empires—strong states with domination projects well beyond their borders—end up suffering overreach and relative decline. Consistent with this pattern, exports and manufacturing in the USA declined noticeably in the 1980s, while federal debt and deficit spending grew. These are typical indicators of decline (Kennedy 1987: 432, 526). Similarly, Bernstein and Adler (1994) note the 1990s stagnation of the U.S. economy, accompanied by "falling real wages, slow productivity growth, and the loss of international competitiveness in major industries." Even U.S. state media (VOA 2022) acknowledges the growing consensus: China is set to overtake the USA as the largest and most powerful economy within a few years. Studies by the British research group CEBR show that the size of China's economy would overtake that of the USA by 2030 and the dynamics of its international infrastructure would also leave it "better placed" (CEBR 2022). That is before any price adjustment is made into purchasing power parity (PPP) terms. By this measurement, China has already surpassed the USA.

The decline of U.S. economic power can be traced back to the late 1960s. However, Washington maintained global influence through the dollar and the post WW2 institutions—NATO, the IMF/World Bank and the WTO—which it still dominates (Shor 2010: 65). Nevertheless, a 2008 National Intelligence Council report predicted that "the United States' relative strength—even in the military realm—will decline and U.S. leverage will become more constrained" (National Intelligence Council 2008: vi).

This relative decline and the concurrent economic rise of China has been spoken of as a 'Thucydides trap,' based on observations of the Greek historian Thucydides about rivalry and pre-emptive war between Athens and Sparta. This 'trap'—also called 'the theory of hegemonic war' (Gilpin 1988)—might be a useful lens to understand U.S.-China relations today (Allison 2017). Allison studied sixteen such rivalries over the past 500 years and concluded that war broke out in 12 of the 16. "Intrinsic" elements of a hegemonic state (e.g., an overvalued currency) are said to shift "the distribution of capabilities" to others, causing instability and potentially war (Gilpin 1981: 109-130; Wohlforth 2014). Layne argues that "accepting the unipolar exit

... will be the United States' "central grand strategic preoccupation" in the near future (Layne 2012: 1, 10). The process has also been framed as "the multipolar world versus the superpower" (Schwenninger 2003).

This dilemma emerged as Washington imagined it had finally gained a long sought after dominance in world affairs after the 1991 collapse of the Soviet Union. With regard to the possible erosion of this position and beginning to see the dilemmas of decline in the late 20th century, Zbigniew Brzezinski argued for a "new type" of hegemony, drawing on 'hegemonic stability' ideas. This doctrine claims that the world needs a single dominant power, to secure the 'public goods' of stability and 'free markets' (Keohane 1984; Schmidt 1998; Grunberg 2009). The Pentagon addressed this challenge in 2000 with its Full Spectrum Dominance doctrine, which saw military strategy linked to communicational, technological, and economic supremacy (USDOD 2000; Engdahl 2009). By this line of reasoning the main task of U.S. foreign policy should be to prevent the rise of any new poles of power, or worse, any aggrupation of poles of power, especially those which build potentially powerful links between Europe and Asia (Brzezinski 1997). After all, the USA remains an American power which, almost by historical accident, gained footholds in Europe and Asia.

Yet conflict is on the rise. The United Nations (2019) speaks of a 'New Era of Conflict and Violence' while Uppsala University (2015) observed a rise in the number of 21st century wars. The increased number of bilateral wars since the late 19th century is sometimes attributed to simply an increase in the number of countries (Dunn-Warwick 2011). In terms of war deaths, absolute numbers have declined—with some post 1945 'spikes' in the early 1950s, early 1970s, the mid 1980s and in the years after 2012 (Roser et al 2016). Yet the decline in wars between the big powers—deterred by the widespread possession of nuclear weapons—has been offset by large numbers of U.S.-driven proxy wars, including more than 100 U.S. military interventions since 1999 (TUFTS 2022). Most are justified on flimsy or fictional pretexts.

At the turn of the 21st century Washington invaded Afghanistan and Iraq. These were part of a 'New Middle East' strategy (Bransten 2006) which envisioned multiple Middle East and North African states being brought under a U.S. 'umbrella.' General Wesley Clark reported that this plan involved the overthrow of "seven states in five years ... starting with Iraq and Syria and ending with Iran" (Conason 2007). However, the form of the interventions shifted, with the emergence of ideas of 'Smart Power' (Lewis 2009), leading to multiple proxy wars reinforced by economic siege warfare. Those measures have been misleadingly termed 'sanctions,' as though such unilateral coercive measures had some foundation in international law. The shift into multiple, semi-secretive proxy wars may have side-stepped the notion that the USA and China were heading for direct war (Allison 2017). Nevertheless, we can chart the rise of proxy wars and economic warfare, and we can trace the sources of most of these to Washington and its allies.

In 2022 former senior Pentagon officials confirmed that a wide range of proxy wars, under the pretext of 'counterterrorism,' were being carried out in near secrecy. Under U.S. Defence Code 127e the U.S. military arms, trains and provide intel to foreign forces in a wide range of countries. Just between 2017 and 2022 there were reports that at least 23 such operations were carried out, mostly in the Middle East (Syria, Lebanon, Egypt, Iraq and Yemen) but also in Africa (Niger, Tunisia, Libya, Mali, Cameroon and Somalia) (Turse and Speri 2022). Another study documents more than 100 international U.S. 'military interventions' since 1999 (TUFTS 2022).

Similarly, economic warfare (usually termed 'sanctions') has become an integral part of contemporary proxy and hybrid warfare. Its use has grown enormously in recent decades (Coates 2019; GAO 2020). Usually practised against whole nations it is necessarily indiscriminate but nevertheless is seen by Washington as a "less expensive alternative to [direct] military intervention" (Felbermayr et al 2020: 1). These sanctions regimes have quadrupled in number since 1980, with 92 listed in 1980 and 407 in 2016 (Felbermayr et al 2020: 54). Of the 1,102 sanctions listed by a Global Sanctions Data Base since 1950, only 77 (or 7%) were imposed by the United Nations; the other 93% were mostly by the USA, the EU, and its western European allies (Felbermayr et al 2020: appendix). These days sanctions are discussed in North American and European terms mainly as to how effective they are as tools of coercive foreign policy.

Yet unilateral sanctions have no basis in international law, as they typically are deployed by one or more states in an attempt to achieve political objectives by coercion. International law prohibits such coercion, by the principle of non-intervention and an implied ban in the UN Charter. This is supplemented by customary and treaty law in areas such as trade, shipping and telecommunications (Anderson 2019: Chapter 3). The illegality is obvious when there is an 'unlawful intent,' such as damaging the economy of another nation or retaliation to enforce political change (Shneyer and Barta 1981: 468, 471-475). For these reasons the widespread use of 'unilateral coercive measures' (UCMs) became a theme of concern at the United Nations in the late 1990s (OHCHR 2020). The UN Special Rapporteur on the Human Rights impact of UCMs has reported that illegality was widespread in these unilateral 'sanctions.' The major offenders were the NATO states. Most UCMs "indiscriminately" harmed entire populations and secondary sanctions against third parties also damaged human rights (OHCHR 2021).

UCMs are often linked to interventions and proxy wars. It is no coincidence that UCMs by the USA against Iran, Iraq, Syria, Lebanon and Yemen correlate with the proxy wars Washington wages against these same countries (see Table 1). This form of hybrid warfare also correlates to the stated U.S. use of 'smart power,' where proxies wage war and third parties pay for it (Barzehar 2008). Such hybrid warfare often relies on 'human rights' pretexts.

If we look at the countries against which the USA and EU have applied unilateral sanctions, only in some cases are there parallels in UN resolutions and international law. Table 1 gives some idea of the extent of these UCMs. The picture is complicated by the fact that UNSC sanctions are mostly against individuals and entities, while Washington's UCMs are more often against entire countries. In the case of Syria, for example, there are UNSC sanctions against some individuals (from the Democratic People's Republic of Korea and certain terrorist groups) but no UN sanctions against the Syrian state (UNSC 2022); despite lacking UNSC approval, powerful UCMs against the Syrian state and the Syrian people are nonetheless imposed by the USA and the EU.

This increased conflict and warfare is not simply "technical"—to do with climate change and water wars (BBC 2021; Vohra 2021)—but is rather rooted in social power dynamics, principally hegemonic ambitions. This is a pattern of conflict quite distinct from the major wars of the twentieth century, where great powers and empires engaged in

Table 1: Countries 'sanctioned' by the U.S.A and the E.U.		
	No.	Of which:
USA	20	**Non-UN**: Balkans (6 countries), Belarus, Burundi, Cuba, Nicaragua, Syria, Ukraine, Venezuela, Zimbabwe
EU	34	**Non-UN**: Belarus, Bosnia & HZ, Burundi, China, Egypt, Guinea, Haiti, Maldives, Moldova, Montenegro, Myanmar (Burma), Russia, Serbia, Syria, Tunisia, Ukraine, USA, Venezuela, Zimbabwe
UN	16	**UN backed**: Afghanistan, CAR, DR Congo, Eritrea, Guinea-Bisseau, Iran, Iraq, Lebanon, Libya, Mali, DPRK (Nth Korea), Somalia, South Sudan, Sudan, Yemen
Sources: European Union 2019, US Dept. of Treasury 2019a, UNSC 2022		

direct confrontations. The current form of warfare seems to substitute for that earlier pattern.

Revised doctrines of intervention

Increased engagement in war and proxy war damages the veneer of "western democracy," despite new pretexts for intervention. After WW2 it did seem that a new set of post-colonial norms were being established. First the United Nations Charter (1945) recognised a system of notionally equal sovereign states, with law prohibiting intervention, in the name of securing the peace and preventing war. Second, decolonisation norms were affirmed and incorporated, as 'the right of peoples to self-determination,' into the twin International Covenants on human rights (1966). Human societies and human development depend on accountable and participatory social structures, yet those structures and processes are always damaged by foreign interventions.

However, at the turn of the 21st century, the U.S. State Department drove a new doctrine of a 'responsibility to protect' (R2P) through a UN committee. The International Commission on Intervention and State Sovereignty in 2001 posed the idea of 'sovereignty as responsibility,' with a focus on violence within weak or fragile states. The World Summit of 2005 declared that states had the responsibility to prevent great crimes but if they failed to do so, the international community should be "prepared to take collective action … through the Security Council" (UN 2005: 138-139). Much of this text was adopted in UN Security Council resolution 1674 the following year (UNSC 2006).

Nevertheless, as was soon demonstrated, in its substance the R2P is an imperial doctrine which seeks to normalise war and enhance the prerogatives of the big powers to intervene. Edward Luck argued that there is no necessary contradiction between this doctrine and state sovereignty. However, he admitted that R2P ideas "might be used by powerful states ... to justify coercive interventions undertaken for other reasons" (Luck 2009: 17). Indeed, the R2P did not fundamentally change international law, but it did attract greater attention to the Chapter VII intervention powers of the Security Council. The doctrine promotes 'a new norm of customary international law' (Loiselle 2013: 317-341), even suggesting an obligation to intervene. That is a serious distortion.

Innovation in intervention doctrine has mostly come from the liberal side of U.S. politics, which has been more innovative in crafting 'exceptional' loopholes. Widespread revulsion at the 2003 invasion of Iraq on a notoriously false WMD pretext (Hoeffel 2014) pushed U.S. liberals to further seize the initiative. Greater legitimacy was required for the NME project. Information wars and irregular warfare using proxy terrorist groups assumed greater importance. This multifaceted approach built on humanitarian intervention and Full Spectrum Dominance (USDOD 2000) notions.

The information wars drove what we might call 'vexatious propaganda'--insistent moral narratives which seek to impose limits on public debate. The main agents of this have been the Western and allied corporate and state media, supplemented by an array of special purpose, state funded NGOs. Large NGOs like the U.S.-based Human Rights Watch (HRW) and Amnesty International have little of the accountability, participatory nature, or independence of traditional community-based NGOs. They are narrative corporations which have become embedded with the U.S. State Department and its associated foreign policy elite. Amnesty International spends around 280 million Euros per year (Amnesty 2017); Human Rights Watch, closely aligned to the Democrat side of U.S. politics, boasts over US$220 million in assets (HRW 2017: 5). Other more specific agencies, purpose-built for the NME wars, have also received hundreds of millions of dollars from those same powerful states (see Anderson 2018).

Contemporary hybrid war thus draws on liberal idealism, albeit distorted towards traditional hegemonic ends (Anderson 2022): to elevate the mission of the aggressor and disqualify resistance, in particular from existing state governments defending their own sovereign territories and peoples. It includes co-opting the contemporary, popular norms of human rights and subsuming them in imperial-modernist language, such that all such human rights problems are globally the West's to protect. The delicate matter of the right of self-determination of peoples and nations is thus collapsed into insistent narratives of 'failed' or 'fragile' states, from which such peoples must be rescued from their very own 'dictators,' whether or not they had been democratically elected.

This open abuse of the R2P doctrine caused some academic dismay, with analysts saying that NATO's disastrous Libyan intervention (Kuperman 2015) undermined the idea of an R2P 'norm,' as NATO shifted from imposing a 'no fly zone' to open attacks on the Libyan government, thus 'betraying' the UN trust by partisan intervention (Dunne and Gelber 2014: 327-328). Brown agreed, saying that the Libyan intervention demonstrated that the suggested 'apolitical nature' of a responsibility to protect "is a weakness not a strength ... the assumption that politics can be removed from the picture is to promote an illusion and thus to invite disillusionment" (Brown 2013: 424-425). The doctrine lost its intellectual gloss but at a popular level was a considerable success. Many Western liberals seem to like the idea of 'saving' other people from their own social systems, and very few Western media organisations denounced the implausible idea that the U.S. and its allies had intervened in Libya, Syria, and Iraq to fight the very terrorist groups they admitted their 'close allies' had financed and armed (Biden in RT 2014; Usher 2014; Dempsey in Rothman 2014). Certainly, the long proxy wars against Iraq and Syria attracted far less western protest than did the earlier invasions. The idea of 'Western saviours' was successfully marketed.

Yet amongst the target populations the 'New Middle East' wars destroyed millions of human lives, human capital, indigenous social structures and accountability processes as well as causing ongoing physical and psychological damage. In the interventionist states these wars killed far fewer numbers of military personnel, but they privileged war economies and undermined domestic social support and trust through sustained deceptions. They damaged genuine internationalism and human solidarity, Western citizenship and democracy. Imperial war is an assault on citizenship and accountability at home and abroad; but the wars of hegemonic decline also signal an important global transition.

References

Allison, Graham. *Destined for War: Can America and China Escape Thucydides's Trap?* Boston: Houghton Mifflin Harcourt, 2017.

Amnesty International. "Global Financial Report 2016." Amnesty International (2017). https://www.amnesty.org/en/2016-global-financial-report/

Anderson, Tim. "Syria: the Human Rights Industry in Humanitarian War." Centre for Counter Hegemonic Studies. January 2018. https://counter-hegemonic-studies.net/humanitarian-war-rp-1-18/

———. *Axis of Resistance: Towards an independent Middle East.* Atlanta: Clarity Press, 2019.

———. "Hegemonic Neoliberalism: A historical re-evaluation," *Journal of Australian Political Economy,* no. 90 (December 2022): 49–74

Barzehar, Kayhan. (2008) "Joseph Nye on Smart Power in Iran-U.S. Relations." Belfer Centre. July 11, 2008. https://www.belfercenter.org/publication/joseph-nye-smart-power-iran-us-relations

BBC. "How water shortages are brewing wars." August 17, 2021. https://www.bbc.com/future/article/20210816-how-water-shortages-are-brewing-wars

Bello, Walden. *China: An Imperial Power in the Image of the West?* Focus on the Global South. October 2, 2019. https://focusweb.org/publications/china-an-imperial-power-in-the-image-of-the-west/

Bernstein, Michael A., and David E. Adler (Editors). *Understanding American Economic Decline.* Cambridge University Press, 1994.

Bransten, Jeremy. "Middle East: Rice Calls For A 'New Middle East.'" *Radio Free Europe/Radio Liberty.* July 25, 2006. https://www.rferl.org/a/1070088.html

Brown, Chris. "The Anti-Political theory of Responsibility to Protect." *Global Responsibility to Protect* 5, no. 4 (2013): 423–442

Brzezinski, Zbigniew. *The Grand Chessboard.* New York: Basic Books, 1997.

CEBR. "Chosun Ilbo—China's Economy Could Overtake U.S. Economy by 2030." Centre for Economics and Business Research. January 5, 2022. https://cebr.com/reports/chosun-ilbo-chinas-economy-could-overtake-u-s-economy-by-2030/

Coates, Benjamin. "A Century of Sanctions." *Origins*. The Ohio State University. December 2019. https://origins.osu.edu/article/economic-sanctions-history-trump-global

Conason, Joe. "Seven countries in five years." *Salon*. October 12, 2007. https://www.salon.com/2007/10/12/wesley_clark/

Cooley, Alexander, and Daniel H. Nexon. *Exit from Hegemony Ends: The Unravelling of American Power.* New York: Oxford University Press, 2020.

Dunne, Tim, and Katherine Gelber. "Arguing Matters: The responsibility to protect and the Case of Libya." *Global Responsibility to Protect* 6 (2014): 326–349

Dunn-Warwick, Peter. "130+ years of steadily increasing war." Futurity. June 29, 2011. https://www.futurity.org/130-years-of-steadily-increasing-war/

Engdahl, F. William. *Full Spectrum Dominance: Totalitarian Democracy in the New World Order.* Boxborough, Mass.: Third Millennium Press, 2009.

European Union. "EU Sanctions Map." March 2019. https://www.sanctionsmap.eu/#/main

Felbermayr, G., A. Kirilakha, C. Syropoulos, E. Yalcin, and Y.V. Yotov. "The Global Sanctions Data Base." *European Economic Review* 129 (2020). Working paper: https://ideas.repec.org/p/ris/drxlwp/2020_002.html

GAO. "The growing use of economic sanctions." June 18, 2020. https://www.gao.gov/blog/growing-use-economic-sanctions

Gilpin, Robert. *War and Change in World Politics.* New York: Cambridge University Press, 1981.

———. (1988) "The Theory of Hegemonic War." *The Journal of Interdisciplinary History* 18, no. 4, *The Origin and Prevention of Major Wars* (Spring 1988): 591–613. https://doi.org/10.2307/204816

Grunberg, Isabelle. (2009) "Exploring the 'myth' of hegemonic stability." *International Organization* 44, no. 4 (Autumn 1990): 431–477. Published online by Cambridge University Press, May 22, 2009. https://doi.org/10.1017/S0020818300035372

Gul, Ayaz. "Western-Led Pressure Grows on Pakistan to Condemn Russia's Invasion of Ukraine." *Voice of America.* March 1, 2022. https://www.

voanews.com/a/western-led-pressure-grows-on-pakistan-to-condemn-russia-s-invasion-of-ukraine/6465104.html

Hoeffel, Joseph. *The Iraq Lie: How the White House Sold the War.* San Diego: Progressive Press, 2014.

Human Rights Watch Financial Statements, year ended 30 June 2016. Human Rights Watch Inc., 2017. https://www.hrw.org/sites/default/files/supporting_resources/financial-statements-2016.pdf

Kennedy, Paul. *The Rise and Fall of the Great Powers.* New York: Random House, 1987.

Keohane, Robert O. *After Hegemony: Cooperation and Discord in the World Political Economy.* Princeton, N.J.: Princeton University Press, 1984.

Kuperman, Alan. "Obama's Libya Debacle." *Foreign Affairs* (March/April 2015). Published online February 18, 2019. https://www.foreignaffairs.com/articles/libya/2019-02-18/obamas-libya-debacle

Kushi, Sidita, and Monica Duffy Toft. "Introducing the Military Intervention Project: A New Dataset on U.S. Military Interventions, 1776–2019." *Journal of Conflict Resolution* (August 2022). https://counter-hegemonic-studies.site/kushi-toft-war-22/

Layne, Christopher. "This Time It's Real: The End of Unipolarity and the Pax Americana," *International Studies Quarterly* 56, no. 1 (March 2012): 203–213. https://doi.org/10.1111/j.1468-2478.2011.00704.x

Lewis, Paul. "Hillary Clinton backs 'smart power' to assert U.S. influence around world." *The Guardian.* January 14, 2009. https://www.theguardian.com/world/2009/jan/13/hillary-clinton-confirmation-hearing-senate

Loiselle, Marie-Eve. "The Normative Status of the Responsibility to Protect After Libya." *Global Responsibility to Protect* 5, no. 3 (2013), 317–341.

Luck, Edward C. "Sovereignty, Choice, and the Responsibility to Protect." *Global Responsibility to Protect* 1 (2009): 10–21

National Intelligence Council. *Global Trends 2025: A transformed world?* Washington: U.S. Government Printing Office, 2008. https://www.files.ethz.ch/isn/94769/2008_11_global_trends_2025.pdf

OHCHR. Reports on unilateral coercive measures from the Office of the UN High Commissioner for Human Rights, 2020. https://www.ohchr.org/en/unilateral-coercive-measures/reports-unilateral-coercive-measures-office-un-high-commissioner-human-rights

OHCHR. A/76/174/Rev.1: Report on the targets of unilateral coercive measures: Notion, categories and vulnerable groups. September 13, 2021. https://www.ohchr.org/en/documents/thematic-reports/a76174rev1-report-targets-unilateral-coercive-measures-notion-categories

Pasricha, Anya. "Resisting U.S. Pressure, India Stays Neutral on Russia." *Voice of America.* March 4, 2022. https://www.voanews.com/a/resisting-us-pressure-india-stays-neutral-on-russia-/6470494.html

Porter, Gareth. Why Iran must remain a U.S. enemy." *Al Jazeera,* May 4, 2015. https://www.aljazeera.com/opinions/2015/5/4/why-iran-must-remain-a-us-enemy

Roser, Max, Joe Hasell, Bastian Herre, and Bobbie Macdonald. "War and Peace." *Our World In Data* (2016). https://ourworldindata.org/war-and-peace

Rothman, Noah. "Dempsey: I know of Arab allies who fund ISIS" September 16, 2014. Video, 00:52. https://www.youtube.com/watch?v=nA39iVSo7XE

RT. "Anyone but US! Biden blames allies for ISIS rise" October 3, 2014. Video. https://www.youtube.com/watch?v=1118nLZNPSY

Schmidt, Helmut. "The Grand Chessboard: American Primacy and Its Geostrategic Imperatives." Review of Zbigniew Brzezinski, *The Grand Chessboard: American Primacy and Its Geostrategic Imperatives* (1997). *Foreign Policy* (Spring 1998). https://ciaotest.cc.columbia.edu/olj/fp/schmidt.html

Schwenninger, Sherle. "The Multipolar World vs. The Superpower." The Globalist. December 5, 2003. https://www.theglobalist.com/the-multipolar-world-vs-the-superpower/

Shneyer, Paul A., and Virginia Barta. "The legality of the U.S. Economic Blockade of Cuba under International Law." *Case Western Reserve Journal of International Law* 13 no. 3 (1981): 450–482

Shor, Francis. "War in the Era of Declining U.S. Global Hegemony." *Journal of Critical Globalisation Studies,* Issue 2 (2010). http://financeandsociety.ed.ac.uk/ojs-images/financeandsociety/JCGS_2_4.pdf

Tufts University. *Military Intervention Project* (MIP). Fletcher Centre for Strategic Studies, 2022. https://sites.tufts.edu/css/mip-research/

Turse, Nick, and Alice Speri. "How the Pentagon uses a secretive program to wage proxy wars." *The Intercept.* July 1, 2022. https://theintercept.com/2022/07/01/pentagon-127e-proxy-wars/

United Nations. 2005 World Summit Outcome, 60/1. October 24, 2005. http://www.un.org/womenwatch/ods/A-RES-60-1-E.pdf

United Nations. "A New Era of Conflict and Violence." 2019. https://www.un.org/en/un75/new-era-conflict-and-violence

UNSC. United Nations Security Council. Resolution 1674. 2006. http://www.securitycouncilreport.org/atf/cf/%7B65BFCF9B-6D27-4E9C-8CD3-CF6E4FF96FF9%7D/Civilians%20SRES1674.pdf

UNSC. United Nations Security Council. "Sanctions." July 20, 2022. https://scsanctions.un.org/kpvzwen-all.html

Uppsala University. "Sudden rise in the number of wars." Phys.org. January 9, 2015. https://phys.org/news/2015-01-sudden-wars.html

U.S. Department of Defense. *Joint Vision 2020.* U.S. DoD, 2000. At Matt Cegelske, "Joint Vision 2020: America's Military—Preparing for Tomorrow [Strategy]." A Cyber Fellow. May 21, 2012. https://mattcegelske.com/joint-vision-2020-americas-military-preparing-for-tomorrow-strategy/

U.S. Department of Treasury. (2019a). "Active Sanctions Programs." March 2019. https://www.treasury.gov/resource-center/sanctions/programs/pages/programs.aspx

Usher, Barbara Plett. "Joe Biden apologised over IS remarks, but was he right?" *BBC News.* October 7, 2014. http://www.bbc.com/news/world-us-canada-29528482

Voice of America. "China's Economy Could Overtake U.S. Economy by 2030." January 4, 2022. https://www.voanews.com/a/chinas-economy-could-overtake-us-economy-by-2030/6380892.html

Vohra, Anchal. "The Middle East Is Becoming Literally Uninhabitable." *Foreign Policy.* August 24, 2021. https://foreignpolicy.com/2021/08/24/the-middle-east-is-becoming-literally-uninhabitable/

Wohlforth, William C. "Hegemonic decline and hegemonic war revisited." In G. John Ilkenberry (Ed.), *Power, Order, and Change in World Politics.* Cambridge University Press, 2014.

4. The Roots of Western Fascism

The U.S.-backed Azov Battalion in Ukraine uses the Nazi Wolfsangel symbol as its logo. Its founder Andriy Biletsky (centre) wants to "lead the white races of the world in a final crusade ... against Semite-led Untermenschen [sub-humans]." Source: Azov/Twitter.

In view of the western claims to humanitarian intervention in other countries, let's recall the roots of fascism in European and North American imperial culture. Amidst the 'Western values' and 'human rights' justifications for the many recent wars one simple fact is hidden: European imperialism lies at the root of the great historical crimes of genocide, colonialism and slavery, and in turn formed the cradle for contemporary fascism. The heavily militarised, anti-democratic and racist regimes of 20th century Europe drew on their imperial and colonial traditions.

In recent years NATO—essentially the USA and Western Europe—has laid bare its fascist roots through multiple interventions across four continents. The NATO states backed fascist coups in Venezuela, Honduras and Bolivia, imposed blockades on dozens of nations, and fomented al Qaeda/ISIS/Boko Haram sectarian terrorism to destabilise Libya, Iraq, Syria, Somalia, Nigeria and several other African states while arming Neo-Nazis in the Ukraine.

All this seems at odds with the NATO states' heavily promoted self-image as models of liberalism and democratic values (NATO 2022), even lecturing other countries on that theme. They claim to have fought both fascism and communism. Yet it was European and North American imperialism that laid the foundation for 20th century fascism.

Since the Second World War—a massive 20th century conflict which robbed more than 70 million lives—both Washington and the Western Europeans have made great efforts to hide the anti-fascist contributions and sacrifices of the Soviet Union and China, nations which lost more lives in WW2 than any other (World Population Review 2022).

Indeed, in 2019 the European Parliament went so far as to blame the Soviet Union under Joseph Stalin, alongside Nazi Germany under Adolf Hitler, as being jointly responsible for WW2. That resolution claimed that "the Second World War … was started as an immediate result of the notorious Nazi-Soviet Treaty of Non-Aggression of 23 August 1939" (European Parliament 2019). If it was not entirely cynical, then this was an extraordinary self-deception, and the culmination of a long campaign where socialist leaders Joseph Stalin and Mao Zedong were presented, over decades, as the moral equivalents of the European fascist, Adolf Hitler.

That deceit made use of false claims that Stalin and Mao had instigated famines which killed many millions. In fact, the famines in both Ukraine and China were the last in a long cycle of famines of the pre-socialist era. U.S. historian Grover Furr has debunked the myth that the Ukrainian famine—which killed 3-4 million in Ukraine and another million elsewhere in the Soviet Union—was a deliberate genocidal act, a 'Holodomor,' by Stalin (Furr 2017). At least five independent U.S. historians (Alexander Dallin, Moshe Lewin, Lynne

Viola, J. Arch Getty and Mark Tauger) reject the claim that this famine was a deliberate act (Furr 2014: 45-50).

Similarly, the claim that WW2 was the "immediate result" of the Soviet-German non-aggression pact is an utter falsehood. There were a number of similar European agreements with Nazi Germany before this, and several were more substantial. The Anglo German Naval Agreement of 1935, for example, helped Germany rebuild its fleet (Yeager 2013), while Britain, France and Italy conceded Berlin's claim to part of Czechoslovakia in the 1938 Munich Pact (Britannica 2022). Then there were the active fascist collaborations between Germany, Spain, and Italy, including the Italian-German Pact of Steel (WW2Database 2009).

Much of Europe's fascist collaboration coalesced under an Anti-Comintern Pact created by Nazi Germany and Japan in 1936, to oppose communist states (Presseisen 1958). This pact later drew in support from Italy, Hungary, Spain and—during the war—from Bulgaria, Croatia, Denmark, Finland, Romania and Slovakia (National WW2 Museum 2021). Fascism was aflame across Europe in the 1930s and 1940s. Key European agreements with Nazi Germany are set out below, in Table 1.

What is fascism? The term is used far too frequently but it has real meaning. We cannot be trapped by particular 20th century histories of fascism: specific conceptual elements must be identified.

Fascism is a heavily militarised, anti-democratic and often racist-colonial regime which engages with a private, capitalist oligarchy. While primary fascism is an imperial project, there is also a subordinate or client fascism in former colonies like Brazil and Chile, which integrates itself with the imperial power of the day. Fascist regimes are especially hostile to socialist and independent states and peoples. They differ from extreme right regimes only by openly crushing any semblance of social and political democracy. Imperial cultures and interventions, which always and everywhere negate the possibility of local democracy or accountability, remain the driving force of contemporary fascism.

Table 1: Key European agreements with Nazi Germany		
1933 July 20	Concordat with the Vatican	Mutual recognition and non-interference https://www.concordatwatch.eu/reichskonkordat-1933-full-text--k1211
1933 August 25	Haavara agreement with German Jewish Zionists	Agreement to transfer capital and people to Palestine. https://www.jewishvirtuallibrary.org/haavara
1934 January 26	German-Polish Non-Aggression Pact	To ensure that Poland did not sign a military alliance with France. https://avalon.law.yale.edu/wwii/blbk01.asp
1935 June 18	Anglo-German Naval Agreement	Britain agreed to Germany expanding its navy to 35% the size of the British. https://carolynyeager.net/anglo-german-naval-agreement-june-18-1935
1936 July	Nazi Germany aids fascists in Spain	Hitler sent air and armoured units to assist General Franco. https://spartacus-educational.com/SPgermany.htm
1936	Rome-Berlin Axis agreement	Italian - German fascist and anti-communist alliance. https://www.globalsecurity.org/military/world/int/axis.htm
1936 Oct.-Nov.	Anti-Comintern Pact	Anti-communist treaty, initiated by Nazi Germany and Japan in 1936, it drew in 9 European states: Italy, Hungary, Spain, Bulgaria, Croatia, Denmark, Finland, Romania and Slovakia https://doi.org/10.1007/978-94-017-6590-9_4
1938 Sept. 30	Munich Pact	Britain, France and Italy concede Germany's Sudetenland (Czech) claims. https://www.britannica.com/event/Munich-Agreement
1939 May 22	Pact of Steel	Consolidates 1936 Italian German agreement. https://ww2db.com/battle_spec.php?battle_id=228
1939 June 7	German–Latvian Non-Aggression Pact	Sought peace with Nazi Germany. https://www.jstor.org/stable/43211534
1939 July 24	German–Estonian Non-Aggression Pact	Sought peace with Nazi Germany. https://www.jstor.org/stable/43211534
1939 August 23	USSR (Molotov-Ribbentrop) Non-Aggression Pact	Sought peace with Nazi Germany, protocol defined spheres of influence. https://universalium.en-academic.com/239707/German-Soviet_Nonaggression_Pact

NATO's fascism was built by the imperial and colonial history of many (but not all) of the European states, where the crushing of local communities and nations was justified by fabricated theories of race and racial superiority. The West's denial of this colonial-fascist history has led to suggestions that, as a Russian documentary put it, the rise of Hitler was "something atypical of European democracies; the Fuhrer's doctrine of superior and inferior races rather appeared out of thin air in Europe due to an unlucky turn of events" (RT 2021).

In fact, the fascism of Nazi Germany had deep roots in European imperial history. Further, as Gerwin Strobl's book *The Germanic Isle* points out, Adolf Hitler himself was a great admirer of the "ruthlessness" of the British Empire and dreamt of such achievements (Strobl 2007). For its part the USA built myths of 'liberty' while running the largest slave economy in human history (Hardy 2017). As the great Latin American resistance leader Simon Bolivar said two centuries ago, "The United States appear to be destined by Providence to plague America with misery in the name of liberty" (Bushnell 2003).

Beyond the European 'appeasement' of Nazi Germany there was active European and North American collaboration with fascists before, during and after WW2.

First of all the Anglo-German Naval Agreement of 1935 helped re-arm Nazi Germany, breaking with the 1919 Versailles Treaty limits on German ships and submarines while pretending to keep the German navy a fraction of the British navy (Yeager 2013). The following year, 1936, Germany began construction of some of the largest battleships in the world (Koop 1998). Then several North American companies, notably General Motors, Ford and IBM, invested directly in the Nazi regime's economy, infrastructure and military. There were many influential North American and British admirers of the Nazis (Ruggerio 2018). On the verge of WW2, British bankers funnelled third party (Czech) gold into Nazi controlled banks (LeBor 2013).

Ford assisted the Nazi war machine before and into WW2 through motor vehicle factories in Germany and occupied Vichy France (Imlay and Horn 2014). It made use of German slave labour from Nazi concentration camps, though the company later complained that it had no control over these labour regimes (JTA 2001). While the Ford company struggled to escape these allegations, Polish officials and former inmates named Ford as "one of 500 firms which had links with [slave labour from the Nazi death camp at] Auschwitz" (Borger 1999). IBM, a 'New Deal' company close to the Roosevelt administration, also invested in Nazi Germany through the 1930s and into the early years of the war, helping build Nazi information systems (Beatty 2001).

The Swiss sold millions in arms to the Nazis, both before and during WW2 (Cowell 1997). Despite pretensions at neutrality, between 1940 and 1944 "84 per cent of Swiss munition exports went to Axis countries" (Summerton 2002). Yet, according to researcher Bradford Snell, "General Motors [GM] was far more important to the Nazi war machine than Switzerland … GM was an integral part of the German war effort" (Dobbs 1998).

North American and European investment in and collaboration with the Nazis continued well into WW2. One aspect of this was a desire to participate in what was, between 1940 and 1942, "a spectacular investment boom, primarily directed towards widening the industrial base for war" (Scherner 2006). No doubt that encouraged Ford and GM to keep relations with Hitler.

After 1939-40, when Nazi Germany had invaded much of western Europe, Berlin counted on the support of many European fascist and collaborationist states, as well as civilian volunteers. Alongside its alliance with fascist Italy, Nazi Germany could count on the support of fascist Spain, despite General Franco's alleged policy of neutrality (Marquina 1998).

Then there were the pro-fascist statelets set up by the Nazis, Vichy France (Boissoneault 2017) and the Quisling regime in Norway (Brady 2018). The Germans created multiple SS divisions, with tens of thousands of willing pro-fascist volunteers, in the Netherlands, in Croatia and in Albania (McGregor 2017; NWM 2022a; NWM 2022b). Vichy France under WWI hero Marshall Petain enacted a racist anti-Jew law (AFP 2010) which made Jews second-class citizens in France and so more readily subject to Nazi predations. The regime of Vidkun Quisling similarly encouraged participation in local SS divisions (Primidi 2017), helping deport Jewish people and execute Norwegian patriots.

Danish King Christian X may have been friendly with the Jewish community, but he did not stand up to the Nazis. It has been falsely claimed that King Christian "donned the Star of David in solidarity with the Danish Jews" (Schere 2018). In reality, the Danish regime opposed resistance activities and shared intelligence with the Nazis. One of the factors in this collaboration was that Denmark was "technically an ally of Germany" (Lund and Deák 1990). Under pressure, they had signed the Anti-Comintern Pact. Despite great efforts to sanitise this history, in 2005 Danish PM Rasmussen apologized on behalf of Denmark for the extradition of minorities and resistance figures to Nazi Germany (Deutsche Welle 2005), many of whom were sent to their death.

Substantial Nazi collaboration took place in all the Baltic states: Latvia, Lithuania and Estonia all had Waffen SS divisions (Bubnys, Kott and Kraft 2016). They, along with ultra-nationalist Nazi collaborators in the Ukraine, played a key role in local massacres of communists, Poles, Russians, Jews and Roma/Gypsies.

Between 1941 and 1944 hundreds of thousands were slaughtered in the Ukraine, many by local ultra-nationalist Nazi collaborators like Stepan Bandera (Rossoliński-Liebe, Grzegorz 2014). Russian historian Lev Simkin says "in practice, the Holocaust of the Jews began in Ukraine," with the June 1941 invasion of the Soviet Union (Tabarovsky 2016). These mass killings were linked to Hitler's paranoid view of dangerous Bolshevik Jews and German Jews who allegedly undermined Germany during and after WW1. Mass killings of Jews in Kiev, Lviv, Kherson and other parts of Ukraine have been well mapped out (IHRA 2020). These are some of the sites of recent Russian fighting with Ukrainian NeoNazis. During WW2 most of the Ukraine's pre-war Jewish population of about 1.5 million "was wiped out" (Auyezov 2011).

Academic studies have shown a "massive participation of Baltic nationals in the murder of Jews in the Holocaust" (Levin 1990). Many tens of thousands of Jews were killed in Latvia, Lithuania and Estonia, much of this at local hands (Yad Vashem 2022). There has been a strong reaction to exposure of this ugly history of fascist collaboration. Lithuania, for example, is said to want to hide its "ugly history of Nazi collaboration" by accusing Jewish partisans of war crimes (Brook 2015). Across Europe there was large scale participation in the fascist slaughter. In Hungary Nazi leader Adolf Eichmann was said to be "reliant on the collaboration of the Hungarian authorities" to deport more than 400,000 Hungarian Jews to the death camps (WHL 2022).

All this underlines the fact that WW2, from the European and North American side, was not fundamentally a fight against fascism, even though those states fought a fascist 'Axis.' The war was more a competition between imperial blocks, with the Hitler-led coalition determined to colonise 'living space' (Rosenberg 2020) in the east. The struggle of patriots in eastern Europe and Russia, as well as much of the Western resistance, was certainly anti-fascist. Those leading the Western states, however, were not idealists.

After WW2 the USA immediately took advantage of Nazi science and technology in their subsequent 'cold war' against the emerging socialist bloc. The allied powers smashed anti-fascist forces in Greece (Fontaine 2017) and militarily occupied western Germany. The Soviet Union, for its part, ensured that it dominated those close neighbours which had been most deeply embedded with its fascist enemies: in particular, the Baltic states, Ukraine and eastern Germany.

The U.S. began a project of secretly recruiting Nazi scientists to its war machine (Lewis 2016). North American use of German rocket specialist Werner Von Braun is often cited with reference to the peaceful Apollo space project. However, Von Braun was an SS officer who had hand-picked slave labour from concentration camps. The U.S. military wanted him for his expertise with military rockets and missiles. In the once secret but now notorious Operation Paperclip, thousands of Nazi scientists were recruited and given safe haven in the USA (Lichtblau 2010) for their value in building up the capacity of the U.S. military. The Pentagon was particularly interested in the Nazi development of a "whole arsenal of nerve agents" and in Hitler's work towards "a bubonic plague weapon" (NPR 2014).

While Operation Paperclip, by the time it became public, could claim civil scientific benefits, the secret Operation Gladio was less easy to sanitise. With Nazi collaborators, Gladio ('Sword') carried on the Nazi anti-communist mission and its very existence shows that the real enemy of the European elites was not fascism but rather communism (Charles 2022). Through Gladio, fascist tactics—including torture, coup d'états, election fraud, assassinations, disinformation, provocation and false flag operations—were justified so as to "prevent the spread of Communism" (Ganser 2004). In 1990 Italian Prime Minister Giulio Andreotti felt obliged to admit the existence of these NATO linked groups, using fascist methods and under CIA and MI6 control, but also under groups called Absalon in Denmark, ROC in Norway and SDRA8 in Belgium (Ganser 2004).

Soon after WW2 the Nazi SS had been branded a criminal organisation and was dissolved, but in 1953 the U.S. 10th Special Forces Group set up its first overseas base at an SS building in Bad Tolz, Bavaria, then later others in Panama and Okinawa (Ganser 2004). The U.S. side trained fascist regimes in Latin America and the European side carried out 'black operations.' For example, in 1961 between 48 and 200 Algerians demonstrators in Paris were massacred, under the supervision of Nazi collaborator Police Chief Maurice Papon (Hamza 2021).

For all their later complaints about other states possessing weapons of mass destruction (WMDs), the U.S. military wanted every type of WMD at its disposal. And Washington was prepared to use these WMDs on civilian populations, as their biological and chemical attacks in Korea (Immerwahr 2020) and in Vietnam (Roul 2010) showed, and as the gratuitous and horrific nuclear 'demonstration' attacks on the civilian Japanese cities of Hiroshima and Nagasaki demonstrated (Hayes 2015). Masters of double speak, and with a doctrine of 'plausible deniability' (NSA 2019), U.S. officials hid their own atrocities, so far as possible.

Washington emerged as the dominant power after WW2. It began to use the same fascist tactics it had used against most countries of the Americas—invasions, coups, dirty wars (Becker 2011)—on other continents. So the terrible war in Korea led to a permanent U.S. military occupation in the south of the peninsula, the democratic government of Iran was overthrown and replaced by a dictatorship in 1953 and the next terrible 'anti-communist' war against the people of Vietnam failed (Caleb 2018), only after many years and after millions had been slaughtered.

In the 21st century Washington backed multiple coup attempts against Venezuela, the biggest oil producer in the Americas and historically important for fuelling the U.S. war machine. In 2002 the USA and Spain backed coup plotters (Blum 2004) who kidnapped elected President Hugo Chavez, falsely claimed that he had resigned, tore up the constitution, dismissed the elected National Assembly and announced the head of the Chamber of Commerce, Pedro Carmona, as President (Forero 2022). Carmona only lasted two days, but multiple coup attempts followed. This was pure fascism. Venezuela decided that a strong state, with a large civilian militia, was necessary to defend itself from the relentless U.S.-backed fascism.

At the same time, fearing the loss of its dominant role in the world, Washington launched multiple wars in the Middle East, in futile attempts to contain the growing influence of Iran, post-Soviet Russia and China (Anderson 2019). The wars against Palestine, Afghanistan, Iraq, Lebanon, Libya, Syria, and Yemen are not the subject of this chapter. However we should observe the U.S.-NATO use of massive proxy armies, al Qaeda and ISIS styled, infused with sectarian Saudi ideology (Clapper 2016), across the West Asian region and similarly into Africa, in the shape of Boko Haram and al Shaabab (Shuriye 2012; Hiraan 2020; IUVM 2022).

In Russia's 2022 retaliatory war on Ukraine—provoked by a sustained assault after 2014 on the Russian speaking population of south-eastern Ukraine and by a NATO military build-up intended to destabilise and weaken Russia (Bloomberg 2022)—we see a combination of U.S. fascist method and older European colonial mentality. The U.S. maintains its double speak over 'liberty,' while the Europeans speak of lesser human classes. In the Ukraine, ultra-nationalists such as Azov and Right Sektor describe themselves as Nazis who want to kill Russians, Jews and Poles (Dean and Duff 2022). NATO and its embedded media try to hide this ugly reality.

German and European Union official Florence Gaub, for example, uses racist rhetoric to dehumanize Russian people: "Even if Russians look European, they are not European, in a cultural sense. They think differently about violence or death. They have no concept of a liberal, post-modern life, a concept of life that each individual can choose. Instead, life simply can end early with death" (Norton 2022). Critics called this a very German reversion to the Nazi concept of *untermenschen* or inferior races (Pakistan Defence 2022).

Twenty-first century fascism has arisen in new circumstances but carries the key elements of the 20th century project: an imperial, heavily militarised, deeply anti-democratic and racist-colonial regime embedded in a private, capitalist oligarchy. It spawns subordinate fascisms, every bit as venomous as their parent. It is a global imperial project which remains the key enemy of all free and democratic peoples.

References

AFP. "STATUT DES JUIFS – Ce document qui accable le maréchal Pétain." *Le Point.* October 3, 2010. https://www.lepoint.fr/societe/statut-des-juifs-ce-document-qui-accable-le-marechal-petain-03-10-2010-1244322_23.php

Anderson, Tim. *Axis of Resistance.* Atlanta: Clarity Press, 2019.

Arūnas Bubnys, Matthew Kott, and Ülle Kraft. "The Baltic States: Auxiliaries and Waffen-SS soldiers from Estonia, Latvia, and Lithuania." Chapter 5 in Jochen Böhler and Robert Gerwarth (Eds.). *The Waffen-SS: A European History.* Oxford University Press, 2016.

Auyezov, Olzhas. "Ukraine Holocaust massacre presaged modern genocide." Reuters. September 29, 2011. https://www.reuters.com/article/uk-ukraine-babiyyar-idUKTRE78S1H220110929

Beatty, Jack. "Hitler's Willing Business Partners." *The Atlantic* (April 2001). https://www.theatlantic.com/magazine/archive/2001/04/hitlers-willing-business-partners/303146/

Becker, Marc. "History of U.S. Interventions in Latin America." Yachana. 2011. https://yachana.org/teaching/resources/interventions.html

Bloomberg. "U.S. Defense Sec. Austin: We Want to See Russia Weakened." April 25, 2022. https://www.bloomberg.com/news/videos/2022-04-25/u-s-defense-sec-austin-we-want-to-see-russia-weakened-video

Blum, William. "US coup against Hugo Chavez of Venezuela, 2002." *Freeing the World to Death: Essays on the American Empire.* Common Courage Press, 2004. https://williamblum.org/chapters/freeing-the-world-to-death/us-coup-against-hugo-chavez-of-venezuela-2002

Boissoneault, Lorraine. "Was Vichy France a Puppet Government or a Willing Nazi Collaborator?," *Smithsonian.* November 9, 2017. https://www.smithsonianmag.com/history/vichy-government-france-world-war-ii-willingly-collaborated-nazis-180967160/

Borger, Julian. "Nazi documents reveal that Ford had links to Auschwitz." *The Guardian.* August 20, 1999. https://www.theguardian.com/world/1999/aug/20/julianborger1

Brady, M. Michael. "The coining of quisling." The Norwegian American. October 31, 2018. https://www.norwegianamerican.com/the-coining-of-quisling/

Britannica. "Munich Agreement, Europe [1938]." Updated March 31, 2023. https://www.britannica.com/event/Munich-Agreement

Brook, Daniel. "Double Genocide." *Slate.* July 26, 2015. https://slate.com/news-and-politics/2015/07/lithuania-and-nazis-the-country-wants-to-forget-its-collaborationist-past-by-accusing-jewish-partisans-of-war-crimes.html

Bushnell, David. *El Libertador: Writings of Simón Bolívar.* Oxford University Press, 2003. http://www.historyisaweapon.com/defcon7/simon-bolivar-el-libertador-writings-of-simon-bolivar-david-bushnell-editor-1.pdf

Caleb G. "The Unspeakable Brutality of the U.S. War Against Vietnam Must Never Be Forgotten." US Hypocrisy. April 30, 2018. https://ushypocrisy.com/2018/04/30/the-unspeakable-brutality-of-the-u-s-war-against-vietnam-must-never-be-forgotten/

Charles, Julien. "Resurrecting the Ghouls." Hampton Think. May 31, 2022. https://www.hamptonthink.org/read/resurrecting-the-ghouls-on-the-wests-history-of-hating-russians-while-rehabilitating-nazis

Clapper, Lincoln. "Wahhabism, ISIS, and the Saudi Connection." Geopolitical Monitor. January 31, 2016. https://www.geopoliticalmonitor.com/wahhabism-isis-and-the-saudi-connection/

Cowell, Alan. "New Records Show the Swiss Sold Arms Worth Millions to Nazis." *New York Times.* May 29, 1997. https://www.nytimes.com/1997/05/29/world/new-records-show-the-swiss-sold-arms-worth-millions-to-nazis.html

Dean, Jim, and Gordon Duff. "Belligerent Rhetoric & SS-Style Regalia: Who are Right Sector and Neo-Nazi Azov?" *Veterans Today.* February 28, 2022. https://www.veteranstoday.com/2022/02/28/belligerent-rhetoric-ss-style-regalia-who-are-right-sector-and-neo-nazi-azov/

Dobbs, Michael. "Ford and GM Scrutinized for Alleged Nazi Collaboration." *Washington Post.* November 30, 1998. https://www.washingtonpost.com/wp-srv/national/daily/nov98/nazicars30.htm

Deutsche Welle. "Denmark Apologizes for Aiding Nazis." May 5, 2005. https://www.dw.com/en/denmark-apologizes-for-aiding-nazis/a-1573618

European Parliament. "European Parliament resolution of September 2019 on the importance of European remembrance for the future of Europe" [2019/2819(RSP)]. https://www.europarl.europa.eu/doceo/document/TA-9-2019-0021_EN.html

Fontaine, Jöelle. "How Churchill Broke the Greek Resistance." *Jacobin.* August 5, 2017. https://www.jacobinmag.com/2017/05/greece-world-war-two-winston-churchill-communism

Forero, Juan. "Uprising in Venezuela: Man in the News; Manager and Conciliator—Pedro Carmona Estanga." *New York Times*. April 13, 2002. https://www.nytimes.com/2002/04/13/world/uprising-venezuela-man-manager-conciliator-pedro-carmona-estanga.html

Furr, Grover. *Blood Lies*. New York: Red Star Publishers, 2014. https://counter-hegemonic-studies.site/blood-lies-1/

Furr, Grover. "The 'Holodomor' and the Film 'Bitter Harvest' are Fascist Lies," *CounterPunch.* March 3, 2017. https://www.counterpunch.org/2017/03/03/the-holodomor-and-the-film-bitter-harvest-are-fascist-lies/

Ganser, Daniele. *NATO's Secret Armies: Operation Gladio and Terrorism in Western Europe.* Oxfordshire: Routledge, 2004.

Hamza, Assiya (2021). "October 17, 1961: A massacre of Algerians in the heart of Paris." France 24. https://webdoc.france24.com/october-17-1961-massacre-algerians-paris-france-police-history/

Hardy, James. "Slavery in America: United States' Black Mark." History Cooperative. March 21, 2017. https://historycooperative.org/slavery-in-america-a-black-mark/

Hayes, Peter. "Hiroshima and Nagasaki: There were other choices," Nautilus Institute. September 28, 2015. https://nautilus.org/napsnet/napsnet-special-reports/hiroshima-and-nagasaki/

Hiraan. "Somali Intelligence Chief accuses Qatar of links with Al-Shahbaab: Saudi Influence?" May 16, 2020. https://hiiraan.com/news4/2020/May/178160/omali_intelligence_chief_accuses_qatar_of_links_with_al_shahbaab_saudi_influence.aspx

IHRA (2020). "Creating an online map of Holocaust killing sites in Ukraine." International Holocaust Remembrance Alliance. https://www.holocaustremembrance.com/news-archive/creating-online-map-holocaust-killing-sites-ukraine

Imlay, Talbot, and Martin Horn. *The Politics of Industrial Collaboration during World War II: Ford France, Vichy and Nazi Germany.* Cambridge University Press, 2014.

Immerwahr, Daniel. "The Great Germ War Cover-Up." *New Republic.* July 13, 2020. https://newrepublic.com/article/158008/germ-warfare-book-nicholson-baker-baseless-review

IUVM (2022). "Boko Haram: Saudi Arabia and state-sponsored terrorism on the African Continent." https://www.iuvmarchive.org/en/article/boko-haram-saudi-arabia-and-state-sponsored-terrorism-on-the-african-continent

JTA. "Report: Ford Had No Control over Slave Labor at Its German Subsidiary." Jewish Telegraph Agency. December 7, 2001. https://www.jta.org/archive/report-ford-had-no-control-over-slave-labor-at-its-german-subsidiary

Koop, Gerhard. *Battleships of the Bismarck Class: Bismarck and Tirpitz, culmination and finale of German battleship construction.* Annapolis: Naval Institute Press, 1998.

LeBor, Adam. "How bankers helped the Nazis." *Sydney Morning Herald.* August 1, 2013. https://www.smh.com.au/business/how-bankers-helped-the-nazis-20130801-2r1fd.html

Levin, Dov. "On the Relations between the Baltic Peoples and Their Jewish Neighbors before, during and after World War II." *Holocaust and Genocide Studies* 5, no. 1 (1990): 53–66. https://doi.org/10.1093/hgs/5.1.53

Lewis, Danny. "Why the U.S. Government Brought Nazi Scientists to America After World War II." *Smithsonian.* November 16, 2016. https://www.smithsonianmag.com/smart-news/why-us-government-brought-nazi-scientists-america-after-world-war-ii-180961110/

Lichtblau, Eric. "Nazis Were Given 'Safe Haven' in U.S., Report Says." *New York Times.* November 14, 2010. https://www.nytimes.com/2010/11/14/us/14nazis.html

Lund, Jens, and István Deák. "The Legend of King Christian: An Exchange." *New York Review.* March 29, 1990. https://www.nybooks.com/articles/1990/03/29/the-legend-of-king-christian-an-exchange/

Marquina, Antonio (1998). "The Spanish Neutrality during the Second World War." *American University International Law Review* 14, no. 1 (Article 10). https://digitalcommons.wcl.american.edu/cgi/viewcontent.cgi?referer=&httpsredir=1&article=1304&context=auilr

McGregor, Andrew. "In the Uniform of the Enemy: The Dutch Waffen-SS." HistoryNet. December 21, 2017. https://www.historynet.com/in-the-uniform-of-the-enemy/

National WW2 Museum. "Nazi Germany, Imperial Japan, and the Anti-Comintern Pact." November 17, 2021. https://www.nationalww2museum.org/war/articles/nazi-germany-imperial-japan-anti-comintern-pact

NATO (2022). "What is NATO?" https://www.nato.int/nato-welcome/index.html

Norton, Ben. "German EU official uses racist rhetoric claiming Russians don't value life." Multipolarista. April 15, 2022. https://multipolarista.com/2022/04/15/german-eu-official-russians-dont-value-life/

Norton, Benjamin, and Asa Winstanley. "Inside Operation Gladio: How NATO supported Nazis and terrorists." Multipolarista. May 6, 2022. https://multipolarista.com/2022/05/06/operation-gladio-nato-nazis-cia/

NPR. "The Secret Operation To Bring Nazi Scientists To America." February 15, 2014. https://www.npr.org/2014/02/15/275877755/the-secret-operation-to-bring-nazi-scientists-to-america

NSA (2019). "Understanding the CIA: How Covert (and Overt) Operations Were Proposed and Approved during the Cold War." National Security Archive. https://nsarchive.gwu.edu/briefing-book/intelligence/2019-03-04/understanding-cia-how-covert-overt-operations-proposed-approved-during-cold-war

NWM (2022a). "The 13th Waffen SS Mountain Division 'Handschar' (Croatian Nr.1)." https://www.nevingtonwarmuseum.com/german-volunteers---13th-waffen-ss-mountain-division-handschar-croatian-nr1.html

NWM (2022b). "21st Waffen Mountain Division of the SS Skanderbeg (1st Albanian)." https://www.nevingtonwarmuseum.com/21st-waffen-mountain-division-of-the-ss-skanderbeg-1st-albanian.html

Pakistan Defence. "German EU Official Uses Racist Rhetoric Claiming Russians Don't Value Life." April 22, 2022. https://defence.pk/pdf/threads/german-eu-official-uses-racist-rhetoric-claiming-russians-dont-value-life.740637/

Presseisen, Ernst L. "The Anti-Comintern Pact." In *Germany and Japan: A Study in Totalitarian Diplomacy 1933–1941* (International Scholars Forum book series. Dordrecht: Springer, 1958): 87–123. https://doi.org/10.1007/978-94-017-6590-9_4

Primidi (2017). "Collaboration During World War II – By Country—Norway." https://www.primidi.com/collaboration_during_world_war_ii/by_country/norway

Rosenberg, Jennifer. "Lebensraum: Hitler's Search for More German Living Space." ThoughtCo. March 23, 2020. https://www.thoughtco.com/lebensraum-eastern-expansion-4081248

Rossoliński-Liebe, Grzegorz. *Stepan Bandera: The Life and Afterlife of a Ukrainian Nationalist: Fascism, Genocide, and Cult* (Ibidem Press, 2014).

Roul, Animesh. "State Actors and Germ Warfare: Historical Perspective." *CBW Magazine* (July-December 2010). https://idsa.in/cbwmagazine/StateActorsandGermWarfare_aroul

RT. "A History of European Fascism." Centre for Counter Hegemonic Studies. September 2, 2021. Video, 54:54. https://www.youtube.com/watch?v=X_ra2VHjNAk

Ruggerio, Bob. "A Cautionary Tale of Hitler's American Friends." *Houston Press*. September 27, 2018. https://www.houstonpress.com/arts/the-nazis-admirers-in-the-united-states-10890545

Schere, Daniel. "Danish royal family was courageous during Holocaust." *Washington Jewish Week*. February 28, 2018. https://www.washingtonjewishweek.com/danish-royal-family-was-courageous-during-holocaust/

Scherner, Jonas. "Industrial Investment in Nazi Germany: The Forgotten Wartime Boom" (2006). https://www.semanticscholar.org/paper/Industrial-Investment-in-Nazi-Germany%3A-The-Wartime-Scherner/740b34dc8120e0e8b167b99a09d77d3b4530be2c

Shuriye, Abdi O. "Research: Al-shabaab's Leadership Hierarchy and Its Ideology." *Horn Affairs*. May 7, 2012. https://hornaffairs.com/2012/05/07/research-al-shabaabs-leadership-hierarchy-and-its-ideology/

Strobl, Gerwin. *The Germanic Isle*. Cardiff: University of Wales, 2007.

Summerton, Jonathan. "Swiss supplied arms to Nazi war machine." Swiss Info. March 22, 2002. https://www.swissinfo.ch/eng/swiss-supplied-arms-to-nazi-war-machine/2613736

Tabarovsky, Izabella. "Lev Simkin: 'The Holocaust Began in Ukraine.'" Wilson Centre. June 20, 2016. https://www.wilsoncenter.org/article/lev-simkin-the-holocaust-began-ukraine

World Population Review (2022). "World War II Casualties by Country." https://worldpopulationreview.com/country-rankings/world-war-two-casualties-by-country

WHL (2022). "German occupation and alliances." The Weiner Holocaust Library. https://www.theholocaustexplained.org/life-in-nazi-occupied-europe/occupation-case-studies/

WW2Database (2009). "The Pact of Steel, 22 May 1939." https://ww2db.com/battle_spec.php?battle_id=228

Yad Vashem (2022). "Murder of the Jews of the Baltic States." https://www.yadvashem.org/holocaust/about/final-solution-beginning/baltic-states.html

Yeager, Carolyn. "Anglo-German Naval Agreement of June 18, 1935." Carolyn Yeager. June 15, 2013. https://carolynyeager.net/anglo-german-naval-agreement-june-18-1935

5. Zionist Cancel Culture: Turning "Racism" on Its Head

The anti-semitism "trick" tries to hide vicious Israeli racism.
Source: SOTT

In recent times Western left-liberalism has been criticised for its 'cancel culture,' its obsession with language and individual identity politics. Yet reactionary cancel culture has been around much longer, witness the McCarthyist purges in the USA. To this reactionary camp we should add Zionist cancel culture (ZCC), where those critical of the Israeli colony in Palestine are purged from political, academic and media platforms.

These purges carry with them intimidation of public debate. After accusations of antisemitism, many are driven to avoid criticism of Israeli apartheid and ethnic cleansing in favour of safe moral equivalence clichés, like the 'Arab-Israeli conflict,' calling for 'even handed' treatment or 'mutual restraint' in face of the massacres and dispossession which remain central to the colonising process.

ZCC is characterised by its artificial charges of anti-Jewish 'racism' (anti-semitism, in its European usage) against those who dare to criticise the colony. What was once viewed in Europe as an issue of deep discrimination and even genocide has become a global cliché used to defend the Israeli colony. This 'racism' claim is peculiar, as most deep-seated racism arises from the crimes of colonisers who (like the Israelis) seek to degrade and disqualify the original inhabitants of the colonised land. In the case of Israel, the mostly European and North American colonisers masquerade as victims of racism, even as they ethnically cleanse the indigenous Palestinian people.

This peculiar phenomenon arose because Jewish communities which had suffered centuries of discrimination in Europe, mostly under the Christian empires, were encouraged by a new wave of European colonialism in the late 19th century to spawn their own colonial movement and imposed a reign of terror on the people of Palestine. The extreme 21st century efforts to cover up this simple historical fact tell us that the battle over Israel's legitimacy matters.

But why is so much effort expended in this battle, at this time? I suggest it has to do with the vulnerability of the colony and its strategic importance to Washington, the principal author of the New Middle East wars of the 21st century. Israel sits at the eye of a storm of multiple wars.

Many imagine that, through its military domination of Palestine and its powerful allies, Israel is in a strong position. This is a misunderstanding. In the 1980s Apartheid South Africa also had nuclear weapons, seemed invincible in the region and was backed by the USA and the UK. Yet within a few years that system collapsed (Eby and Morton 2017).

As Israeli leaders are well aware, the roots of the South African collapse lay in the linked elements of resistance and illegitimacy. Former Israeli Prime Ministers Ehud Barak and Ehud Olmert have both said that, once the illusion of a 'two states' solution disappears—given ongoing, substantial resistance—Israel will face an unwinnable anti-apartheid campaign (McCarthy 2007; Sommer 2017). So, it is worth looking more closely at resistance and legitimacy in order to understand the strenuous efforts of Zionist cancel culture.

21st century Zionist cancel culture

Zionist cancel culture is a concerted effort to extinguish voices which expose the apartheid nature of the alleged 'only democracy in the Middle East.' The main targets are those who actually side with the resistance.

The use of fake claims of anti-semitism to purge political leaders has its best recent example in the ejection of British Labour Party leader Jeremy Corbyn. Although leftist Corbyn was disliked by the British oligarchy for other reasons, it is no coincidence that alleged anti-semitism was central to the pretext used by his successor, Keir Starmer, to 'suspend' Corbyn from the party he once led (Scott 2020).

The move against Corbyn was part of a broader purge of critics of Israel within the alternate wing of the British state (Winstanley 2020; MEMO 2020). While Britain was the 'mother' of the zionist colony it is no longer the key hegemon in the West Asia. Nevertheless, a British government committed to the rights of the disenfranchised Palestinian people would have been a bitter blow to the colony. That threat has been removed for now.

In academia the purges have been most intense in the UK, France, and the USA—the NATO and permanent UNSC members—which matter most to the Israel lobby. The aim has been to remove platforms for critical voices in support of Palestine and of the regional resistance.

A recent *Guardian* article cited several British academics on the problem of university managers trying to "silence academics on social media." This was said to be part of a tension between the corporate university and social media, where "on the one hand unis are pushing their staff to be more active online … but when that individual voice is in conflict with the official brand it creates a tension … about brand protection" (Reidy 2020). The corporate media has also discovered it can use this tension to goad management to move against select academics.

The Israel lobby has spent time and effort in this territory, in particular by trying to vilify public figures who criticise Israel. It is claimed that the critics are acting in a 'racist' manner against Jewish people. The International Holocaust Remembrance Alliance (IHRA) has had some success in its attempts to extend the definition of anti-semitism "to criticism of Israel and support for Palestinian rights" (England 2017). This document is discussed below.

An Israel lobby group in the USA, under the guise of 'protecting Jewish students,' targeted as 'biased' more than 200 academics who supported the boycott against Israel (AMCHA 2014). Academics and teachers have been hounded from their positions in the USA, the UK, Australia, and New Zealand because of their comments on Israel, including those who have raised legitimate academic questions about the crimes of 'ethno-nationalist settler colonialism' and of 'victims becoming perpetrators' (Flaherty 2016; Sales 2020).

Jewish writers have not been immune from these attacks, and some have hit back, confirming that "unfounded allegations of anti-Semitism [are used] to cover up Israeli apartheid" (Handmaker 2019; Weiss 2019). More recently, sixty Jewish and Israeli academics criticised the German parliament for its attempts to equate the Boycott, Divestment and Sanctions movement with anti-semitism (O'Malley and Gardner 2019).

Similarly, a 2017 letter signed by more than 200 British academics complained of the Israel lobby's repeated attempts to link academic criticism of Israel and support for the Palestinian people with anti-semitism. These moves were deemed "outrageous interferences with free expression" and "direct attacks on academic freedom." The group said "we wish to express our dismay at this attempt to silence campus discussion about Israel, including its violation of the rights of Palestinians for more than 50 years. It is with disbelief that we witness explicit political interference in university affairs in the interests of Israel under the thin disguise of concern about anti-semitism" (Rosenhead 2017; England 2017)

Hegemonic states reinforce this process. In the USA President Donald Trump signed an executive order to withhold funds from universities which did not do enough to stop "anti-Semitic practices," specifically including criticism of Israel (Basken 2019).

Increasingly corporatised universities, for their part, feel vulnerable to possible damage to their reputation, and that is compounded by special interest (or funding) group sponsorship plus foreign influence laws which seek to bring academies into line with official government policy.

Importantly, the Western corporate and state media, for the most part, systematically exclude commentators critical of Israel, along with those who support resistance to Washington's New Middle East wars. This was well illustrated by CNN's severing of its connection with U.S. academic commentator Marc Lamont Hill (AP 2018).

When strong denunciations of Israeli apartheid are removed, Western debate more readily moves back into moral equivalence clichés, alongside demands to avoid alleged antisemitism which targets the apartheid colony. That has led to delusional campaigns against supposed anti-Jewish racism in the (post-Jeremy Corbyn) British Labour Party, simply because of that party's strong pro-Palestinian sentiment (Winstanley 2020).

Decline of the Zionist colony

The current state of Israel grew from demands of the late 19th century European and Russian zionist movement, in reaction to centuries of discrimination and periodic repression. While a concession was secured from Britain at the end of the First World War, based on land taken from the Ottomans, zionism was not popular even amongst European Jews until the Nazis' attempted genocide of 1941-45 (Black 1984). After the Second World War, in reaction to the Nazi Holocaust and the death camps, liberal Jews joined the Zionists, thinking that a Jewish refuge might be created, so long as it was not at the expense of the native Palestinians.

Yet the idea of cooperation and two states was always a myth. As Israeli historian Ilan Pappe pointed out in his book, *The Ethnic Cleansing of Palestine,* the chief architect of the colony, David Ben Gurion, wanted to seize "eighty to ninety percent" of British occupied Palestine, removing most of the Arab population. "Only a state with at least 80% Jews [would be] a viable and stable state," Ben Gurion told the party faithful in 1947 (Pappe 2006: 26, 48). Consequently, the final Plan Dalet of 1948 aimed at "destroying villages," wiping out armed resistance and making sure any resisting Arab "population [was] expelled outside the borders of the state" (Pappe 2006: 39). There followed multiple massacres, including the infamous razing of the village of Deir Yassin (McGowan and Hogan 1999).

More than seven decades later—still lacking its own state, and despite ongoing ethnic cleansing in the occupied West Bank plus the continued occupation of the Syrian Golan and parts of south Lebanon—the Palestinian Arab population has not diminished. Rather, it has begun to outnumber the Jewish Israeli population. Palestinians refused to disappear. Despite the denials of some zionist writers (Faitelson 2009; Eldar 2018), the Palestinian population has grown relative to the Jewish-Israeli population, notwithstanding the efforts of the colony to recruit immigrant Jews, mainly from eastern Europe and the USA.

Israeli sources confirm the pro-Palestinian shift. The Jewish Virtual Library shows that the Jewish population of Israel (called '1948 Palestine' by most Arabs) declined from a peak of 88.9% in 1960 to 74.7% in 2017 (JVL 2017). In parallel, officials from Israel's Central Bureau of Statistics and the military-run civil administration of the Occupied Territories (COGAT) say that the Arab population of Gaza, the West Bank and Arab citizens of Israel, along with residents of the annexed East Jerusalem municipality, add up to 6.5 million, about the same number as "Jews living between the Jordan Valley and the Mediterranean" (Heller 2018). So by the early 21st century Jewish Israelis and Palestinian Arabs were in equal numbers; and this is before we include the millions of exiled, refugee Palestinians.

Further, the Palestinian cause has grown in legitimacy, helped by Israeli brutality and arrogance. In 2018 an Israeli journalist published details of 2,700 assassinations carried out by zionist secret services: "more people [murdered] than any other country in the western world" (Bergman 2018: xxii). The open arrogance over such "achievements," the journalist says, blinds the colony's leadership to its strategic failures (Bergman 2018: 629). Despite a powerful Israel lobby in Europe, which tries to sanitise the occupation, 65% of Europeans recognise that Israel engages in religious discrimination (Abdullah and Hewitt 2012: 41-42, 279). The zionist argument that opposing Israel is seen as racist or anti-semitic is losing ground in Europe. Just over half (53%) of Europeans over 55 years of age still believe this but only 45% of 18–24-year-olds (Abdullah and Hewitt 2012: 292).

Recognition of Palestine at the UN level has grown while that of Israel has weakened. In 1988 the UNGA acknowledged the proclamation of the state of Palestine and began to use 'Palestine' in place of the

PLO for the delegation. In 2011 Palestine was admitted to UNESCO (MSPUN 2013). In reaction, in 2017, both Israel and the USA withdrew as members of UNESCO, citing anti-Israel bias (Beaumont 2017). When the UN's Human Rights Council passed several motions against Israel, including the call for an arms embargo, the zionist state's foreign minister reacted by calling for Israel to withdraw from that body (JPost 2018).

In 2012 the UNGA accorded 'Non-member observer state' status to the Palestinian delegation, marking the first time that the General Assembly considered Palestine to be a state (UNGA 2012). By 2018 137 UN member states recognised the State of Palestine (MSPUN 2018). One of the advantages of this advance has been the new capacity of the Palestinian Authority to recognise and adopt treaties such as the Statute of Rome, allowing Palestine to refer the zionist slaughter of civilians to the International Criminal Court as 'crimes against humanity' (Morrison 2018). That was not possible before 2012.

Yet the ongoing colonisation of the West Bank, despite occasional feeble European and U.S. protests, has undermined any real possibility of a two-state solution. All that is possible now is a type of fragmented Bantustan solution, such as that presented by Apartheid South Africa in the 1980s, just before that system crumbled (Swift 2020). The seven-decade fiction of an Arab state is maintained because, as former Prime Ministers Olmert and Barak recognised, without the two-state illusion the colony will face an unwinnable anti-apartheid campaign (McCarthy 2007; Sommer 2017).

The move towards some form of single state will almost certainly be through that anti-apartheid campaign, drawing on Palestinian resistance, further strengthening the international illegitimacy campaign alongside (in the best-case scenario) relative unity amongst Palestinian and regional resistance forces and relative disunity amongst the sponsors of the Israeli colony (Anderson 2018). Yet even dismantling the Apartheid regime would not solve all problems of the colony. As UN rapporteur Francesca Albanese (2022) has pointed out, even if equal citizenship were instituted that would not necessarily address the questions of war crimes, land theft and the millions of Palestinian refugees.

The survival of Israel as an apartheid state is not simply a matter of concern to the zionists, who strongly influence but do not control

Washington. The colony was facilitated by Britain but then inherited by the USA, which has used it as a means of destabilising and controlling the Middle East region. Its strategic role has become particularly acute as Washington fears a loss of influence in both Europe and Asia.

Former top U.S. official Zbigniew Brzezinski, in his 1997 book *The Grand Chessboard: American Primacy and Its Geostrategic Imperatives*, outlined Washington's need to block the impending peaceful integration of Eurasia, as that would put an end to U.S. global power. The extreme U.S. consternation at the rise of China and the role of Russia, alongside the multiple New Middle East wars of the 21st century (Anderson 2019), should be seen in this light. These considerations remain valid, notwithstanding Brzezinski's own realist adjustments, before his death, stating that "as its era of global dominance ends, the United States needs to take the lead in realigning the global power architecture" (Whitney 2016).

The Israeli regime (previously alongside Saudi Arabia, the key U.S. regional agent for sectarian terrorism—though this may change after the 2023 Saudi-Iranian rapprochement, facilitated by China) remains the central tool of U.S. influence in the Middle East region. That relationship was highlighted more than once by U.S. president Joe Biden. In 1986 the then Senator Biden said that Israel was "the best three billion dollar investment [per year] we make. Were there not an Israel the United States of America would have to invent an Israel, to protect our interests in the region" (Candidate Research 2019). In 2013 he repeated much the same argument: "if there were not an Israel, we would have to invent one to make sure our interests were preserved" (HDN 2013).

It is in this context—the desperation of the Israeli colony to avoid facing an open anti-apartheid campaign and the urgency of Washington, in face of the rise of China and Eurasian integration, to not lose control of West and Central Asia—that we can best understand the intense anti-semitism witch-hunts by the Israeli lobby.

This artificial attempt to redefine racism is complemented by the deeply racist campaign to pretend that the Palestinian people and Palestine simply do not exist (Greenfield 2019; Harsanyi 2019, MEE 2019). This is an adjunct to the constant ethnic cleansing of the West Bank, which succeeds in stealing land but fails to displace most of the colony's non-citizens.

The IHRA "definition," a.k.a. the anti-semitism "trick"

On 26 May 2016 the International Holocaust Remembrance Alliance (IHRA), a group which had previously focussed on opposing 'Holocaust Denial,' adopted a working definition of anti-Semitism. The document is said to have gained the endorsement of a number of European governments, as well as support from Israel and the USA. However, it is a misguided document which tries to link anti-Jewish racism with erroneous 'illustrations' mostly focused on Israel. These constant accusations of anti-zionism as anti-semitism attempt to shield the real racism of the Zionist colony.

More than a decade ago former Israeli minister Shulamit Aloni admitted that linking criticism of Israeli to anti-Jewish racism ('anti-semitism') was "a trick" used by the Israeli lobby. Calling someone anti-semitic for criticising Israel "is a trick," she said, "we always use it." When criticism comes from Europe "then we bring up the holocaust"; when Israel is criticised from the USA "then they are anti-semitic." The Israeli lobby has "power, media and other things and their attitude is, Israel my country right or wrong … they are not ready to hear criticism. … So to bring up the holocaust and the suffering of the Jewish people, that justifies everything we do to the Palestinians" (Aloni 2010).

That deceptive tradition is carried on by the IHRA, which has presented a working definition of anti-semitism as follows: "Antisemitism is a certain perception of Jews, which may be expressed as hatred toward Jews. Rhetorical and physical manifestations of antisemitism are directed toward Jewish or non-Jewish individuals and/or their property, toward Jewish community institutions and religious facilities" (IHRA 2016).

So far it might seem reasonable, if we accept that 'anti-Semitic' means anti-Jewish. However, as this is a Eurocentric concept which excludes many other groups of 'Semites,' not least Arabic speakers, a better term might be 'anti-Jewish.' There are at least two good reasons to clarify anti-Jewish racism, the first has to do with the long European history of discrimination against European Jews, the second concerns the mistaken conflation of Israel with the Jewish people.

However, the IHRA paper hopelessly confuses the matter by its appended illustrations, which conflate Jewish people with Israel and seek thereby to disqualify criticism of Israel. Eight of the twelve (at times contradictory) IHRA illustrations refer to the state of Israel, showing the IHRA's priorities and diverting the document from its stated purpose, of identifying anti-Jewish racism.

Racism and racial discrimination, as clarified by the 1965 Race Discrimination Convention, refer to discriminatory actions against 'human beings' (OHCHR 1965). That is, discrimination is something inflicted on people, not states. The subjects of rights are human beings (Yeatman 2000) and, in the case of collective rights such as the right to self-determination, 'peoples' (ICCPR 1966: Article 1; Mello 2004). 'Human rights' do not attach to any state. However, when states ratify international treaties, they "assume obligations and duties under international law to respect, to protect and to fulfil human rights" (UN 2019). Criticism of a state, therefore, should never be confused with prejudice or discrimination against a people.

While 'race' is a fictitious concept, as there are no intrinsic differences between human communities, as affirmed by the UN's Durban Declaration (OHCHR 2002: 11), and while Jewish people do not constitute an ethnicity (most are European), they certainly can be subject to racial discrimination or racism, as a religious community. The Durban Declaration reaffirms this in its rejection of "racial and violent movements based on racism and discriminatory ideas against Jewish, Muslim and Arab communities" (OHCHR 2002: 28).

The roots of anti-Jewish discrimination in Europe go back many centuries and appear to have grown in strength from the concepts and practices of the early Christian empires, beginning with Constantine (Carroll 2002; Julius 2010; Seaver 1952). From there, many European regimes practised systematic discrimination against Jewish people, excluding them from citizenship, taking their property or outright expulsions of entire populations, for example from France, England and Spain (Dahan 2004; Singer 1964; Beinart 2005). At other times Jews in medieval Europe, despite facing periodic discrimination, did well and their communities grew (Chazan 2010). Nevertheless, false stories of European Jews engaging in ritual murder were invented (Johnson 2012; Teter 2019).

Stereotypes developed in European literature helped reinforce prejudice against Jewish people. Shakespeare's character Shylock, in The Merchant of Venice, and Charles Dickens' Fagin, in *Oliver Twist*, both reflected and drove ugly stereotypes of hooked-nose old Jewish money lenders, either after their 'pound of flesh' (Shylock) or as criminal manipulators of children (Fagin). That sort of prejudiced imagery remains in many European cultures.

Periods of Christian revival and fanaticism, such as the crusades and the Spanish Inquisition (Kamen 2014), helped build strong anti-Jewish prejudice in Europe and drive practices of social exclusion and expulsion. All that preceded the great crimes of Nazi Germany against the European Jews, a history which deserves separate study. Millions of European Jews were murdered in a concerted campaign, promoted by multiple Nazi leaders, in a terrible campaign to 'annihilate' the Jewish people (Berben 1975; Van Pelt 2002; Friedländer 2009). Efforts to deny this great crime are ignorant and deplorable.

Yet that history has little to do with the zionist colonisation of Palestine, a British project which shares much of its racial history with other European colonisations, such as that of the Americas and Australia. In all these cases racial ideologies were developed in attempts to legitimise large scale ethnic cleansing and racial massacres. It is this imperial and colonial practice which lies at the root of the most serious forms of racism, including that inflicted on the Palestinian people.

Past imperial massacres led the Polish-Jewish lawyer Rafael Lemkin to coin the term 'genocide' as a 'recurring' feature of human history such as that seen in the destruction of Christian communities under the Ottomans (in Moses 2010: 8). Later, as the Nazi holocaust was underway, Lemkin wrote of genocide as "a coordinated plan … aiming at the destruction of essential foundations of the life of national groups, with the aim of annihilating the groups themselves" (Lemkin 1944: 79). When images of the death camps emerged in 1945, the term was correctly applied to Nazi Germany's systematic slaughter of the European Jews.

As shocking as that great crime was, similar genocides and mass killings had been carried out, many times, in the European colonies, for example the forced starvation of millions in Bengal over 1942-43, and the slaughter of millions by the Belgians in the Congo. The greatest recorded genocide occurred during the colonisation of the Americas, where 95% of the 75 to 100 million indigenous Americans were wiped out (Stannard 1992: 266-268; Churchill 1997).

Let's return to the IHRA 'working definition' and its appended 'illustrations.' On the positive side, an initial reference suggests recognition of equality before the law, a key legal and human rights theme. "Criticism of Israel similar to that levelled against any other country cannot be regarded as anti-semitic," the document says. Later on, confusing a people with a state, the document suggests that anti-Semitism may include: "applying double standards by requiring of it a behavior not expected or demanded of any other democratic nation." Were this a reference to Jewish people it may be correct. But the notion of equality before the law is negated by much of which follows, especially about the state of Israel.

The document suggests that the following criticisms of Israel are effectively prohibited, as an anti-semitic form of racism:

- "The targeting of the state of Israel, conceived as Jewish collectivity";
- "Denying the Jewish people their right to self-determination, e.g. by claiming that the existence of the state of Israel is a racist endeavour"; and
- "Drawing comparisons of contemporary Israeli policy to that of the Nazis."

The idea that Israel cannot be targeted or criticised as a "racist endeavour" is an absurd suggestion, contradicting the IHRA's citation of equality before the law. Any state that practices ethnic cleansing and civilian massacres, based on racial ideology, should be criticised severely. No state can claim immunity from criticism, as that would encourage more great crimes. The foundation of the state of Israel through ethnic cleansing has been well documented (Pappe 2006); an Israelis-Palestinian civil rights group has documented more than 65 racist laws created by the zionist state (Adalah 2017).

It is true that recourse to comparisons with Nazi Germany are made too often. Nevertheless, when a state (i) demonstrates a racial ideology which dehumanises a supposedly distinct race, (ii) carries out massacres based on such ideology and (iii) engages in systematic ethnic cleansing, comparisons with prior fascist regimes including that of Nazi Germany may be justified. Indeed, such comparisons may be valuable in highlighting great crimes and inducing shame in their apologists. None of this is unique to Israel, but all elements apply to contemporary Israel, a largely European Jewish colony which, by blocking all possibilities of a contiguous Arab state, has become an apartheid state (CCHS 2022).

Naturally many Jewish people who support Israel (often expressed as a haven for Jews who suffered persecution in Europe) will not like comparisons between Israel and the fascist German state which carried out genocidal practices against their own religious community. But this is often the consequence of colonial practice, and Israel is not unique in that regard. Other persecuted and impoverished European minorities came to Australia, Canada and the Americas only to take part in the ethnic cleansing and genocide of indigenous populations. Many liberal Jews imagined that the Israeli colony might serve as a refuge for persecuted European Jews. But, like the late Albert Einstein, they naively dreamed this might happen without prejudice to the native population of Palestine (Jerome 2009).

The question of genocidal practice against the Palestinian people by the Israeli state is an important theme of international debate. The U.S.-based Center for Constitutional Rights set out some terms of this debate, citing several scholars for the affirmative—Martin Shaw, Francis Boyle, Ilan Pappe and the late Michael Ratner. They observed that the *Journal of Genocide Studies*, while presenting opposing positions, rejected complaints that this was an "illegitimate" question to pose or debate (CCR 2016: 3-5). The CCR also noted that even "dozens of [Jewish] Holocaust survivors" had accused Israel of "genocide" over its attacks on Gaza and cited Amnesty International's call for the ICC to investigate and "break the culture of impunity" in Israel "which perpetuates the commission of war crimes" (CCR 2016: 6-7).

In 2002 the UN's Durban Declaration (of the 'World Conference Against Racism, Racial Discrimination, Xenophobia and Related Intolerance') expressed concerns about "the plight of the Palestinian people under foreign occupation and recognised the right of the Palestinian people to self-determination under an independent state" (OHCHR 2002: 2, 29, 101). Yet the possibility of such an independent Arab state has been buried by successive Israeli administrations, creating an effective apartheid state, where half the population, by reason of their ethnic or religious community have no equal rights, and in most cases, no citizenship. The Durban Declaration condemned the crimes of apartheid and genocide as crimes against humanity (OHCHR 2002: 9, 17, 20, 37-38) and several authoritative reports—such as that from U.S. lawyers Richard Falk and Virginia Tilley (2017)—now make it clear that Israel has indeed become an apartheid state and, therefore, as a crime against humanity, its system of apartheid must be dismantled (Falk, Dugard, and Lynk 2023).

Former Israeli Prime Minister Ehud Olmert (2007) recognised that "if the day comes when the two-state solution collapses, and we face a South African-style struggle for equal voting rights … the State of Israel is finished." The extensive Israeli ethnic cleansing in recent years has created that very circumstance. In this context, seeking to exempt Israel from criticism of its racist practice is an affront to the principles of anti-racism and equality before the law. Such efforts try to cover up the crimes of colonialism.

Some of the IHRA's other suggested 'racist' practices have to do with banning 'holocaust denial' and exempting Jewish communities from criticism:

- Denying the fact, scope, mechanisms (e.g. gas chambers) or intentionality of the genocide of the Jewish people at the hands of National Socialist Germany and its supporters and accomplices during World War II (the Holocaust).
- "Accusing the Jews as a people, or Israel as a state, of inventing or exaggerating the Holocaust";
- "Accusing Jewish citizens of being more loyal to Israel … than to the interests of their own nations"; and
- "Holding Jews collectively responsible for actions of the state of Israel."

There should be no doubt that the Nazi German attempt at genocide of European Jews was a terrible crime which should be remembered. However, whether 'denial' should be criminalised (as is the case in several European states) is another matter. There may well be short term exigencies in suppressing the resurgence of fascism in Europe. However, declaring state-sanctioned 'official truth' (e.g. EUVSDISINFO 2020), jailing the odd person and suppressing debates on history is likely to create adverse reactions. What is wrong with states assisting in popular education by extensive museum display—and school study—of the evidence of these great crimes and their associated racial ideologies? New generations learn better through investigation, reason and evidence, than by decreed dogma.

As for a ban on discussion of criticism of Jewish communities and their organisations, while this may address negative stereotypes, there are good reasons why religious communities and their secret and public organisations should not be exempt from scrutiny. If, for example, the secret Mossad run 'sayanim' group cannot be discussed, because it is a secret Jewish network, why should we not also ban discussion of secretive Catholic networks like Opus Dei, or secretive Muslim groups like the Muslim Brotherhood? Similarly, if discussion of the German peoples' responsibility for the rise of the Nazi regime in Germany may be discussed (e.g. Johnson and Reuband 2006), why not the support of Jewish communities for the rise of apartheid Israel?

Privileging certain communities in the name of human rights and anti-racism has serious problems. Several honest writers, not unsympathetic to Jewish people, have pointed out that a racialised Israel is the greatest contemporary source of anti-Jewish prejudice. That was the theme of *Zionism: the real enemy of the Jews*, by British journalist Alan Hart, a confidant of the late Israeli Prime Minister Golda Meir. His argument was that the crimes of Israel against the people of Palestine help inflame rising anti-Jewish feelings in Europe and the Americas. In a related way, anti-zionist religious Jews complain that they are blamed for the crimes of Israel. Rabbi Yaakov Shapiro says that the recent declaration of Israel as 'the nation-state of the Jewish people' is "a bogus notion and dangerous for Jews around the world" (TTJ 2018).

The IHRA statement has come under attack from scholars of Jewish history and anti-semitism, notably Professor David Feldman, who observes "three fatal problems" with the IHRA statement: there is no reference to the universal fight against all forms of discrimination and bigotry, the core of the statement is widely misrepresented, and it serves as a basis for "conflating the interests of Israel" with "the struggle against antisemitism" (Feldman 2022). Feldman says "we lose our way when the struggle against antisemitism, a movement intended to protect Jewish minorities from intolerance and violence, becomes closely aligned with the political interests of the state of Israel." He and others have promoted another statement, The Jerusalem Declaration, which aims to join struggles against anti-semitism with wider struggles against 'all forms of racial discrimination.'

The history, myths and evils of European anti-Jewish racism certainly deserve attention. But racism more broadly stems from imperialism and colonialism. To link the essentially colonial and racist state of Israel with a definition of anti-Jewish racism is a travesty. Attempts to ban discussions of victims becoming perpetrators and re-colonisation are going nowhere. Meanwhile we are presented with distorted discussions about racism, from relatively privileged European and North American zionists, backed by billionaires. They secure their second passports and cry 'racism' when attacked for dispossessing indigenous Palestinians. That is the perverse narrative zionist cancel culture has helped create, another aspect of what the late Eduardo Galeano called the "upside down world."

References

Abdullah, Daud, and Ibrahim Hewitt. *The Battle for Public Opinion in Europe*. London: MEMO Publishers, 2012.

Adalah. "The Discriminatory Laws Database." September 25, 2017. https://www.adalah.org/en/content/view/7771

Albanese, Francesca. "Report of the Special Rapporteur on the situation of human rights in the Palestinian territories occupied since 1967, Francesca Albanese (A/77/356) [EN/AR]." Relief Web. October 22, 2022. https://reliefweb.int/report/occupied-palestinian-territory/report-special-rapporteur-situation-human-rights-palestinian-territories-occupied-1967-francesca-albanese-a77356-enar

Aloni, Shulamit. "Anti-semitic, it's a trick we always use it." stevenbennett100. June 26, 2010. Video, 1:21. https://www.youtube.com/watch?v=D0kWAqZxJVE

AMCHA (2014). "AMCHA Publishes List of Over 200 Anti-Israel Middle East Studies Professors." https://amchainitiative.org/amcha-publishes-list-of-over-200-anti-israel-middle-east-studies-professors/

Anderson, Tim. "The Future of Palestine." Centre for Counter Hegemonic Studies. August 7, 2018. https://counter-hegemonic-studies.site/future-palestine-1/

———. *Axis of Resistance.* Atlanta: Clarity Press, 2019.

———. "What's wrong with the IHRA 'working definition'of Anti-Semitism?" *Black Agenda Report.* January 29, 2020. https://www.blackagendareport.com/whats-wrong-ihra-working-definition-anti-semitism

AP. "CNN ends contract with contributor Mark Lamont Hill after speech on Israe." *The Guardian.* November 30, 2018. https://www.theguardian.com/media/2018/nov/29/cnn-marc-lamont-hill-israel

Basken, Paul. "Trump tells universities to halt campus criticism of Israel." Times Higher Education. December 12, 2019. https://www.timeshighereducation.com/news/trump-tells-universities-halt-campus-criticism-israel

Beinart, Haim. *The Expulsion of the Jews from Spain.* Liverpool: Littman Library of Jewish Civilization, 2005.

Berben, Paul. *Dachau: The Official History 1933–1945.* London: The Norfolk Press, 1975.

Bergman, Ronan. *Rise and Kill First.* New York: Random House, 2018.

Beaumont, Peter. "UNESCO: Israel joins US in quitting UN heritage agency over 'anti-Israel bias.'" *The Guardian.* October 13, 2017. https://www.theguardian.com/world/2017/oct/12/us-withdraw-unesco-december-united-nations

Black, Edwin. "The Transfer Agreement: The Untold Story of the Secret Pact Between the Third Reich and Jewish Palestine." Exton: Revaluation Books, 1984.

Brzezinski, Zbigniew. *The Grand Chessboard: American Primacy and Its Geostrategic Imperatives.* New York: Basic Books, 1997.

Candidate Research. "Joe Biden says if Israel didn't exist, the US would have to invent one to protect US interests" (Senate Session, June 5, 1986). Candidate Research. March 3, 2019. Video clip, 0:33. https://www.youtube.com/watch?v=FYLNCcLflkM

Carroll, James. *Constantine's Sword: The Church and the Jews, A History.* Boston: Houghton Mifflin Harcourt, 2001.

CCR. "The Genocide of the Palestinian People: An International Law and Human Rights Perspective." Centre for Constitutional Rights. August 25, 2016. https://ccrjustice.org/

genocide-palestinian-people-international-law-and-human-rights-perspective

CCHS. "SIX (6) important reports on Israeli Apartheid." February 24, 2022. https://counter-hegemonic-studies.site/israeli-apartheid-6/

Chazan, Robert. *Reassessing Jewish Life in Medieval Europe.* Cambridge University Press, 2010.

Churchill, Ward. *A Little Matter of Genocide: Holocaust and Denial in the Americas, 1492 to the Present.* San Francisco: City Lights Books, 1997.

Dahan, Gilbert. *L'Expulsion des Juifs de France: 1394.* Paris, Le Cerf, 2004.

Dickens, Charles. *Oliver Twist.* 1937.

Eby, John C., and Fred Morton. *The Collapse of Apartheid and the Dawn of Democracy in South Africa, 1993.* Chapel Hill, N.C.: Reacting Consortium Press, 2017.

Eldar, Shlomi. "Israelis, Palestinians both use demography as political tool." Al-Monitor. March 27, 2018. http://www.al-monitor.com/pulse/originals/2018/03/israel-palestinians-west-bank-gaza-strip-demography-abbas.html#ixzz5GHEEjBy2

England, Charlotte. "Free speech on Israel is under threat from groups conflating criticism of country with anti-Semitism, say academics." *The Independent.* March 1, 2017. https://www.independent.co.uk/news/uk/home-news/free-speech-israel-anti-semitism-university-academics-criticisms-jews-palestinian-rights-international-holocaust-remembrance-alliance-a7605306.html

EUVSDISINFO (2020). "EUvsDisinfo database." https://euvsdisinfo.eu

Faittelson, Yakov. "The Politics of Palestinian Demography." *Middle East Quarterly* 16, no. 2 (Spring/March 2009). https://www.meforum.org/articles/2009/the-politics-of-palestinian-demography

Falk, Richard, and Virginia Tilley. "Israeli Practices towards the Palestinian People and the Question of Apartheid." *Palestine and the Israeli Occupation, Issue No. 1.* Beirut: UN Economic and Social Commission for Western Asia (ESCWA), 2017. https://counter-hegemonic-studies.site/wp-content/uploads/2018/03/Falk-Tilley-un_apartheid_report_15_march_english_final_.pdf

Falk, Richard, John Dugard, and Michael Lynk (2023) *Protecting Human Rights in Occupied Palestine: working through the United Nations.* Atlanta: Clarity Press, 2023.

Feldman, David. "9th UNAOC global forum—Breakout Session 3" [video 1:33:33]. *UN Web TV.* November 22, 2022. https://media.un.org/en/asset/k1y/k1y7rnpl8e

Flaherty, Colleen. "Oberlin Ousts Professor." Inside HigherEd. November 16, 2016. https://www.insidehighered.com/news/2016/11/16/oberlin-fires-joy-karega-following-investigation-her-anti-semitic-statements-social

Friedländer, Saul. *Nazi Germany and the Jews.* London: Phoenix, 2009.

Greenfield, Daniel. "Peace doesn't exist; neither do the Palestinians." *Arutz Sheva 7.* July 25, 2019. https://www.israelnationalnews.com/Articles/Article.aspx/24206

Handmaker, Jeff. "Unfounded allegations of anti-Semitism cover up Israeli apartheid." *MondoWeiss.* March 4, 2019. https://mondoweiss.net/2019/03/unfounded-allegations-apartheid/

Harsanyi, David. "Sorry You're Offended, But 'Palestine' Does Not Exist." *The Federalist.* April 2, 2019. https://thefederalist.com/2019/04/02/sorry-palestine-does-not-exist/

Hart, Alan. *Zionism: The Real Enemy of the Jews,* Volume 1. Neha Publishers & Distributors, 2005.

HDN (2013) "If there were no Israel, we'd have to invent one: Biden." *Hurriyet Daily News.* October 2, 2013. https://www.hurriyetdailynews.com/if-there-were-no-israel-wed-have-to-invent-one-biden-55494

Heller, Jeffrey. "Jews, Arabs nearing population parity in Holy Land: Israeli officials." Reuters. March 27, 2018. https://www.reuters.com/article/us-israel-palestinians-population/jews-arabs-nearing-population-parity-in-holy-land-israeli-officials-idUSKBN1H222T

IHRA (2016). "Working Definition of Antisemitism." https://www.holocaustremembrance.com/working-definition-antisemitism

JDA (2021). "The Jerusalem Declaration on antisemitism," https://jerusalemdeclaration.org

Jerome, Fred. *Einstein on Israel and Zionism.* London: St Martin's Press, 2009.

Johnson, Eric A., and Karl-Heinz Reuband. *What We Knew: Terror, Mass Murder, and Everyday Life in Nazi Germany.* New York: Basic Books, 2006.

Johnson, Hannah. *Blood Libel: The Ritual Murder Accusation at the Limit of Jewish History.* University of Michigan Press, 2012.

JPost. "Lieberman: Israel must immediately withdraw from U.N. Human Rights Council." *Jerusalem Post.* May 17, 2018. https://www.jpost.com/Breaking-News/Liberman-Israel-must-withdraw-immediately-from-UN-Human-Rights-Council-556701

JVL (2017). "Demographics of Israel: Jewish & Non-Jewish Population of Israel/Palestine (1517–Present)." Jewish Virtual Library. http://www.jewishvirtuallibrary.org/jewish-and-non-jewish-population-of-israel-palestine-1517-present

Julius, Anthony. *Trials of the Diaspora: A History of Anti-Semitism in England.* Oxford University Press, 2010.

Kamen, Henry. *The Spanish Inquisition.* Yale University Press, 2014.

Lemkin, Raphael (1944). *Axis Rule in Occupied Europe.* Clark, NJ: The Lawbook Exchange, 2005.

McCarthy, Rory. "Israel risks apartheid-like struggle if two-state solution fails, says Olmert." *The Guardian.* December 1, 2007. https://www.theguardian.com/world/2007/nov/30/israel

McGowan, Daniel A., and Matthew C. Hogan. *The Saga of Deir Yassin: Massacre, Revisionism, and Reality.* Geneva, New York: Deir Yassin Remembered, 1999. https://www.deiryassin.org/SAGA.html

MEE. "Yair Netanyahu says Palestine does not exist because there is no 'P' in Arabic." *Middle East Eye.* April 23, 2019. https://www.middleeasteye.net/news/yair-netanyahu-says-palestine-does-not-exist-because-there-no-p-arabic

Mello, Brian. "Recasting the Right to Self-Determination: Group Rights and Political Participation." *Social Theory and Practice* 30, no. 2 (April 2004): 193–213.

MEMO. "Britain's Labour Party accused of purging members critical of Israel." *Middle East Monitor.* June 17, 2020. https://www.middleeastmonitor.com/20200617-britains-labour-party-accused-of-purging-members-critical-of-israel/

Morrison, David. "The ICC Prosecutor Warns Israel about Gaza Killings." *American Herald Tribune.* June 9, 2018. https://ahtribune.com/world/north-africa-south-west-asia/palestine/2295-icc-prosecutor-gaza-killings.html

Moses, A. Dirk (Editor). Empire, Colony, Genocide. Oxford: Berghahn Books, 2010.

MSPUN. "Status of Palestine." Mission of the State of Palestine to the UN. Aug. 1, 2013. http://palestineun.org/status-of-palestine-at-the-united-nations/

OHCHR (1965). "International Convention on the Elimination of All Forms of Racial Discrimination." Office of the High Commissioner for Human Rights. https://www.ohchr.org/en/professionalinterest/pages/cerd.aspx

——— (1966). "International Covenant on Civil and Political Rights." Office of the High Commissioner for Human Rights. https://www.ohchr.org/en/professionalinterest/pages/ccpr.aspx

——— (2002). "World Conference Against Racism, Racial Discrimination, Xenophobia and Related Intolerance: Declaration and Programme of Action" [Durban Declaration]. New York: United Nations. https://www.ohchr.org/Documents/Publications/Durban_text_en.pdf

O'Malley, Brendan, and Michael Gardner. "Academics oppose motion against Israel boycott campaign." *University World News*. May 25, 2019. https://www.universityworldnews.com/post.php?story=20190523080603l2

Olmert, Ehud. "Olmert to Haaretz: Two-state Solution, or Israel Is Done For." Haaretz, November 29, 2007. https://www.haaretz.com/1.4961269

Pappe, Ilan. *The Ethnic Cleansing of Palestine.* Oxford: One World, 2006.

Ranciere, Jacques. "Who is the subject of the rights of man?" *The South Atlantic Quarterly* 103, no. 2/3, (Spring 2004): 297–310.

Reidy, Tess. "'Naked intimidation': How universities silence academics on social media." *The Guardian.* Feb. 12, 2020. https://www.theguardian.com/education/2020/feb/12/naked-intimidation-how-universities-silence-academics-on-social-media

Rosenhead, Jonathan. "Free speech on Israel under attack in universities." *The Guardian.* February 28, 2017. https://www.theguardian.com/education/2017/feb/27/university-wrong-to-ban-israeli-apartheid-week-event

Sales, Ben. "Elite NYC prep school fires Jewish teacher who posted anti-Zionist tweets." *Times of Israel.* January 10, 2020. https://www.timesofisrael.com/elite-nyc-prep-school-fires-jewish-teacher-who-posted-anti-zionist-tweets/

Scott, Jennifer. "Why was Jeremy Corbyn suspended from the Labour Party?" *BBC.* October 30, 2020. https://www.bbc.com/news/uk-politics-54746452

Seaver, James Everett. *The Persecution of the Jews in the Roman Empire (300–428).* Lawrence, KS: University of Kansas Pubs., 1952.

Shakespeare, William. *The Merchant of Venice.* 1599.

Singer, Sholom A. "The expulsion of the Jews from England in 1290." *The Jewish Quarterly Review* 55, no. 2 (October 1964): 117–136.

Sommer, Allison Kaplan. "Ehud Barak Warns: Israel Faces 'Slippery Slope' Toward Apartheid." *Haaretz,* June 21, 2017. https://www.haaretz.com/israel-news/ehud-barak-warns-israel-on-slippery-slope-to-apartheid-1.5486786

Stannard, David E. *American Holocaust: The Conquest of the New World.* New York: Oxford University Press, 1992.

Swift, Robert (2020) "Legacy of South African Bantustans hangs over Trump deal." *+972 Magazine.* February 9, 2020. https://www.972mag.com/apartheid-bantustans-palestinian-statehood/

Teter, Magda. *Blood Libel: On the Trail of an Antisemitic Myth.* Cambridge, Mass.: Harvard University Press, 2019.

TTJ. "Rabbi Yaakov Shapiro on Israel's Nation State Law." True Torah Jews. August 22, 2018. Instructional video, 4:49. https://www.youtube.com/watch?v=2XJsisX4Umk

UN (2019). "The Foundation of International Human Rights Law." United Nations. https://www.un.org/en/sections/universal-declaration/foundation-international-human-rights-law/index.html

UNGA. "General Assembly Votes Overwhelmingly to Accord Palestine 'Non-Member Observer State' Status in United Nations." November 29, 2012. https://www.un.org/press/en/2012/ga11317.doc.htm

Van Pelt, Robert Jan. *The Case for Auschwitz: Evidence from the Irving Trial* (Bloomington: Indiana University Press, 2002).

Weiss, Phillip. "Don't blame the Israel lobby on Christians and Republicans." *MondoWeiss,* February 12, 2019. https://mondoweiss.net/2019/02/israel-christians-republicans/

Whitney, Mike. "The Broken Chessboard: Brzezinski Gives Up on Empire." *CounterPunch.* August 25, 2016. https://www.counterpunch.org/2016/08/25/the-broken-chessboard-brzezinski-gives-up-on-empire/

Winstanley, Asa. "New Labour purge against Israel critics." Electronic Intifada. May 20, 2020. https://electronicintifada.net/blogs/asa-winstanley/new-labour-purge-against-israel-critics

Yeatman, Anna. "Who is the subject of human rights?" *The American Behavioral Scientist* 43, no. 9, (Jun/Jul 2000): 1498–1513.

6. The Kurdish Card in Syria

On the streets of Qamishli (2021) Christian and Syrian nationalist images compete with those of Kurdish separatism

From Manbij

Late 2019. We are sitting at a joint military command centre in Arima (northern Syria, just west of Manbij) with three Syrian Arab Army (SAA) colonels and two uniformed Kurdish SDF 'koval' (comrades). There are Russians here too, but they do not enter our conversation. Yet even in the friendly chat, as we wait for permission to travel on to Manbij and Ayn al Arab (Kobane), some tensions are apparent.

Sharing coffee and food, both the SAA officers and the SDF (Syrian Democratic Forces, a Kurdish separatist group, QSD in Arabic) comrades acknowledge they are fighting and dying together against an invading Turkish army and its proxy militias. The frontline is just a few kilometres away.

When I ask what differences there are between DAESH, Nusra and the 'Free Army,' they all respond derisively. "There is no difference, it is a money game, the fighters go back and forwards depending on the pay rates." "Any difference between groups in the numbers of foreigners?" I ask. "No difference," they repeat. SDF Comrade B passes me a recent video of 'Free Army' fighters at Tal Abiad, to the north-east, protesting pay and conditions and demanding their return to HTS/Nusra controlled Idlib.

But we all know they fight for a different cause. The SAA officers are fighting for a liberated and united Syria, while the SDF comrades still dream of an independent 'Kurdistan' cut out from parts of contemporary Turkey, Syria, Iraq and possibly also Iran. Conveniently, the later three are all states Washington wants to divide and weaken.

Separatist Kurds collaborated with U.S. occupation forces in pursuit of their 'Rojava' (western Kurdistan) dream, even though Washington has never openly supported the project. Many Syrians see these Kurds as traitors. But Damascus is patient, dealing with one enemy at a time and, for the moment, the common enemy in north Syria is Erdogan and his gangs.

The 'Rojava' dream is effectively dead. As both Afrin (in March 2018) and Manbij (in October 2019) demonstrated, no Kurdish militia can defend itself from Ankara, which correctly sees any 'Rojava' statelet as a steppingstone for the bigger game, a large slice of Turkey. Protection by U.S. occupation forces will not last forever. Moreover, Kurdish groups have no exclusive historical claims over any parts of northern Syria. Many other peoples live there. In most of north and east Syria Kurds are a small minority.

Despite these tensions there is a close, even affectionate, relationship in the room. The SAA colonels are all older men in their 40s and 50s, while the SDF comrades are younger men, around 30 years old. Colonel H offers more coffee to Comrade A while Comrade B tells of Kurdish conquests. "We lost 850 martyrs liberating Manbij," he says, and "2,000 in Kobane." And what about all those in your prisons? one of the colonels asks. "They are reformatories," Comrade B replies.

Between Aleppo and Manbij (in 2021) there was a switch from checkpoints controlled by the Syrian Arab Army to those controlled by the Kurdish SDF, even though the SAA and Russia provided the main security from Erdogan's Islamist militia.

What Comrade B does not say about the "liberation" of Manbij is that (1) the 2016 battle was effectively a transfer of the city from one U.S. proxy (ISIS/DAESH) to another (SDF), and (2) there were and are very few Kurds in that mostly Arab city. After major battles with ISIS, many from surrounding areas fled to the city, swelling its population. A recent estimate put its population at 700,000, of which 80% are Arab (Najjar 2019). Of the rest there are other non-Arab minorities, including Assyrians, Circassians and Armenians. There is no real social base for a separatist Kurd regime in Manbij.

Yet even after the departure of U.S. occupation forces from this part of northern Syria, and even though the Syrian and Russian presence constrains Turkish ambitions, the SDF has been allowed to maintain its former administration of both the city and the region.

The bizarre and unsustainable nature of this regime is made apparent when my Syrian journalist colleague, asks one of the colonels to show us where we are. Colonel A happily rolls out a military map, with friend and enemy troop placements. The first thing apparent is that six Syrian armoured units protect Manbij to the north. Second, although Syrian forces have resumed control of more than 200km of the northern border, it is depressing to see how much of northern Syria remains occupied by Erdogan and his proxies.

The picture seemed even more grim when we later spoke with a Manbij councillor and his lawyer friend. They complained of many held in prison and tortured under the SDF regime. They said there were only two Kurd villages in rural Manbij.

Nevertheless, it seemed that a transition was slowly taking place. Over November-December both Syrian and Russian flags were raised over previous SDF positions in Hassakah, Ayn al Arab, Jarablus and Tal Jemaa (Syrian Observer 2019; Semenov 2019; SOHR 2019), with suggestions that the SDF was involved in negotiations with Damascus "to reach conclusive solutions." However, SDF leader Mazloum Abadi said that the group wanted "Syrian unity … [with] decentralised self administration" including maintenance of the separate SDF militia (Syrian Observer 2019). Damascus is unlikely to accept such terms.

A Kurdish homeland?

The claim for a Kurdish homeland in Syria is not an indigenous movement claiming the return of ancestral lands. Nor does the debate over Kurds as historical migrants (Yildiz 2005) or long-standing inhabitants (Hennerbichler 2012: 77-78) resolve the question. While Kurdish languages are of Iranian origin, and their longer history passes through Mesopotamia (Iraq) and the Ottoman empire, Kurds are certainly part of the native Syrian population. However, numbered at 1.5 million Kurds, Syria hosts the smallest group in the region, with around 20 million in Turkey (Gürbüz 2016: 31) and another 6-8 million each in Iran and Iraq.

The idea of a 'Rojava' statelet in Syria has been compromised in three ways. First, the Kurdish groups in north and north-east Syria are only one of several groups (amongst Assyrians, Circassians, Armenians and Arabs), and in some areas, they are small minorities. Second, the Kurdish separatist movement in Syria has been over-determined by the politics of and migration from Turkey. Rojava was seen as the steppingstone for a larger Kurdistan project, driven from the north. Third, intervention by the imperial power raised separatist expectations and reciprocal fears, damaging Kurdish relations with other Syrian groups. These social contradictions are often not well recognised by the many self-referential studies of Kurdish identity (e.g. Al Kati 2019).

In the longer history of Syria, a traditional refuge for minorities, there have been many Kurds, including famous personalities, who did not buy into the separatist dream. Two of them are buried inside the grounds of the Ummayad Mosque in Damascus: the 12th century ruler, Sala'addin, and the Quranic scholar, Sheikh Mohammad al Bouti (murdered by Jabhat al Nusra in 2013). Many Syrians of Kurdish origin embraced the idea of a wider identity. Before the 2011 conflict Tejel (2009: 39-46) classified Syrian Kurdish identities as comprising Arab nationalists, communists and Kurdish nationalists, with Syrian Kurd leaders Husni Za'im and Adib al-Shishakli campaigning for a non-sectarian 'Greater Syria.'

The Turkish Kurd influence began early in the 20th century, as Kurdish culture was repressed by post-Ottoman Turkish nationalism. Turkish Kurds first took refuge in Syria, including in Damascus, after their failed rebellion in 1925. The very idea of a Syrian Kurdish party first arose in 1956 from the Turkish refugee Osman Sabri; another Turkish refugee Nûredîn Zaza, became president of that party (al Kati 2019: 45, 47).

There were multiple splits in subsequent years. The Democratic Union Party (PYD) emerged in the 1980s as a branch of the Kurdistan Workers Party (PKK), loyal to its leader Abdallah Öcalan, who in 1996 acknowledged that "most of the Kurds of Syria were refugees and migrants from Turkey and they would benefit from returning there" (in Allsop 2014: 231). Many of the claims about 'stateless' Kurds in Syria have to be read in light of this Turkish influx. However, Öcalan departed in 1998, following Syria's Adana agreement with Turkey (al Kati 2019: 49-52).

The big powers, conscious of the potentially divisive role of separatist Kurds, have used them for decades to divide and weaken Arab governments. U.S. regional allies Israel and Iran (pre-1979) joined in, with Iran's Shah in 1962 ordering his SAVAK secret police to help finance the Kurdish insurgency in northern Iraq, so as to undermine Baghdad. The Israelis joined in two years later. The CIA offered further help to the Barzani-led Kurds in 1972. One result was that Iraq was unable to join the Arab resistance against Israeli expansion in 1967 and 1973 because a large part of its military was deployed against the Kurds in northern Iraq (Gibson 2019).

The U.S.-led hybrid war on Syria in 2011 presented new separatist opportunities. Peoples Protection Units (YPG) were reactivated in 2012, at first with support from Damascus so that Syrians in the north could fight ISIS. However, the U.S. occupation of parts of north and east Syria in late 2015 led to the reorganisation of many YPG units into the U.S.-sponsored 'Syrian Democratic Forces' (SDF) (Martin 2018: 96). These were sometimes referred to as a 'Rojava' force, while at other times the Kurdish component was played down.

According to one U.S. military report in 2017 the SDF in Manbij was only 40% Kurd (Townsend in Humud, Blanchard and Nikitin 2017: 12), addressing the embarrassing reality that Manbij had a very small Kurdish population. In late 2016 U.S. Col. John Dorrian gave a different estimate, saying that the SDF "consists of approximately 45,000 fighters, more than 13,000 of which are Arab" (USDOD 2016). Many of the latter came from the fragments of an earlier U.S. proxy militia in Syria.

However Syrian Colonel Malek from Aleppo confirmed to me that the bulk of SDF members were always Kurdish, including many from Turkey and Iraq. The size of the non-Kurd and foreigner contingents varied according to the money on offer. A report from the London-based International Centre for the Study of Radicalisation and Political Violence (ICSR) recognised that both the YPG and SDF ground forces remained largely arms of the Turkish PKK (Holland-McCowan 2017: 10).

Turkish Kurd leader Abdullah Öcalan is at the head of the Kurdish separatist movement in Syria, Source SDF

The failure of a September 2017 separatist referendum in Iraq dealt a serious blow to the Kurdish regional project. Iraq's KDP and PUK put aside their rivalry to hold an independence referendum (having already pushed for federal status) even though it was not authorised by Baghdad. The proposal was said to have gained 92% approval but was immediately rejected by the Iraqi Government and Army, which drove Peshmerga forces out of Kirkuk in just a few hours (Gabreldar 2018; ICG 2019). For the first time in decades the Iraqi Army took control of the NE region. Baghdad was showing a political will that had been lacking for many years, since the 2003 invasion.

In Syria, U.S. forces did nothing to stop the YPG's ethnic cleansing of non-Kurds in areas over which they laid claim. In October 2015, the Western aligned NGO Amnesty International accused the YPG (just before the U.S. rebranded them as 'Syrian Democratic Forces') of forcibly evicting Arabs and Turkmens from areas they took, after displacing ISIS. Amnesty produced evidence to show instances of forced displacement, and the demolition and confiscation of civilian property, which constituted war crimes (AI 2015). Similar accusations had come from Turkish government sources (Pamuk and Bektas 2015) but also from refugees who said that "YPG fighters evicted Arabs and Turkmens from their homes and burned their personal documents" (Sehmer 2015; Al Masri 2015).

However, after U.S. forces became the direct patrons of the SDF in late 2015, a UN commission, co-chaired by U.S. diplomat Karen Koning AbuZayd, continued its quest to place most of the blame for abuses on Syrian Government forces. The Commission admitted the YPG/SDF had forcibly displaced communities "[but only] in order to clear areas mined by ISIL," and had engaged in forcible conscription, but "found no evidence to substantiate claims that YPG or SDF forces ever targeted Arab communities on the basis of ethnicity, nor that YPG cantonal authorities systematically sought to change the demographic composition of territories" (IICISAR 2017: 111 and 93).

Nevertheless, in 2018 there were ongoing reports of the ethnic cleansing of Assyrian Christians from U.S.-SDF held areas in NE Syria. Young men in the Qamishli area were reported to have been arrested and forcibly conscripted into Kurdish militia, alongside property theft by those same militia (Abed 2018). In 2019 the SDF were reported to have closed more than 2,000 Arabic-teaching schools in the Hasaka region (*Syria Times* 2019) and to have shot, killed, wounded, and jailed displaced people who were trying to escape from al-Hawl Refugee Camp in South-Eastern Hasaka (FNA 2019). Regardless, once U.S. forces created and adopted the Kurdish-led 'SDF,' Amnesty International and most of the Western media muted their earlier criticisms.

Washington in 2012 had looked favourably on the ISIS plan for a sectarian 'Salafist principality' in eastern Syria, so as to weaken Damascus (DIA 2012). As late as September 2016 U.S. air power, supported by some Europeans and Australia, was used to attack and kill more than 120 Syrian soldiers at Mount Tharda behind Deir Ezzor airport, to help ISIS efforts to take over the mountain and threaten the city (Anderson 2017). But when Russia, Syria and Iraq began wiping out these Saudi clones, U.S. forces simply rescued their best commanders and replaced ISIS with a Kurdish-led SDF (Anderson 2019: Chapters 5 and 7), once again to undermine and weaken Damascus.

However, U.S. occupation forces did not wait around to sponsor the ill-fated Rojava project. In October 2019 President Trump gave the order for a partial withdrawal from northern Syria. Former U.S. diplomat Robert Ford had warned in 2017 that the U.S. would abandon the SDF (O'Connor 2017). So, stripped of U.S. military protection and their main source of arms and finance, sections of the SDF were forced to rapidly put together a new alliance with Damascus and Russia to prevent their annihilation by Erdogan's forces. The Turkish leader (for all his other crimes) correctly saw the Öcalan-led YPG/SDF groups as building steppingstones for their larger separatist project in Turkey (Demircan 2019).

Western liberals complained the U.S. was 'betraying' its Kurdish allies, but they were placing great faith in romantic myths. Ünver (2016), for example, had presented separatist Kurds as recipients of unplanned opportunities in Syria's "civil war" in an "age of shifting borders," as though the big power were not once again using the 'Kurdish card' to divide and weaken both Iraq and Syria. Schmidinger (2018: 13, 16-17) tried to twist Syria's historic diversity into an argument for the Rojava sectarian division—instead of an inclusive unitary state. But, as has been said many times before, imperial powers never have real allies, only interests. Lebanese Resistance leader Hassan Nasrallah told Kurdish separatists in February 2018: "In the end they will work according to their interests, they will abandon you and … sell you in a slave market."

Meanwhile, with Washington's blessing, Erdogan persisted with his plan to control large parts of northern Syria, with the aim of settling many of the Syrian refugees in Turkey under a Muslim Brotherhood–style regime, controlled by sectarian Islamist militia. In late 2019 retired Syrian Major General Mohammad Abbas Mohammad told this writer that Turkey's leader had not given up his ambition of becoming a modern-day 'Caliph' of Muslim nations and was working to colonise Syrian minds with his constant Islamist slogans.

Kobane: Between Erdogan, Washington, and Damascus

Nevertheless, with the help of its allies, Syria has been winning the long war. ISIS and Nusra are virtually defeated, the crisis actors of the 'White Helmets' are gone and the chemical weapons stunts have been exposed. But the Washington-driven economic war now targets all independent countries of the region, aggravating the occupation and terrorism.

The then–Director of the Syrian Arab Army's Political Department, Major General Hassan Hassan, told this writer that the U.S. "has the power to destroy the world many times over, but it has not been able to turn that power into capabilities." That is why U.S. wars are failing across the region. While we are indeed heading for a multi-polar world, he says, we are not there yet. "Syria still faces the unipolar regime." Erdogan, ISIS, Israel and the SDF are all "puppets" of this dying world order. Authorised by the U.S., he claimed, Erdogan still wants to set up a Muslim Brotherhood region in north and east Syria. This is a dying but a "most dangerous" order, General Hassan says. "The U.S. deep state knows that its unipolarity is failing, but that has not yet been announced. The new world system is born but is not yet recognised. The U.S. wants to prolong this conflict as long as possible, to punish the Syrian people."

In that transitional phase we are seeing some collaboration between the SAA and the SDF, e.g. in the extraordinary anomaly of an SDF-run Manbij and the ongoing experiment of Kobane, the SDF controlled border town which most Syrians call Ayn al Arab.

Traveling from rural Aleppo to rural Raqqa on the M4 highway we cross the Furat (Euphrates) river, a huge, semi-dammed expanse of fresh water which appears particularly sweet between two deserts. Turning north we arrive in Ayn al Arab, at the Turkish border, in less than an hour. Although Erdogan's gangs are attacking Ayn al Issa deeper inside Syria on the M4, there is no sign of fighting near Ayn al Arab itself. Syrian Major General Abbas Mohammad explains this as Erdogan looking at narrow incursions, which might later be widened.

This small city of perhaps 45,000 people was evacuated during earlier fighting and still shows signs of great destruction, especially on the eastern and northern sides. Less than a tenth the size of Manbij it is now said to have a majority of Kurds and, in contrast, the SDF comrades here seemed well organised. We are taken to their small headquarters, a three-story building, to await further security checks and an escort to one of their schools and one of their hospitals.

At the secondary school, as in the headquarters, they seem wary of a foreigner accompanied by a Syrian colonel and a Syrian journalist. That breaks down a little as I ask about their curriculum and the children, who have clearly gone through substantial trauma. The headmaster says they are developing programs to help students deal with their war experiences. The threat is not over, as Erdogan's troops, including sectarian Islamist gangs, are only a few kilometres to the north.

The Kurdish nationalist curriculum has made a break with the centralised Arabic-based system set in Damascus. The headmaster explains that their syllabus is carried out 60% in the Kurdish language, 20% in Arabic and 20% in English. For children from Arab families the syllabus is said to be 60% in the Kurdish language, 20% in Arabic and 20% in English. They speak of four 'nationalities' in Kobane: Kurd, Arab, Yazidi and Christian. That is how they see their small town.

The management of the small hospital is also strongly Kurd nationalist. I ask where they get their support, and they mention the Americans and some international NGOs. Of course, there is nothing from Ankara. "What about Damascus?" I ask. "Nothing and we want nothing," says one of the managers.

That may be true for this hospital. However Syrian colleagues told me that most of the health centres in SDF controlled areas still get finance and supplies from Damascus. So not only is their security guaranteed by the Syrian state, so are some of their basic services.

From left: Syrian journalist Nihad Roumieh, a female teacher, the headmaster (red jacket), this writer, then other staff at the Dibistana Şehîd Bêrîtan Batman (Batman Martyrs High School) in Kobane/Ayn al Arab (2019).

It remains to be seen how much Kurdish autonomy will remain, under a final political settlement. A federal system is not part of the discussion. It is clear that Damascus sees that as an Iraqi style path which would dismember and weaken the country. While the SAA and the SDF jointly fight Erdogan's gangs, Damascus has been calling on Arab leaders in the north and north east, who had collaborated with the U.S. occupation force and the SDF, to return to the Syrian Arab Army. On the other side, SDF Commander General Mazloum Abdi opposes incorporation of the SDF into the SAA (Van Wilgenburg 2019) and wants to hold onto as much local administration as possible (*Syrian Observer* 2019). The continued illegal U.S. presence and its sponsorship of SDF units in Hasaka, Qamishli and Deir Ezzor (Ahval 2019), serves to maintain the illusions of autonomy.

In the Russian media there is some pessimism about an SDF-Damascus reconciliation. One observer suggests that "Russia will eventually force most (if not all) of Turkey's forces to leave Syria … [but Damascus] and the Syrian Kurds have opposing political and military goals that will not be easily reconciled" (Stein 2019).

However, Damascus has some other cards. The YPG/PKK/SDF grew its influence through U.S. sponsorship and, as that declines, other voices in the north, including Kurdish voices, are likely to re-emerge, especially through the constitutional process in Geneva. Major General Abbas Mohammad points out that there are now dozens of Kurdish parties in the north east (*Syria Times* 2018). Given the intransigence of the U.S.-dependent SDF, Russia is said to be recruiting Syrian Kurd youth to a rival group (Duvar 2019), which is likely to be incorporated into the SAA.

In my view there may be some accommodation of Kurdish nationalist demands at the cultural and local administrative levels, but alongside efforts to ensure this does not privilege Kurds above other Syrian groups. That might appear in an amended constitution.

Education in the shallow occupation

In late 2021 this writer again visited the nominally SDF/QSD controlled areas, this time in Hasakeh province. Several things stood out. First, unlike NW Idlib and the Syrian Golan, where the Syrian state is excluded, the Syrian state, including the Syrian Arab Army, is present and active in most of the Hasakeh region. This is not apparent from the many international 'yellow zone' maps of eastern Syria, which—despite rhetoric at the UN about supporting the "territorial integrity" of Syria—Western governments and media call the 'Autonomous Administration of North and East Syria.' U.S. forces are generally not present in the cities and towns, and the SDF/QSD grip appears weak.

Second, as we were told several times, the Kurdish leadership is dominated by Turkish PKK, which collaborates with the U.S. military in Erbil (Iraq) to train Kurdish troops. Erbil has become a base for dividing Iraq and for training separatist militia for both Syria and Iran. Third, and most dramatically, I was able to witness the results of a collapse in the Kurdish education system (Drwish 2017) and the displacement of tens of thousands of Syrian children, who had joined classes in Syrian state schools across Hasakeh province (Xinhuanet 2020).

Children assemble at the change of shifts, Syrian state school, "Martyr Ablahad Moussa," Hasakeh city

The Syrian education system in the northeast is under severe pressure because the U.S. occupation has confined state schools to small 'security zones' protected by the Syrian Arab Army, in particular those in the province's major cities of Qamishli and Hasakeh.

That means that these schools have thousands of students and huge classes, at times a hundred children in each class. Nevertheless, Syria has a remedial curriculum for children who have missed years of school, the mass closure of schools means there are sufficient teachers, and UNICEF is helping with some portable buildings and schoolbooks.

The regional director of education, Ms. Elham Sourkhat, told this writer that of the 2,189 schools in Hasakeh province, most had been closed, with many used for SDF/QSD militia purposes. However, the Syrian state was running 145 schools, including 22 larger ones in Hasakeh city and 20 in Qamishli city.

She estimated that the U.S.-backed SDF is running another 50 schools, where they teach mainly in the Kurdish language and with their own curriculum, as in Kobane. However, these have few well trained teachers, and their curriculum is not recognized in Syria or the region. The result is that most families now seem to have rejected or abandoned this system and are sending their children to Syrian schools. Most parents want their children to receive a decent education, to help with their future lives. Teachers in Hasakeh and Qamishli told me that even a number of SDF/QSD leaders have been sending their children to Syrian schools.

Primary school children, Hasakeh city

Kurds are one of several minorities in NE Syria, even if that Kurdish minority has swollen in recent decades through immigration from Iraq and Turkey. Back in 1939, near the end of the French colonial period, Kurds in Qamishli and Hasakeh were counted as about 30%, while the mainly Christian Assyrians and Armenians were 29% and Arab clans were 39% (Altug 2011).

Some ethnic cleansing took place in the middle years of the current U.S.-led war, but substantial Christian communities are still present. George, active in the semi-dormant local council of occupied Qamishli city, told me that Christians numbered about 62,000 before the war but are down to about 50,000 today. Arab clans remain the largest group in the province.

There are far fewer Kurds in the other parts of the wider U.S.-created 'autonomous administration' area—including parts of Aleppo, Raqqa, and Deir Ezzor provinces—all controlled by the U.S. military and its SDF/QSD clients.

The failure of the Rojava project was evident in Hasakeh province, where families have been voting with their children's feet in search of a decent education. Education Director Sourkhat, escorted by some Syrian army officers, took us to see three schools in the 'security zones' of Hasakeh city: 1. Martyr Waleed Nofd school (using UNICEF temporary classrooms since June 2021), 2. Martyr Edwar Iwas school, 3. Martyr Ablahad Moussa school (with over 4,000 students, many in the catch-up curriculum). In the classrooms we visited, we saw between 50 and 100 students, usually with three teachers and often 4 or 5 students per desk. Some of the little ones were standing. Nevertheless, they had Syrian workbooks and were making their way through the primary curriculum.

Primary school children, Hasakeh city

Ms. Sourkhat told us that the province had about 140,000 children enrolled in the Syrian curriculum, but only about 25% of these could attend school regularly. Nevertheless, the other 75% were able to submit exams, after informal schooling at home, in makeshift classes, or sometimes after internet private classes from volunteer teachers. Many other children were simply not in any school system.

We were told many times that the SDF/QSD militia had been obstructing delivery of schoolbooks and harassing students and teachers, claiming that the students are supporting Damascus. Teachers and students faced obstacles in traveling long distances to school. Transport had become expensive, and incomes were very low, mostly due to the U.S. economic blockade.

The SDF has indeed been kidnapping hundreds of young men including boys over 14 years of age (Relief Web 2019), plus those in displaced persons camps, for 'compulsory service' in their militia (SJAC 2020). Such cases are regularly reported in the Syrian media. This was a serious cause of friction between families and the SDF. There had been a number of revenge attacks on SDF militia and occasional attacks on the U.S. occupation (The Cradle 2021b), which has been openly stealing Syrian oil to sell and thus fund its 'autonomous zone' project.

Primary school children return home, crossing a rail line to avoid the SDF/QSD checkpoint (far left), Hasakeh city

A senior Syrian officer confirmed to us reports that the SDF/QSD had been helping the U.S. occupation move ISIS fighters around eastern Syria, to carry out more attacks on the Syrian Army (The Cradle 2021a). Several Syrians told us they believed that QSD was deliberately destroying the school system to keep the next generation illiterate and ignorant. They also complain of the group's links to and parallels with Israel. Indeed the Western image of a heroic 'socialist feminist' Kurd group is reminiscent of the 1970s Western myth of Israeli Kibbutzniks 'farming the desert,' with little mention of the ethnic cleansing of Palestinian people (Dossett 2020). A Jacobin article even borrows the Israeli 'blooming in the desert' phrase and uses it for the U.S.-sponsored 'autonomous administration' in Raqqa (Orsini 2021).

In Qamishli city we visited the Al Orouba selective school for distinguished students (SANA 2021). Hundreds of female secondary students in pink blouses were beginning their afternoon shift. Deputy Principal Ms. Nagah Ali told us that there were previously 300 in this school, but those numbers had grown to 600 and the school was now running morning and afternoon shifts. Students came from all over the region and included the children of some SDF/QSD leaders.

On the day of our visit, the SDF militia had detained the school's librarian and her assistant. Ms. Ali said this sort of thing was a regular occurrence. The boys had stopped wearing their blue uniform shirts to avoid harassment from the U.S.-backed militia, who saw these uniforms as the sign of a Syrian state presence.

Indeed the Syrian state is present and active in most of the Hasakeh region, contrary to the international 'yellow zone' maps of eastern Syria. The Syrian Army is deployed throughout the province and in the major cities, around most major infrastructure (e.g. Qamishli's airport and hospital) and across 90% of the northern border. Damascus backs Qamishli's public hospital and most of the damaged education system. The U.S. military occupation, based east of the cities, controls the NE border crossings to Iraq. Local councils were still in place, carrying out some limited functions and ready to resume their duties.

A Syrian general told me he believed SDF would last "only days" after a U.S. withdrawal. Fearing this, Washington has had talks with the Russians over the future of its client militia. Meanwhile, separatist Kurd leaders, fearing abandonment and new military offensives by Erdogan (Erdimir and Edesnik 2021), were themselves looking to the Russians, British, and Europeans. But many know they will have to turn back to Damascus.

References

Abed, Sarah. "Kurdish Militias in Northeastern Syria Turn to Kidnapping, Conscription, ISIS-like Tactics." *MintPress*. February 12, 2018. https://www.mintpressnews.com/kurds-in-conflict-ridden-northeastern-syria-turn-to-kidnapping-conscription-isis-like-tactics/237466/

Ahval. "Syrian Kurdish military commander announces SDF deal with Russia." December 2, 2019. https://ahvalnews.com/northern-syria/syrian-kurdish-military-commander-announces-sdf-deal-russia

AI. *Syria: 'We had nowhere to go' – Forced displacement and demolitions in Northern Syria*. London: Amnesty International, October 2015. https://www.amnesty.org/download/Documents/MDE2425032015ENGLISH.PDF

Al-Kati, Mohannad (2019) "The Kurdish Movement in the Arab World: The Syrian Kurds as a Case Study." *AlMuntaqa* 2, no. 1; Arab Center for Research & Policy Studies (April/May 2019): 45–61.

Al Masri, Abdulrahman. "Is there 'systematic ethnic cleansing' by Kurds in north-east Syria?" *Middle East Monitor*. June 21, 2015. https://www.middleeastmonitor.com/20150621-is-there-systematic-ethnic-cleansing-by-kurds-in-north-east-syria/

Allsop, Harriet. *The Kurds of Syria: Political Parties and Identity in the Middle East*. New York: I.B. Tauris, 2014.

Altug, S. *Sectarianism in the Syrian Jazira: Community, land and violence in the memories of World War I and the French mandate (1915–1939)* (Dissertation). Utrecht University Repository, 2011. https://dspace.library.uu.nl/handle/1874/205821

Anderson, Tim. "Implausible Denials: The Crime at Jabal al Tharda." *Global Research*. December 17, 2017. https://www.globalresearch.ca/implausible-denials-the-crime-at-jabal-al-tharda-us-led-air-raid-on-behalf-of-isis-daesh-against-syrian-forces/5623056

Chomani, Kamal. "Oil dispute reignites Baghdad-Erbil tensions." *Al-Monitor*. May 29, 2019. https://www.al-monitor.com/pulse/originals/2019/05/iraq-kurdistan-oil-kirkuk.html

Cradle, The (2021a). "Report: US forces move ISIS fighters from prison to northern Syria." August 7, 2021. https://thecradle.co/Article/news/850

——— (2021b). "Illegal US military base in Syria's Al-Hasakah governorate hit by rocket attack: Report." September 30, 2021. https://thecradle.co/Article/news/2288

Demircan, Davut. “Evidence points to nexus between YPG/PKK.” Andalou Agency. October 23, 2019. https://www.aa.com.tr/en/middle-east/evidence-points-to-nexus-between-ypg-pkk/1624238#

DIA (2012) ‘14-L-0552/DIA/288,’ Defence Intelligence Agency, Washington, 12 August, online: https://www.judicialwatch.org/wp-content/uploads/2015/05/Pg.-291-Pgs.-287-293-JW-v-DOD-and-State-14-812-DOD-Release-2015-04-10-final-version11.pdf

Dossett, Will. “Making the Desert Bloom: Fact or Fiction?” December 12, 2020. https://www.alfusaic.net/blog/antiquity/making-the-desert-bloom-fact-or-fiction

Drwish, Sardar Mlla. “The Kurdish School Curriculum in Syria: A Step Towards Self-Rule?” Atlantic Council. December 20, 2017. https://www.atlanticcouncil.org/blogs/syriasource/the-kurdish-school-curriculum-in-syria-a-step-towards-self-rule/

Duvar. “Russia ‘seeks to build local force from ethnic Kurds to replace SDF.” December 24, 2019. https://www.duvarenglish.com/world/2019/12/24/russia-seeks-to-build-local-force-from-ethnic-kurds-in-syrias-northeast-report/

Erdimir, Aykan, and David Edesnik. “Turkey Threatens New Military Offensive in Northern Syria.” FDD. October 18, 2021. https://www.fdd.org/analysis/2021/10/18/turkey-threatens-new-offensive-northern-syria/

FNA. “US-Backed SDF Kills Civilians Trying to Escape Hasaka Refugee Camp.” *Fars News Agency.* May 24, 2019. https://en.farsnews.com/newstext.aspx?nn=13980303000377

Gabreldar, Bushra. “Kurdish independence in Iraq.” *Harvard International Review* 39, no. 1, Athletic Diplomacy: The intersection of sports and culture (Winter 2018): 7–9.

Galbraith, Peter. “The Betrayal of the Kurds.” *New York Review of Books.* November 21, 2019. https://www.nybooks.com/articles/2019/11/21/betrayal-of-the-kurds/

Gibson, Bryan. “The Secret Origins of the U.S.-Kurdish Relationship Explain Today’s Disaster.” *Foreign Policy.* October 14, 2019. https://foreignpolicy.com/2019/10/14/us-kurdish-relationship-history-syria-turkey-betrayal-kissinger/

Gunter, Michael. “The KDP-PUK Conflict in Northern Iraq.” *Middle East Journal* 50, no. 2 (Spring 1996): 224–241.

Gürbüz, Mustafa. *Rival Kurdish Movements in Turkey.* Amsterdam University Press, 2016.

Hennerbichler, Ferdinand. "The Origin of Kurds." *Advances in Anthropology* 2, no. 2 (2012): 64–79.

Hoffman, Sophia. *The Politics of Iraqi Migration to Syria.* New York: Syracuse University Press, 2016.

Holland-McCowan, John. *War of Shadows: How Turkey's Conflict with the PKK Shapes the Syrian Civil War and Iraqi Kurdistan.* International Centre for the Study of Radicalisation and Political Violence (ICSR), August 2017. https://icsr.info/wp-content/uploads/2017/08/ICSR-Report-War-of-Shadows-How-Turkey's-Conflict-with-the-PKK-Shapes-the-Syrian-Civil-War-and-Iraqi-Kurdistan.pdf

Humud, Carla E., Christopher M. Blanchard, and Mary Beth D. Nikitin. *Armed Conflict in Syria: Overview and U.S. Response.* Congressional Research Service, April 26, 2017. https://www.refworld.org/pdfid/591c08bc4.pdf

Hunt, Edward. "The US Is Trying to Undermine the Kurds' Revolutionary Ambitions." *Jacobin.* January 8, 2021. https://www.jacobinmag.com/2021/01/kurds-revolution-syria-turkey-rojava-us-trump

Ibrahim, Shivan. "Syria's Kurdish parties do not see eye to eye." *Al-Monitor.* December 9, 2019. https://www.al-monitor.com/pulse/originals/2019/12/kurds-syria-pyd-national-council-russia-syrian-regime.html

ICG. "After Iraqi Kurdistan's Thwarted Independence Bid." International Crisis Group, Report no. 199 / Middle East & North Africa. March 27, 2019. https://www.crisisgroup.org/middle-east-north-africa/gulf-and-arabian-peninsula/iraq/199-after-iraqi-kurdistans-thwarted-independence-bid

IICISAR (2017) "Human rights abuses and international humanitarian law violations in the Syrian Arab Republic, 21 July 2016 - 28 February 2017": Conference room paper of the Independent International Commission of Inquiry on the Syrian Arab Republic (A/HRC/34/CRP.3). UNHCR. March 10, 2017. At Reliefweb: https://reliefweb.int/report/syrian-arab-republic/human-rights-abuses-and-international-humanitarian-law-violations-syrian

Kutschera, Chris. "Mad Dreams of Independence: The Kurds of Turkey and the PKK." *Middle East Report,* no. 189, The Kurdish Experience (July-August 1994): 12–15.

Martin, Kevin. "Syria and Iraq ISIS and Other Actors in Historical Context." In Feisal al-Istrabadi and Sumit Ganguly (Editors). *The Future of ISIS: Regional and International Implications.* Brookings Institution Press, 2018.

Najjar, Faray. "New front in Syria's war: Why Manbij matters." *Al Jazzera.* October 16, 2019. https://www.aljazeera.com/amp/news/2019/10/front-syria-war-manbij-matters-191015143157365.html

Öcalan, Mehmet. "Öcalan: People of Northern Syria must struggle more for their freedoms." ANHA Hawar News Agency. June 7, 2019. https://hawarnews.com/en/haber/ocalan-people-of-northern-syria-must-struggle-more-for-their-freedoms-h9499.html

O'Connor, Tom. "U.S. will lose Syria to Iran and abandon Kurdish allies, former Ambassador says." *Newsweek.* June 29, 2017. https://www.newsweek.com/us-military-kurds-lose-iran-syria-former-ambassador-627395

Orsini, Margherita. "The Women of Raqqa Are Rebuilding Their Future." *Jacobin.* May 30, 2021. https://www.jacobinmag.com/2021/05/raqqa-women-blooming-in-the-desert-film

Pamuk, Humeyra, and Umit Bektas. "Turkey sees signs of 'ethnic cleansing' by Kurdish fighters in Syria." Reuters. June 17, 2015. https://www.reuters.com/article/us-mideast-crisis-kurds-turkey-idUSKBN0OW1SA20150616

Relief Web. "SDF kidnaps dozens of orphans and hundreds of youths in eastern Syria." September 18, 2019. https://reliefweb.int/report/syrian-arab-republic/sdf-kidnaps-dozens-orphans-and-hundreds-youths-eastern-syria

SANA. "The difficult academic conditions did not prevent the students of Al-Hasakah Governorate from achieving excellence in the basic education certificate." *The Limited Times.* July 15, 2021. https://newsrnd.com/news/2021-07-15-the-difficult-academic-conditions-did-not-prevent-the-students-of-al-hasakah-governorate-from-achieving-excellence-in-the-basic-education-certificate.r1-LdWjTpO.html

Schmidinger, Thomas. *Rojava: Revolution, War and the Future of Syria's Kurds.* London: Pluto, 2018.

Sehmer, Alexander. "Thousands of Arabs flee from Kurdish fighters in Syria's north." *The Independent.* June 1, 2015. https://www.independent.co.uk/news/world/middle-east/thousand-of-arabs-flee-from-kurdish-fighters-in-syrias-north-10289475.html

Semenov, Kirill (2019) 'Russia faces Dilemmas in northeastern Syria,' Al Monitor, 21 November, online: https://www.al-monitor.com/pulse/originals/2019/11/russia-syria-us-turkey-kurds.html

SJAC. "One Year After Banning the Practice, the SDF is Still Recruiting Children." Syria Justice and Accountability Centre. July 23, 2020. https://syriaaccountability.org/updates/2020/07/23/one-year-after-banning-the-practice-the-sdf-is-still-recruiting-children/

SOHR. "Lens of SOHR monitors the rise of the Syrian flag and the flag of Syriac Military Council affiliated to 'SDF,' in Tal Jemma north of Tal Tamr town." Syrian Observatory of Human Rights. December 4, 2019. http://www.syriahr.com/en/?p=149576

Stein, Aaron. "Temporary and Transactional: The Syrian Regime and SDF Alliance." Valdai Club. November 29, 2019. https://valdaiclub.com/a/highlights/temporary-and-transactional-the-syrian-regime/

Syrian Observer. "Russia takes over SDF Base in northern Hassakeh." December 2, 2019. https://syrianobserver.com/EN/news/54623/russia-takes-over-sdf-in-northern-hassakeh.html

Syria Times (2018). "Syrian officer to ST: forces in Syria." December 31, 2018. http://syriatimes.sy/index.php/editorials/opinion/39606-syrian-officer-to-st-forces-in-syria

——— (2019). "SDF militia closes 2154 Syrian schools and gives some of them to US occupation army." September 27, 2019. http://syriatimes.sy/index.php/news/local/43878-sdf-militia-closes-2154-syrian-schools-and-gives-some-of-them-to-us-occupation-army

Tejel, Jordi. *Syria's Kurds: History, Politics and Society.* New York: Routledge, 2009.

Ünver, H. Akin. "Schrödinger's Kurds: Transnational Kurdish Geopolitics in the Age of Shifting Borders." *Journal of International Affairs* 69, no. 2, Shifting Sands: The Middle East in the 21st Century (Spring/Summer 2016): 65–100.

USDOD. "Department of Defense Press Briefing by Col. Dorrian via teleconference from Baghdad, Iraq." U.S. Department of Defense, December 8, 2016. https://www.defense.gov/News/Transcripts/Transcript-View/Article/1025099/department-of-defensepress-briefing-by-col-dorrian-via-teleconference-from-bag

Wilgenburg, Wladimir van. "SDF leadership meets with Arab tribes in response to Damascus call to defect." *Kurdistan24.* December 11, 2019. https://www.kurdistan24.net/en/news/09be9fde-3988-4307-be32-ab161da48412

Xinhuanet. "Feature: Syrian children pursue education despite danger." Nov. 20, 2020. http://www.xinhuanet.com/english/2020-11/20/c_139530905.htm

Yildiz, Kerim. *The Kurds in Syria: The Forgotten People.* Pluto Press, 2005.

7. Inside Syrian Idlib

Syrian frontline post against HTS (al Qaeda) in Ma'arat al Numan, southeast Idlib

As at 2023, North West Idlib remained occupied by the Turkish military, which sheltered large groups of HTS/Nusra/AL Qaeda terrorists. The NATO embedded media often speaks as though this HTS held enclave in two-thirds of Idlib province represents Syria, itself. It is a haven of 'moderate rebels' which, they claim, holds 4 million people. The Syrian government says 1.3 million.

War propaganda themes have become dutifully reported 'facts': this is a 'Syrian Civil War' (even as Syria is occupied by NATO's two largest armies plus Israel, plus thousands of foreign terrorists), the Syrian Government has repeatedly used chemical weapons (i.e. WMDs, meriting NATO retaliation) and (for some unexplained reason) bombs its own schools and hospitals.

But there is another Idlib: that part was liberated at great cost by Syria's national army. From August 2019 through to early 2020, the Syrian Arab Army (SAA) liberated the south-eastern third of Idlib province, including the towns of Khan Shaykhoun, Maarat al Numan and Saraqeb. That opened the M5 highway for all traffic from the south to Aleppo, through Hama and SE Idlib.

The SAA looked for further advances but the NATO powers demanded an end to Syrian operations, in defence of the al Qaeda dominated enclave (NewsWires 2020). That real threat of escalation led Russia to engage in further talks with Turkey and to stall further advances.

Yet this development demonstrated that Syria, with its allies, could have freed the country from all terrorism, were it not for repeated interventions from the NATO-led war coalition, which prefers to dismember and maintain occupied enclaves within Syria: NW Idlib, the NE 'autonomous' zone, the U.S. occupied al Tanf zone and the Israeli occupied Golan.

South East Idlib

In November 2021 this writer visited Syrian Idlib, authorised by the Syrian Army, just as most Western journalists are authorised by U.S. troops when they enter its various war zones. In one day we travelled to Khan Sheykhoun in the south through Ma'arat al Numan, the second largest provincial city, to the strategic crossroads town of Saraqeb.

Khan Sheykhoun is the only liberated Idlib town I saw with a significant civilian population. Mayor Mohammad Iskandar told us that 600 to 700 families have returned, about 10% of the pre-war population. Now far from the frontline, the town is peaceful with some rebuilding and small markets.

Most of those displaced moved to Turkey or north Idlib and some to other parts of Syria. The mayor is in touch with many and says most want to return, but the armed groups (HTS/Nusra) demand large sums of money for them to leave.

We also spoke with Mr Iyad Sukheta, who runs a small grocery store, a small farm, and used to drive a bus. Like the Mayor, Iyad remained in Khan Sheykhoun throughout the conflict. He says the *musalaheen* (armed groups) took many prisoners and killed many local people, including his 17-year-old son. They wanted him to use his bus to drive people north, but he refused.

Asked about the chemical weapons incident of April 2017, Iyad said that the prisoners were not killed to provide victims (as they had been in East Ghouta in 2013) but rather, after a Syrian airstrike, the armed groups attacked the local people directly with chemicals. Many were killed.

Back in 2017 the armed groups blamed the SAA for the chemical attacks, using their own false flag massacre to incite President Trump (who had campaigned against the war) to make his first missile strike on Syria.

Maarat al Numan is a much larger town with an ancient history, sitting on the frontline between Syrian forces and the Turkish backed Nusra/HTS gangs. Even though the SAA has pushed its effective frontline forward three times in the past two years, there are no civilians here. The frontline, about 4km north of the town, is constantly tested by the armed groups.

I visited Ma'arat's museum with its famous Roman and Byzantine mosaics, protected for several years with sandbags. As with many mosques, schools, and hospitals throughout Syria, the HTS/Nusra terrorists used it as a military headquarters, digging tunnels under the Museum.

Jabal Zeitoun (Mountain of Olives) is now at the centre of the frontline, as it occupies the high ground from which the SAA's 9th Division has placed a substantial vanguard of soldiers, tanks, arms, and surveillance equipment. Yet the actual Maarat frontline extends over many kilometres.

Nusra/HTS had built barricades around the town's hospital and placed a small mosque inside. We saw evidence of supplies (medicines and cars) from Qatar, Germany, Sweden, and France. The typical pattern of the armed groups' takeover of Syrian hospitals (for example in Aleppo) has been that they first rob all existing supplies for their war clinics.

Despite nominal support at the UN. for the territorial integrity of Syria, the NATO states had backed a breakaway Idlib enclave called 'North Syria.' In much the same way, and contrary to international law, they still support an 'Autonomous Administration of North and East Syria.' Dismembering a country is a second-best Western war aim, after the failure of regime change.

Further on up the road the crossroads town of Saraqeb is also at the frontline, with Nusra/HTS making daily small arms attacks on, and occasional shelling of, SAA positions. They hide behind, and sometimes in front of, the many Turkish bases which are all across northern and central Idlib. The aim of these attacks, according to General J, has been to provoke retaliation, which might spark direct conflict between Syrian and Turkish forces.

Captain Y took us to the frontline, looking out on the road to Ariha, with a Turkish base 1.7 kilometres ahead. They know these distances quite precisely and are ready to liberate their country from foreign occupation and NATO backed terrorism when the time is right.

Syria could have eliminated terrorism and restored its territorial integrity long ago, were it not for the NATO-led war coalition which prefers to fragment and occupy segments of the country, all along its land borders. In this way they provide safe haven for the internationally proscribed terrorist groups.

The view from Nabi Younis

The author with Syrian General R, looking over the Ghaab plains into northwest Idlib

Syria's pilgrimage site of Nabi Younis (Prophet Jonah) sits atop a 1500m coastal mountain range overlooking, to the west, the Ghaab plains of NW Hama and the hills of western Idlib. The site has been taken over by the Syrian Arab Army's 4th Division, as part of its strategic encirclement of NATO's remaining al Qaeda enclave in NW Idlib.

The range provides a tremendous panoramic view over NW Hama's deep valley, looking down at towns like Jurin, defended by the Syrian Arab Army (SAA), and those held by the armed groups and their Turkish occupation sponsors, like Jisr al Shughur and Sirmaniyeh.

By the end of 2021 large scale terrorism in Syria had been mostly defeated, remaining only in and around the safe havens provided by the occupations of NATO's two largest armies (Turkey and the USA) and the Israeli occupied Golan.

The Syrian Arab Army (SAA) deployment around Nabi Younis is one of several army bases positioned and ready to liberate the remainder of Idlib province from what U.S. official Brett McGurk in 2017 called "the largest Al Qaeda safe haven since 9/11" (MEI 2018), but which the *New York Times* in 2021 revised as "a rebel group once linked to al Qaeda" (Hubbard 2021).

Of course this anomaly is simply an attempt to hide NATO sponsorship of all the terror groups in Syria used, as senior U.S. officials admitted several years ago (CCHS 2021), to provoke regime change or, failing that, the dismemberment of the Syrian nation.

When the time comes to liberate the rest of Idlib this 4th division will be joined by the 9th Division, now based at Ma'arat al Numan, the Republican Guards at Saraqeb and the 25th Division (formerly 'Tiger Forces') stationed in north Hama. These four divisions are all led by commanders with great experience in defeating Nusra, ISIS and their allied 'jihadist' groups across all Syria's various terrains.

NW Idlib remained dominated by al Qaeda (HTS) armed groups. Unlike the *New York Times*, on HTS the UN Security Council does not mince words:

> In January 2017, Al-Nusrah Front created Hay'at Tahrir al-Sham (HTS) as a vehicle to advance its position in the Syrian insurgency and further its own goals as Al-Qaida's affiliate in Syria. Although the emergence of HTS has been

> described in various ways … Al-Nusrah Front has continued to dominate and operate through HTS in pursuit of its objectives (UNSC 2022).

Yet the full liberation of Idlib province from these terrorists was stalled by threats of deeper NATO intervention in support of their proxy 'rebels.'

After more than 30 Turkish troops stationed in Idlib were killed in the 2020 SAA offensive (Gall 2020), Turkish President Erdogan called for NATO support, threatening to release millions more refugees into Europe (Evans and Coskun 2020). With possible U.S. and European air attacks on Syria (for 'humanitarian' reasons), in early March 2020, Presidents Putin and Erdogan agreed to yet another ceasefire (Higgins 2020).

With Idlib only partly liberated, and although Russia had previously accused Erdogan of breaching his commitments in Idlib (News Wires 2020a), the latest ceasefire did not stop the Turkish leader from reinforcing the terrorist groups. He also threatened to use heavy weapons against the Syrian Army, if it sought to liberate its own territory (Press TV 2021).

Since then, the SAA at Nabi Younis and in S.E. Idlib has been actively repelling small arms attacks and occasional shelling from HTS terrorists. In the Ghaab plains NATO's terrorists have repeatedly attacked the civilian village of Jurin (Beeley 2021) and try incursions on SAA positions with tanks.

Yet the gangs have made no ground. On a second visit to Nabi Younis in 2022 Syrian army commanders told this writer that they had killed three Iranian terrorists, from the MEK (see Niknam and Anderson 2021). It had not been well known that the MEK—for decades used by Washington against Iran—was in Syria.

In each SAA position there were soldiers with rifles set on makeshift tripods, ready for the many surveillance drones and the occasional armed drone, which can fly as high as 5,000 metres. The armed groups' expensive technology comes directly from the NATO states.

Up in the range at Nabi Younis General R had intelligence and air power support from the Russians, ready with their war jets at Hmeimim airbase on the coast. There were also several Hezbollah officers in the mountain, acting as intelligence advisers. But the liberation battles have all been fought by Syrians, the General stresses.

There is not much mystery about how the SAA will recapture major towns like Jisr al Shughur and Idlib City. As in Aleppo, Douma and Ma'arat al Numan they will begin with air and artillery attacks, then surround each target, control the exits and carve in at the edges, slice by slice.

The western war media will once again scream that 'civilians and children' are being slaughtered. The sources for their reports will once again be those same throat cutting al Qaeda gangs, universally hated in Syria. But there will be no 'green buses' this time, to take defeated 'jihadists' to a safe haven. More than one commander told me: they will flee to Turkey and Europe or they will be killed.

References

Beeley, Vanessa. "The bombs rain down as I visit the Idlib frontlines, and witness the atrocities committed against civilians by NATO-backed terror." *RT.* July 23, 2021. https://www.rt.com/op-ed/530082-attacked-syrian-civilians-us-weapons/

CCHS. "Syria by Admissions." Centre for Counter Hegemonic Studies. Novemer 6, 2021. Video clips, 5:33. https://www.youtube.com/watch?v=9uBN522X-FA

Evans, Dominic, and Orhan Coskun. "Turkey says it will let refugees into Europe after its troops killed in Syria." Reuters. February 27, 2020. https://www.reuters.com/article/us-syria-security-idUSKCN20L0GQ

Gall, Carlotta. "Turkey Declares Major Offensive Against Syrian Government." *New York Times.* March 1, 2020. https://www.nytimes.com/2020/03/01/world/middleeast/turkey-syria-assault.html

Higgins, Andrew. "Putin and Erdogan Reach Accord to Halt Fighting in Syria." *New York Times.* March 5, 2020. https://www.nytimes.com/2020/03/05/world/europe/putin-erdogan-syria.html

Hubbard, Ben. "In a Syrian Rebel Bastion, Millions Are Trapped in Murky, Violent Limbo." *New York Times.* April 6, 2021. https://www.nytimes.com/2021/04/06/world/middleeast/syrian-war-refugees.html

MEI. "Assessing the Trump Administration's Counterterrorism Policy." Middle East Institute, 2017. https://www.youtube.com/watch?v=UgzqabDYK7I#t=59m03s

NewsWires (2020). "'End this offensive': Europeans call on Syria, Russia to return to 2018 Idlib ceasefire deal." *France 24.* February 26, 2020. https://www.france24.com/en/20200226-end-this-offensive-europeans-call-on-syria-russia-to-return-to-2018-idlib-ceasefire-deal

NewsWires (2020a). "Russia claims Turkey broke Syria deals, rejects Erdogan's accusations of aggression." France 24. February 12, 2020. https://www.france24.com/en/20200212-erdogan-turkey-syria-troops-turkish-idlib-president-bashar-al-assad-putin-russia-sochi-iran-soldier-army-recep-tayyip-rebel-moscow

Niknam, Alireza, and Tim Anderson (2021). "The MEK Has No Future In Iran: The Interview With Prof. Tim Anderson." Terror Spring. https://terrorspring.com/the-mek-has-no-future-in-iran-the-interview-with-prof-tim-anderson/

Press TV. "Erdogan threatens use of heavy weapons against Syrian army in Idlib." October 21, 2021. https://www.presstv.ir/Detail/2021/10/21/668973/Turkish-President-Recep-Tayyip-Erdogan-terrorist-groups-Idlib-Syrian-government-forces

UNSC (2022). "Al-Nusrah Front for the People of the Levant." UN Security Council. https://www.un.org/securitycouncil/sanctions/1267/aq_sanctions_list/summaries/entity/al-nusrah-front-for-the-people-of-the-levant

8. Purging Christians from the "New Middle East"

Maloula, the ancient Christian town in western Syria

Despite its pseudo-Christian 'crusade' of the 21st century (Waldman and Pope 2001), it was Washington that masterminded the purge of Christians from the region in pursuit of its declared aim to create a New Middle East (Bransten 2006).

That purge made use of sectarian Judaism, led by Apartheid Israel (CCHS 2022), the worst of sectarian Islamists, led by the Saudis and Muslim Brotherhood groups (Cockburn 2016), and ethnic cleansing carried out by U.S.-backed Kurdish separatist projects (Barber 2018) in both Iraq and Syria.

Many sources tell of the recent purge of Christians from the Middle East. Members of the oldest Christian communities themselves wrote of the "ethnic cleansing [of] Assyrians from Iraq," soon after the U.S. invasion of 2003 (Betbasoo 2007). Later the terrorist group ISIS was blamed.

In 2015 Pope Francis demanded an immediate end to the "'genocide" of Christians taking place in the Middle East (AFP 2015). In 2018 he repeated this call to ROACO, a group assisting the Eastern Churches, speaking of the risk of "eliminating Christians" from the Middle East and of the "great sin of war" (Wells 2018). Yet he did not point his finger at any particular state or group as responsible, for which failure he was chastised by the Syrian Priest Father Elias Zahlawi (Anderson 2021).

The Western war media has blamed everyone from ISIS to Hamas to Muslims in general for the steady expulsion of Christians from Palestine, Iraq and Syria. But those claims all miss the mark. The USA. and its collaborators, including Australia, are the prime movers of this great crime.

Western liberal society has also played a role, priding itself on giving refuge to 'persecuted minorities,' while ignoring responsibility for the wars which drive these refugees.

The aims of Washington's 'crusade,' initially said to be against 'terrorism,' were made clear in subsequent years. The growing cluster of wars were part of a greater project which former U.S. Secretary of State Condoleezza Rice in 2005 and 2006 called the "creative chaos" (Karon 2006) involved in the "birth pangs" of Washington's vision of a New Middle East (Bransten 2006). That meant "taking out" multiple independent states, which General Wesley Clarke specified, after Afghanistan, as "Iraq, then Syria and Lebanon, then Libya, then Somalia and Sudan, and back to Iran" (Clark 2007).

Those who focus only on the ISIS purges or claim some 'organic' Muslim reaction to the various U.S. invasions and proxy wars, miss the directing hand of Washington. That has been the key driver behind the catastrophe which has fallen on the entire region and in particular on the world's oldest Christian communities in several West Asian countries.

As 'fighting ISIS' became the main false pretext for occupying both Iraq and Syria, let's look first at the evidence of U.S. responsibility for the creation of ISIS, before moving to the purge of Christians in Palestine, Iraq and Syria.

Washington's responsibility for the creation of ISIS

In early 2007 U.S. investigative journalist Seymour Hersh wrote of the redirection in U.S. policy, which would focus on using "moderate Sunni" Muslim states, such as Saudi Arabia, to counter the influence of Shia Muslim Iran (Hersh 2007). Sectarian conflict was at the core of the "creative chaos" idea.

ISIS was created over 2004-05 in Iraq as Al Qaeda in Iraq (AQI) or the Islamic State of Iraq (ISI) (Johnston et al 2011), by the Saudis at Washington's direction, to inflame sectarian violence (Hersh 2007) and in particular to keep apart (post 2003) the governments of Iraq and Iran. The terrorist group committed shocking sectarian atrocities against Iraqi civilians, especially Shia Muslims. By 2007 U.S. Army papers showed that the largest group of foreign ISI/AQI fighters in Iraq had come from Saudi Arabia (Fishman and Felter 2007).

The U.S.-backed death cult was then exported to Syria. In August 2012 a U.S. intelligence agency, the DIA, predicted that a "salafist principality in eastern Syria" was likely, as extremist forces dominated the insurgency, and that was "exactly" what the U.S. wanted, so as "to isolate the Syrian regime" in Damascus (DIA 2012).

The resurgence of ISIS in both Iraq and Syria over 2012-2017 followed the failure of other proxies to overthrow the Damascus government and Washington's fear of the growing ties between Damascus, Baghdad and Tehran, which faced common security threats.

Practising the old 'divide and rule' strategy, Washington sought to maintain barriers between Iran, Iraq and Syria. Yet it was the combined forces of these three neighbours that eventually drove ISIS out of major cities and towns. Former Secretary of State John Kerry made the partial admission that Washington just watched as the terror group grew (Weiss 2017), hoping it could be managed—while ISIS took over the cities of Mosul in Iraq and Raqqa and Palmyra in Syria.

By late 2014 senior U.S. officials, including Vice President Biden and head of the U.S. Military General Martin Dempsey, were admitting that their major allies in the region had been arming and funding all the extremist groups in Syria, including the UN Security Council proscribed groups Jabhat al Nusra and ISIS, in attempts to overthrow the Syrian government. Dempsey acknowledged that "major Arab allies" fund ISIS, while Biden named Turkey, the Saudis and the Emiratis as having poured "hundreds of millions of dollars and thousands of tons of weapons" into "anyone who would fight against Assad" (HOS 2020), disingenuously suggesting that their 'major allies' would take such a course independently.

Despite these admissions, and despite the successful Iran-Iraq-Syria purge of ISIS announced by Iranian General Qassem Soleimani in November 2017 (IFP 2017), U.S. direct military intervention in both Iraq and Syria was maintained under the pretext of "fighting ISIS."

None of Palestine's Christians are Israelis

The only Christian 'residents' (Israel will not recognise them as citizens) in the Israeli colony are Palestinian, and they are subject to the same ethnic cleansing as their majority Muslim brethren. Washington and its NATO allies occasionally complain about the expanding Israeli settlements in Palestine, but in practice Washington is the colony's major foreign funder (USCPR 2022) while the USA, Germany and some other Europeans are the Israelis main weapons providers (Andrews 2021).

Christians are now a very small minority in occupied Palestine, but they were once many more, at least in certain areas. One church source put Christians at 11% of Palestine at the end of the Ottoman era in 1922 (Casper 2020). Yet Ramzy Baroud (2019) says "the most optimistic estimates" today have Palestinian Christians at less than 2% of occupied Palestine.

Some declines have been quite recent. The Christian population of Bethlehem in 2020 was only 22% but was said to have been many more just ten years earlier. Other villages have seen big losses. In Beit Jala, the Christian majority fell from 99% to 61%; in Beit Sahour, from 81% to 65%. A study by Dar al-Kalima University found that the sharp decline of Christians in Beit Jala was due to "the pressure of Israeli occupation ... discriminatory policies, arbitrary arrests, confiscation of lands [which] added to the general sense of hopelessness among Palestinian Christians" (Baroud 2019).

The Israeli media blamed the Islamic resistance party, Hamas, for the decline of Christians in Gaza, while Palestinian Christians blamed Israel (Jacobson 2014). The zionist story was self-serving and misleading. Syrian priest Father Zahlawi posed this question to Pope Francis: "If you want to suggest that the Muslims are the ones who force Christians to leave 'the land they love'… how can you explain their emigration at a worrisome rate since the establishment of Israel while they [Christians] throughout hundreds of years, lived … side by side with the Muslims?" (Anderson 2021).

There can be little doubt that the atrocities committed by Israeli armed forces against Palestinian youth in Bethlehem have contributed to the purge of Christians in that town. Bethlehem, as a Christian holy site, has a relatively high proportion of Christian Palestinian families. In the Dheisheh 'camp,' now an outer suburb of Bethlehem (UNWRA 2015), a young third generation refugee told this writer in early 2018 that the Israeli southern command had a declared practice of systemically shooting Palestinian youth in the legs and knees, to cripple them. Many published reports support his account (e.g. Ashly 2017). This was and is an ongoing and systematic campaign against both Muslim and Christian Palestinians (BADIL 2016).

Purges of Christians in Iraq after the 2003 invasion

While Iraqis feared Saddam Hussein, many Christians also feared his removal, as his government had been "largely tolerant of their faith and included high-ranking Christians" (Daily Press 2003). By late 2004 that generalised fear persisted, with Christians believing they were "high on the target list." They were only 3% of the Iraqi population but their community was "one of the oldest in the Middle East … [and had] long played an important role in Iraqi politics, society and the economy" (Colt 2004).

Just one year after the U.S. invasion of Iraq in March 2003, Islamic extremists were reported to have bombed many Iraqi churches, with 59 Assyrian churches bombed: "40 in Baghdad, 13 in Mosul, 5 in Kirkuk and 1 in Ramadi" (Sveriges Radio 2009). Al Qaeda in Iraq (AQI, later ISI and later still ISIS) was only able to operate after the U.S. invasion.

A 2007 report (revised in 2017) spoke of the "incipient genocide" of Iraqi Assyrians, most of whom were Christians. By then, 118 churches were said to have been attacked or bombed. The report said that "Assyrians comprised 8% (1.5 million) of the Iraqi population in April of 2003. Since then, 50% have fled the country" (BetBasoo 2007). By 2007 there were more than 1.2 million Iraqi refugees in neighbouring Syria (al-Miqdad, Faisal 2007).

The Assyrian report blamed extremist Muslims but also the newly empowered Kurdish administrations. "Kurdish authorities denied foreign reconstruction assistance for Assyrian communities and used public works projects to divert water and other vital resources from Assyrian to Kurdish communities. Kurdish forces blockaded Assyrian villages. Children were kidnapped and forcibly transferred to Kurdish families" (BetBasoo 2007)

This was all part of the U.S. restructuring of Iraq. As early as the 1970s Washington had enlisted the support of Kurdish leaders in north Iraq (PBS 2011), at first as a counter weight to Saddam Hussein (who was also a U.S. collaborator in the 1970s and 1980s) and later as a tool to divide and weaken any government in Baghdad. The Israelis have also had a long standing presence in Iraqi Kurdistan, "more conspicuous" in recent years (Khosravi, Kalhori and Hamehmorad 2016).

The strong 2014 resurgence of ISIS in Iraq, after it had been reactivated and rebadged to help divide both Iraq and Syria, renewed these pressures. A 2015 report wrote that while ISIS had "killed Sunni and Shia Muslims, they are clearly engaged in a systematic campaign to rid Iraq of non-Muslims and ethnic minority communities, including Assyrian Christians" (Johnston 2015). The terror group, essentially an instrument of Washington through the Saudis, gave the Christians in Mosul the 'options' of conversion to Islam, paying a religious levy, or death (Lagos 2019). Many fled.

When the second wave of ISIS attacks hit Iraq in 2014, the terror group seized Mosul and drove thousands of Christians from that large city and from the nearby smaller city of Qaraqosh, near the ruins of ancient Nimrod and Nineveh (BBC 2014). Most of those Assyrians fled north into the Kurdistan region but many others left the country. Cynically, the U.S. had warned of a "humanitarian catastrophe' from the ISIS attacks (BBC 2014), but was more concerned with dismembering the Iraqi and Syrian states.

Before ISIS Mosul had more than 15,000 Christians; by mid-2019 only 40 had returned. A Christian report of 2019 spoke of the "genocide" of Christians and Yazidis, and of a 15 year climate of violence and turmoil following the U.S. invasion (IC 2019). Sargon Donabed's book, *Reforging a Forgotten History*, concludes that the 1.4 million Iraqi Christians in 2005 had been almost halved to 750,000 by 2014 (Donabed 2015).

Kurdish separatists in Iraq and Syria, backed by the U.S. war coalition, added to the pressures on Assyrian and other Christian communities. After the sectarian Islamists, mostly recruited by the Persian Gulf monarchies, Kurdish separatists became Washington's second tool to divide and weaken those independent states. Indeed in north Iraq the notion of a 'second [Kurdish] Israel' was widely touted (Levinson 2017).

In September 2017, when a Kurdish referendum in north Iraq sought to covert federal status into a separate state, this attempt at secession was repudiated by the Iraqi parliament and government (Al Jazeera 2017a). Israel was "the only state to [openly] support the Kurdish secession from Iraq" (Andoni 2017). Iraqi forces moved in and took control of Kirkuk with a matter of hours, crushing the secession plan (Chulov 2017).

Nevertheless, the northern Iraqi region had developed strategic relations with both the U.S. and Israel (MEMO 2015) and became a base for covert operations aimed at dividing Iraq and destabilising both Iran and Syria. But those plans met resistance. From at least 2007 Iran began shelling anti-Iran insurgent groups on its border (EKurd 2007), armed groups which were sheltering in Iraqi Kurdistan. Iranian shelling of these U.S. proxies inside Iraq's northern borders was ongoing in late 2021 (Aldroubi and Gharagozlou 2021).

Washington was thus the prime mover and mastermind of the demise of Iraq's Christians by invading Iraq, destroying the relative protection which had been offered to Christians; then destabilising new Baghdad administrations with terror through the Saudi-styled sectarian Islamist creations (AQI/ISI and later ISIS), which purged Christians and other minorities; and finally by backing a Kurdish controlled northern zone, which further purged indigenous Christians and in particular, Assyrians. That operation was later ported into NE Syria, where Assyrians and Armenians had fled a century back, seeking refuge from the massacres of the Ottoman Empire.

Purging the Christians of Syria

The U.S. role in the purge of Syrian Christians was apparent from the first months of 2011, but warnings came earlier. In 2005 CNN's Christine Amanpour, closely linked to senior Washington officials, told Syrian President Assad: "the rhetoric of regime change is headed towards you" (CNN 2005). At about the same time Iraqi Christians, fleeing into Syria had warned Syrian Christians, "You are next!" They believed that Syria was next in line for "regime change" and that "Christians in particular would be targeted in a planned sectarian war—just as in Iraq" (Hoff 2021). Syria was indeed targeted by the proxy armies which former Vice President Joe Biden and General Martin Dempsey acknowledged in 2014 had been funded and armed by U.S. allies (HOS 2020).

Sectarian violence was apparent from the beginning of the dirty war on Syria (Anderson 2016), as the slogan "Masehi la Beirut wa alawi altabut" (Christians to Beirut, Alawites to the grave) was reported from sectarian Islamists in Homs city over April-May 2011 (Blanford 2011). Indeed, while the Western media blamed all violence on the Syrian Government, Alawis were murdered and many Christians fled to Beirut. Overall, the internationalised assault on Syria displaced half the country's population, creating the world's largest refugee crisis (USA for UNHCR 2022).

Yet in 2011 it was well reported that Syria's Christians had more faith in President Assad than in the U.S., Saudi and Qatari backed armed 'opposition' (Gavlak 2011). In 2011 the U.S. media knew very well, and acknowledged that both Saddam Hussein in Iraq and Bashar al Assad in Syria protected Christians (Tobia 2011). Wingert and Hoff (2021) in their book, *Syria Crucified*, document the suffering of many Christian families "at the hands of radical terrorists" supported by Western countries.

In 2014 Jabhat al Nusra terrorists (called 'moderate rebels' by the NATO media) from Turkey attacked the mainly Armenian-Christian town of Kesab (Kucera 2014), in NW Syria, kidnapping, murdering and desecrating churches (Parliamentary Assembly 2014), with graffiti which reminded the Armenian residents of the Ottoman massacres a century earlier. All 14 churches were burned and vandalised. In December 2021 Kesab Mayor Sebouh Kurkjian told this writer, "We know the Turkish language … they are talking together in the Turkish language … the Turkish government helps them." Priest Father Nareg Iwisyan said the gangs had robbed valuables and graves, and then destroyed all the religious artefacts and books, leaving sectarian graffiti and even human excrement in his church.

ISIS, ported in from Iraq, also terrorised Syria's communities, until Iraqi and Syrian forces backed by Iran and at great cost in lives, drove them out.

Assyrian and other Christians in NE Syria formed a 'Sootoro' militia (Wilgenburg 2016), armed by and allied to Damascus, at first to defend the Christian communities from ISIS. The Syrian government also armed the Kurdish groups, but these began looking for outside support, to serve their regional agenda.

When Washington began to arm separatist Kurds and rally popular support for their romanticised 'Rojava' Kurdish homeland project in Syria (Applebaum 2021), Western histories were rewritten to erase the other minorities of North and Eastern Syria, in particular the Arab, Assyrian, Armenian and other Christian groups.

A key focus became Qamishli, near the Turkish border, a city founded by Christian refugees fleeing the Ottoman Empire's massacres of the early 20th century. Kurdish groups, mostly Muslim, did not suffer Ottoman persecution but did face repression under the modern Turkish state. As a result of that conflict in Turkey, combined with Saddam Hussein's repression in Iraq, and the purges by ISIS, NE Syria received many Kurdish immigrants from Turkey and Iraq.

Yet Kurds never dominated the populations of NE Syria. Near the end of the French occupation the colonial power carried out a census of Qamishli and Hassakeh (Altug 2011), the core of areas claimed by Western states to be some sort of natural Kurdish homeland. That census showed Kurds to have been a small minority in the region's major cities, but a slight majority in countryside Qamishli. In the region as a whole, Kurds were about 31%, while Christians were 40% and Arabs 28%.

In other words, in a region which since the 1940s has been a governorate or province of Syria—but which Washington and its military occupation in about 2015 designated as the heart of an 'autonomous administration' to be handed over to separatist Kurds—Christians had historically been the largest group.

Many recent Western media accounts falsely paint Kurdish separatism in Syria as a heroic indigenous movement, criticising the Syrian government for alleged abuses against Kurds (Allard, et al 2019). However Damascus had granted citizenship to tens of thousands of Kurdish immigrants in early 2011 (CNN 2011). Most likely many came from Iraq and Turkey. Nevertheless, with more than 15 million Kurds in neighbouring Turkey, Syria would always place limits on immigration.

The U.S. aim of dismembering Syria and using parts as a springboard for Turkish-led Kurd agendas was both an illegal blow to the territorial integrity of the Syrian nation and a direct assault on the Christian communities of Syria's northeast. After fighting the U.S.-Saudi sectarians of ISIS, a discriminatory Kurdish project fell upon the Christians and Arabs of the NE region.

In early 2015 Amnesty International accused the Syrian "Kurdish fighters" and their militia, the YPG, of the "forced displacement and home demolitions" of "Arabs and Turkmens" (Zaman 2015). Several U.S. media reports called this the Kurdish "ethnic cleansing" of these other groups (CBS 2015). Yet they made no mention of Kurds purging the Christian communities.

The Amnesty report also claimed that Kurds had been "subject to long term discrimination and human rights violations" in Syria before 2011—in particular by "restrictions on the use of Kurdish language and culture" and their being "denied the rights enjoyed by Syrian nationals." Yet the report later admitted that "the Syrian Government [in April 2011] granted nationality to most of these Kurds" (AI 2015).

Preparations for a 2015 U.S. land invasion of North and East Syria made use of the 'Kurdish Card.' In October 2014 Kurdish forces had gone from Erbil in north Iraq across into north Syria via Turkey, supposedly to bolster YPG efforts against ISIS, and the U.S. began air drops of weapons to the YPG (Cooper 2014). In March the U.S. sent trainers to assist the YPG (MacAskill 2015) and by August, U.S. firepower was reportedly used in support of what it had converted into another anti-Syrian Government militia (BBC 2015). The 'Syrian Democratic Forces' (SDF or QSD in Arabic) were formed from a YPG base in October 2015, including a draft constitution which contained a unilateral separatist Kurd declaration.

After direct U.S. intervention had bolstered this SDF/QSD, Amnesty said no more about Kurdish "forced displacement and home demolitions." Yet Christians still faced expulsion from Qamishli. The SDF was nominally (but not practically) wider than Kurdish separatists, as Washington knew there were precious few Kurds in the cities of Manbij, Raqqa and Deir Ezzor, key centres which were to be included in Washington's SDF-led 'autonomous' region, carved out of Syria.

In October 2021 this writer visited Qamishli and its Christian community. Suheil and George from the former city council told me that the Christian community in Qamishli had been 62,000 before the war but was down to about 50,000. This followed the ISIS terrorism and the seizing of many properties by the U.S.-backed SDF.

Because of its U.S. military backing, SDF controlled most but not the entirety of the northern city. The Syrian Arab Army still protected the airport, the main hospital and several military and 'security zone' areas, which included residences and schools. The Christian militia Sootoro had checkpoints in several adjacent areas. Yet all these facilities faced obstruction from the SDF. The Council still operated in the 'security zone,' the Christian areas, and to some extent outside. An uneasy peace had been in place for some months, with few direct clashes (Hardan 2021).

Christians in Syria have been attacked and purged in the west of the country by U.S. and NATO backed sectarian Islamists ('moderate rebels') and in the east by the death cult ISIS. As Father Elias Zahlawi wrote, in the name of "Freedom, Democracy and Human Rights" Washington "declared war on my home country, Syria, and drove to it, from a hundred countries … jihadis, haunted by the evil of money, blood, avarice, and power" (Anderson 2021). After that the SDF proxy militia in the northeast seized non-Kurd properties, adding to the exodus of Christians.

Australia helped purge Iraqi and Syrian Christians

Under the guise of assisting 'persecuted minorities,' U.S. allies like Australia and Canada helped this purge (Berger 2016). In late 2015 Australian Prime Minister Tony Abbott won media praise for announcing 12,000 new 'humanitarian visas' for 'persecuted groups' in the Middle East. They would mostly come from Iraq and Syria and were mostly Assyrian Christians. Yet at the same time Abbott said that the Australian military would join in U.S. "airstrikes" against ISIS (Hurst 2015).

In fact, in September 2016 the Australian Airforce, alongside that of the U.S., attacked and killed more than 120 Syrian soldiers at the mountain behind Deir Ezzor airport. That carefully planned attack, which allowed ISIS to take control of the mountain, was dismissed by then Australian Prime Minister Malcolm Turnbull as a "mistake" (Daniel and Brown 2016). Yet evidence showed this to have been a well-planned operation, designed to assist ISIS in its efforts to take Deir Ezzor city (Anderson 2020).

There had been more than 40,000 Assyrian immigrants in Australia, the biggest group in the Fairfield suburb of Sydney (Ahern 2016). A new wave came after the U.S. attacks and sanctions on Iraq in the 1990s. Frederick Aprim's book, *The Betrayal of the Powerless,* charts the displacement of Iraqi Assyrians after the 2003 invasion. Initially most came from Iraq but after 2015, many also came from Syria (Aprim 2021).

In January 2017 Australian Prime Minister Malcolm Turnbull told U.S. President Donald Trump, in typical servile style, "We will take more, we will take anyone that you want us to take." Of Turnbull's program to bring in "12,000 Syrian refugees, 90 per cent … will be Christians … it is a tragic fact of life that when the situation in the Middle East settles down—the people that are going to be most unlikely to have a continuing home are those Christian minorities" (Doherty 2017). Of course, it was Washington's successive war projects which deprived them of their homes. In this way collaborators helped Washington with its New Middle East project.

Behind the shallow declarations of Christian values and the cynical claims of humanitarian intervention as pretexts for wars of aggression, Washington has been the central engine behind the purging of the world's oldest Christian communities in Palestine, Syria and Iraq.

Elias Zahlawi: Syrian priest's letters rattle the Vatican

He is troubled that Pope Francis has never pointed a finger at Israel or the USA for their roles in the ethnic cleansing of Christians.

The author with Father Elias Zahlawi

Syrian priest Father Elias Zahlawi reportedly rattled the Vatican over its vague statements on the U.S.-driven Middle East wars (Anderson 2021). Not once has Pope Francis pointed a finger at Israel or the USA for their roles in two decades of slaughter and ethnic cleansing.

While both men are in their 80s, Father Zahlawi has ministered in Damascus since the 1960s and, since 1975, at the Church of Our Lady of Damascus. Syrian-born, he studied in Jerusalem and founded the now famous Damascus Choir of Joy in 1977, a huge choir that has toured Europe.

While Pope Francis attained the highest rank in the Catholic Church after being an Archbishop in Argentina, he is said to be "haunted" by accusations of his involvement in Argentina's dirty war, carried out by a U.S.-backed military dictatorship. No charge was ever laid against him but some years ago the Argentine judiciary found that the Catholic Church was "complicit in abuses" (Hernandez 2013).

Some Syrian Christians told me that Father Zahlawi's accusations over the Pope's meaningless words—in face of the U.S. and Israeli-led atrocities in Palestine, Syria, Iraq, and Yemen—touched a raw nerve. The gentle, humble priest in Damascus, now 90 years old, wrote a series of letters to U.S. and Syrian leaders, to the European Parliament, and to the last two Popes. But his first two letters to Pope Francis, in 2018 and 2019, were probably the most incisive.

On 29 June 2018, Father Zahlawi asked Pope Francis:

> Why don't you decisively and unequivocally adopt this very clear position of Saint Peter, against a western world that has spared nothing in its pursuit of total and absolute world dominance ... including the systematic and continuous killing and destruction of total peoples and countries, including my homeland Syria?
>
> All of that is happening ... either with complete media silence or worse yet, with the roaring noise of fabricated "facts," designed to give credence to the worst obscenities, under the banner of "human rights, democracy, and freedom."
>
> I have continued to read "with sorrow and dismay" ... the *Roman Observer,* hoping that one day I will find in it even one word of activism, [but] to be honest I only find in it ... empty words, of the usual clerical content that we have gotten used to since the Emperor Constantine, with very rare exceptions. Yet outside the Church, in the west, there are many courageous and honorable voices.

On 12 February 2019, he wrote again, after the Pope's address to ROACO, the Board of the Society for Support of the Eastern Churches, where Francis was reported to have denounced the "great sin of war," the thirst for "domination" of great "World Powers" and a refugee crisis which carries with it the risk of "eliminating Christians" from the Middle East (Wells 2018).

This was a more carefully thought-out letter, in which Father Zahlawi raised eight points. He began by asking, gently: *"I wonder if the many grave issues you raised ... did not deserve a clearer stand of more commitment and responsibility?"*

His first point had to do with the Pope's refusal to address the ethnic cleansing in Palestine:

> You say that "In the Middle East there is also a danger ... of eradicating the Christians" ... [but] do you believe that your audience and consequently your readers are ignorant, as your words suggest, of the countries which strive, with open insistence, and since the establishment of Israel, to totally eradicate the Christian existence in the whole Near East at the time they are about to accomplish this in occupied Palestine, which you call "the land of Jesus" and which has become the land of injustice, vengeance and death, and whose true name has been obliterated to become only 'The Holy Land'?

In a second point he referred to the failure of the Pope's generic words about the "pain" of the Middle East, and of land theft by "World Powers," to address the U.S.-led assault on his own country, Syria:

> these 'World Powers,' at the head of which is the United States of America ... forced about 140 member states countries ... to declare war on my home country, Syria, and drove to it, from a hundred countries ... jihadis, haunted by the evil of money, blood, avarice, and power.

Third, Father Zahlawi chastised the Pope for suggesting that the "diminishing" numbers of Christians in the region might be due to pressure from Muslims.

> If you want to suggest that the Muslims are the ones who force Christians to leave 'the land they love' ... how can you explain their emigration at a worrisome rate since the establishment of "Israel" while they [Christians] throughout hundreds of years, lived ... side by side with the Muslims?

In his fourth point, he asked if the Pope, while speaking of the Middle East as 'the cradle of Christianity,' can possibly be ignorant that "the Judaising of occupied Palestine ...will very soon end every presence of Christians in 'the land of Jesus'?"

Fifth, with regard to the Pope's references to "great churches" in the Middle East, and ignoring the role of "Israel," Father Zahlawi noted that "what you are practically doing … shackled by a horrific and sickly guilt complex towards the Jews" is to ignore and close your eyes to "the atrocities that are being committed openly and in flagrant violation of all laws, against all the Arabs, Muslims and Christians equally," while even "some distinguished Jews" speak out against these crimes.

Sixth, he denounced the Pope's overly general words about "the Middle East … [as] a land of death and emigration," as the pontiff says nothing about the displacement of 12 million of the 23 million people in Syria "without pointing an accusing finger at those who are responsible for these planned and inhuman emigrations in a country that was considered, before the so-called Arab Spring, as one of the safest countries on earth?"

In a seventh point, Father Zahlawi cites the Pope's reference to "the grave sin … the sin of war"; But what does this mean, he asked, "without pointing, in the end, an accusing finger to countries such as the United States of America, Britain, and France, on the global scope, and at "Israel" on the scope of the Middle East, as they do not stop exploding totally unjust war … [in the name of] Freedom, Democracy and Human Rights?"

Finally, he refers to the Pope's call that "the Middle East is a hope that we must take care of," linking this to a revelation said to have taken place in Soufaniyeh Alley in Damascus in 2014, in the midst of the war on Syria. This revelation likens the wounds on Syria to those on Jesus. The clear, implicit message is: why has Pope Francis not denounced those who, like Judas, betrayed the people of Syria?

References

AFP (2015) 'Pope Francis calls for end to 'genocide' of Christians in Middle East,' France 24, 10 July, online: https://www.france24.com/en/20150710-bolivia-pope-francis-calls-end-genocide-christians-middle-east

Ahern, Peter (2016) 'AINA Editorial: Australia's Assyrians in Focus, AINA, 1 April, online: http://www.aina.org/releases/20160401023453.htm

AI. "Syria: 'We had nowhere to go'—Forced displacement and demolitions in Northern Syria." Amnesty International. October 13, 2015. Index Number: MDE 24/2503/2015. https://www.amnesty.org/en/documents/mde24/2503/2015/en/

Aldroubi, Mina, and Leila Gharagozlou. "Iran shells Kurdish insurgents in Iraq." *The National.* September 21, 2021. https://www.thenationalnews.com/mena/iraq/2021/09/20/iran-shells-kurdish-insurgents-in-iraq/

Al Jazeera. "Iraq parliament rejects Kurdish independence referendum." September 12, 2017. https://www.aljazeera.com/news/2017/9/12/iraq-parliament-rejects-kurdish-independence-referendum

al-Miqdad, Faisal. "Iraqi refugees in Syria." *Forced Migration Review* (June 2007). DOAJ. https://core.ac.uk/download/pdf/27064698.pdf

Allard, LaDonna Brave Bull, Eve Ensler, Stuart Basden, and others. "We stand in solidarity with Rojava, an example to the world." *The Guardian.* November 2, 2019. https://www.theguardian.com/world/2019/nov/01/we-stand-in-solidarity-with-rojava-an-example-to-the-world

Altug, S. *Sectarianism in the Syrian Jazira: community, land and violence in the memories of World War I and the French mandate (1915–1939)* (Dissertation). Utrecht University Repository, 2011. https://dspace.library.uu.nl/handle/1874/205821

Anderson, Tim (2016). *The Dirty War on Syria.* Montreal: Global Research.

——— (2020). 'Implausible Denials: The Crime at Jabal al Tharda—the Sept. 2016 US-Australian air massacre of Syrian soldiers, to help ISIS/Daesh,' Centre for Counter Hegemonic Studies, 28 December, online: https://counter-hegemonic-studies.site/jat-1/

——— (2021a). "Children in Hasakeh Flock to Syrian Schools After Collapse of Kurdish 'Education.'" *Al Mayadeen.* October 26, 2021. https://english.almayadeen.net/articles/analysis/children-in-hasakeh-flock-to-syrian-schools-after-collapse-o

———(2021) "Father Elias Zahlawi: Syrian Priest's Letters Rattle the Vatican.' *Al Mayadeen.* November 16, 2021. https://english.almayadeen.net/articles/opinion/father-elias-zahlawi:-syrian-priests-letters-rattle-the-vati

Andoni, Lamis. "Why is Israel supporting Kurdish secession from Iraq?" *Al Jazeera.* October 7, 2017. https://www.aljazeera.com/opinions/2017/10/7/why-is-israel-supporting-kurdish-secession-from-iraq

Andrews, Frank. "Arms trade: Which countries and companies are selling weapons to Israel?" *Middle East Eye.* May 18, 2021. https://www.middleeasteye.net/news/israel-palestine-which-countries-companies-arming

Applebaum, Stephen (2021) "The Other Side of the River: The reality of the Kurdish women's movement in Rojava." *The Independent.* November 9, 2021. https://www.independent.co.uk/independentpremium/long-reads/other-side-river-kurdish-women-movement-b1950488.html

Aprim, Frederick. *The Betrayal of the Powerless: Assyrians after the 2003 US Invasion of Iraq.* Xlibris Publishing, 2021.

Ashly, Jaclynn. "How Israel is disabling Palestinian teenagers." *Al Jazeera.* September 21, 2017. https://www.aljazeera.com/features/2017/9/21/how-israel-is-disabling-palestinian-teenagers

BADIL (2016). "The targeting of Palestinian youth in Dheisheh refugee camp continues." PR/EN/260916/42. https://www.badil.org/press-releases/912.html

Barber, Matthew. "Romancing Rojava: Rhetoric vs. Reality." Syria Comment. July 31, 2018. https://www.joshualandis.com/blog/romancing-rojava-rhetoric-vs-reality/

Baroud, Ramzy. "The ethnic cleansing of Palestinian Christians that nobody is talking about." *CounterPunch.* October 31, 2019. https://www.counterpunch.org/2019/10/31/the-ethnic-cleansing-of-palestinian-christians-that-nobody-is-talking-about/

BBC (2014). "Iraq Christians flee as Islamic State takes Qaraqosh." August 7, 2014. https://www.bbc.com/news/world-middle-east-28686998

BBC (2015). "Syria crisis: US 'support fire' to defend American-trained fighters." August 3, 2015. https://www.bbc.com/news/world-middle-east-33762448

Berger, Katya. "Canada: Religious sponsorship of refugees creates controversy." *France 24.* July 25, 2016. https://www.france24.com/en/20160725-focus-canada-syrian-refugees-quebec-christians-muslims-sponsorship

BetBasoo, Peter. "Incipient Genocide: the Ethnic Cleansing of the Assyrians of Iraq." Assyrian International News Agency (AINA). June 12, 2007. http://aina.org/reports/ig.pdf

Blanford, Nicholas. "Assad regime may be gaining upper hand in Syria." *The Christian Science Monitor.* May 13, 2011. https://www.csmonitor.com/World/Middle-East/2011/0513/Assad-regime-may-be-gaining-upper-hand-in-Syria

Bransten, Jeremy. "Middle East: Rice Calls For A 'New Middle East." RFERL. July 25, 2006. https://www.rferl.org/a/1070088.html

Casper, Jayson. "Why Many Christians Want to Leave Palestine. And Why Most Won't." *Christianity Today.* August 4, 2020. https://www.christianitytoday.com/news/2020/august/palestinian-christians-survey-israel-emigration-one-state.html

CBS. "Kurds accused of 'ethnic cleansing' by Syria rebels." CBS News. June 15, 2015. https://www.cbsnews.com/news/kurds-accused-ethnic-cleansing-syria-rebels-isis/

CCHS. "SIX (6) important reports on Israeli Apartheid." Centre for Counter Hegemonic Studies. February 24, 2022. https://counter-hegemonic-studies.site/israeli-apartheid-6/

Chulov, Martin. "Kurds defeated, displaced and divided after Iraq reclaims oil-rich Kirkuk." October 2, 2017. https://www.theguardian.com/world/2017/oct/22/kurds-bitter-defeat-iraq-reclaims-kirkuk

Clark, Wesley. (2007) "Seven Countries in Five Years." Genius. https://genius.com/General-wesley-clark-seven-countries-in-five-years-annotated

CNN. "2005: Amanpour and Assad." November 7, 2012. https://edition.cnn.com/videos/international/2012/07/11/exp-amanpour-assad-2005.cnn

CNN. "Stateless Kurds in Syria granted citizenship." April 8, 2011. http://edition.cnn.com/2011/WORLD/meast/04/07/syria.kurdish.citizenship/

Cockburn, Patrick. "We finally know what Hillary Clinton knew all along—US allies Saudi Arabia and Qatar are funding Isis." *The Independent.* October 15, 2016. https://www.independent.co.uk/voices/hillary-clinton-wikileaks-email-isis-saudi-arabia-qatar-us-allies-funding-barack-obama-knew-all-along-a7362071.html

Colt, Ned. "Iraq's Christian community flees violence." *NBC News.* November 17, 2004. https://www.nbcnews.com/id/wbna6501943

Cooper, Hayden. "Islamic State: Kurdish Peshmerga troops leave Iraq to join battle in Kobane." October 29, 2014. https://www.abc.net.au/news/2014-10-29/iraq-kurd-fighters-leave-base-for-syria-deployment/5849452

Daily Press. "Iraqi Christians Fear Loss of Religious Tolerance." April 18, 2003. https://www.dailypress.com/news/dp-xpm-20030418-2003-04-18-0304180387-story.html

Daniel, Zoe, and Matt Brown. "Syria Air Strike: Malcolm Turnbull 'regrets' Australia's involvement in attack that killed regime soldiers." *ABC News*. September 19, 2016. https://www.abc.net.au/news/2016-09-19/turnbull-regrets-australia-jet-involvement-in-syria-air-strike/7856712

DIA (2012). 14-L-0552/DIA/287-293. Department of Defence, Information report, Iraq. Judicial Watch. August 12, 2012. https://www.judicialwatch.org/wp-content/uploads/2015/05/Pg.-291-Pgs.-287-293-JW-v-DOD-and-State-14-812-DOD-Release-2015-04-10-final-version11.pdf

Doherty, Ben. "What we've learned from the Trump-Turnbull call transcript." *The Guardian*. August 4, 2017. https://www.theguardian.com/us-news/2017/aug/04/what-weve-learned-from-the-trump-turnbull-call-transcript

Donabed, Sargon. *Reforging a Forgotten History: Iraq and the Assyrians in the Twentieth Century*. Edinburgh University Press, 2015.

EKurd. "Iranians shell anti-Iranian Kurdish PEJAK guerrillas in Kurdistan region-Iraq." May 23, 2007. https://ekurd.net/mismas/articles/misc2007/5/irankurdistan248.htm

Fishman, Brian, and Joseph Felter (2007). "Al-Qa'ida's Foreign Fighters in Iraq: A First Look at the Sinjar Records." https://ctc.usma.edu/al-qaidas-foreign-fighters-in-iraq-a-first-look-at-the-sinjar-records/

Gavlak, Dale. "Syria's Christians Back Assad." *Christianity Today*. July 7, 2011. https://www.christianitytoday.com/ct/2011/july/syria-christians-assad.html

Hardan, Mohammed. "Syrian government, Kurdish forces end dispute in Qamishli." *Al-Monitor*. April 30, 2021. https://www.al-monitor.com/originals/2021/04/syrian-government-kurdish-forces-end-dispute-qamishli

Hernandez, Vladimir. "Argentina 'Dirty War' accusations haunt Pope Francis." *BBC*. March 15, 2013. https://www.bbc.com/news/world-europe-21794798

Hersh, Seymour. "The Redirection." *New Yorker*. February 25, 2007. https://www.newyorker.com/magazine/2007/03/05/the-redirection

Hoff, Brad. "Syrian Christians were Quietly Warned Before the War." The Libertarian Institute. November 20, 2021. https://libertarianinstitute.org/articles/syrian-christians-were-quietly-warned-before-the-war/

HOS (2020) "Syria by admissions—revisited." Hands off Syria. https://www.youtube.com/watch?v=fjtdJX2gVmI

Hurst, Daniel. "Abbott praised for Syrian refugee intake amid calls to spell out military exit strategy." *The Guardian.* September 9, 2015. https://www.theguardian.com/australia-news/2015/sep/09/abbott-praised-for-syrian-refugee-intake-amid-calls-to-spell-out-military-exit-strategy

Kucera, Joshua. "Turkey Blamed In Attack On Syrian Armenian Village." EurasiaNet. May 28, 2014. https://eurasianet.org/turkey-blamed-in-attack-on-syrian-armenian-village

IC. "In Iraq, Christians and Yazidis suffer 'ethnic cleansing.'" Info Chrétienne. July 19, 2019. https://en.infochretienne.com/en-irak-les-chretiens-et-les-yezidies-subissent-un-nettoyage-ethnique/

IFP. "Gen. Soleimani to Iran Leader: ISIS Completely Defeated in Iraq, Syria." Iran Front Page. November 21, 2017. https://ifpnews.com/soleimani-leader-isis-defeated

Jacobson, William A. "Gaza ethnic cleansing of Christians." Legal Insurrection. August 2, 2014. https://legalinsurrection.com/2014/08/gaza-ethnic-cleansing-of-christians/

Johnston, Patrick B., Jacob N. Shapiro, Howard J. Shatz, Benjamin Bahney, Danielle F. Jung, Patrick Ryan, and Jonathan Wallace (2011). *Foundations of the Islamic State: Management, Money, and Terror in Iraq, 2005–2010.* Rand. https://www.rand.org/pubs/research_reports/RR1192.html

Johnston, Geoffrey (2015) "Ethnic cleansing in Iraq, Part 1: Extremists need to be confronted." The Whig. March 11, 2015. https://www.thewhig.com/2015/03/11/column-ethnic-cleansing-in-iraq-part-1--extremists-need-to-be-confronted

Karon, Tony. "Condi in Diplomatic Disneyland." *Time.* July 26, 2006. http://content.time.com/time/world/article/0,8599,1219325,00.html

Khosravi, Jamal, Jalal Kalhori, and Loghman Hamehmorad. "The Presence of Israel in Iraqi Kurdistan and its Security Challenges for Iran's National Security." Journal of Politics and Law 9, no. 3 (2016). http://dx.doi.org/10.5539/jpl.v9n7p169

Lagos, Ioannis. "Expulsion of Christians from Mosul." Parliamentary question – E-002838/2019. European Parliament. September 17, 2019. https://www.europarl.europa.eu/doceo/document/E-9-2019-002838_EN.html

Levinson, Adam Valen. "The 'second Israel' dream: Kurdistan and 21st century secessions." *Salon*. November 12, 2017. https://www.salon.com/2017/11/12/the-second-israel-dream-kurdistan-and-21st-century-secessions/

MacAskill, Ewen (2015) 'UK to send 75 military trainers to help moderate Syrian rebels,' The Guardian, 27 march, online: https://www.theguardian.com/uk-news/2015/mar/26/uk-military-trainers-help-syrian-rebels

MEMO. "Strategic dimensions of the relationship between Israel and Iraqi Kurdistan." *Middle East Monitor.* September 1, 2015. https://www.middleeastmonitor.com/20150901-strategic-dimensions-of-the-relationship-between-israel-and-iraqi-kurdistan/

New Arab. "Syria Kurds adopt constitution for autonomous federal region." December 31, 2016. The New Arab. https://english.alaraby.co.uk/news/syria-kurds-adopt-constitution-autonomous-federal-region

Parliamentary Assembly. "Kesab: Condemning terrorist attack against civilians in Syria." Council of Europe. April 7, 2014. https://assembly.coe.int/nw/xml/XRef/Xref-XML2HTML-en.asp

PBS (2011). *Kurds at the Crossroads.* https://www.pbs.org/frontlineworld/stories/iraq203/crossroads02.html

Sveriges Radio (2009). "Church Bombings in Iraq Since 2004." Assyrian International News Agency. https://sverigesradio.se/diverse/appdata/isidor/files/83/6810.pdf

Tobia, P. J. "Why Did Assad, Saddam and Mubarak Protect Christians?" *PBS News Hour.* October 14, 2011. https://www.pbs.org/newshour/world/mid-easts-christians-intro

UNWRA (2015). "Dheisheh Camp." https://www.unrwa.org/where-we-work/west-bank/dheisheh-camp

USA for UNHCR (2022). "Syria Refugee Crisis Explained." July 8, 2022. https://www.unrefugees.org/news/syria-refugee-crisis-explained/

USCPR (2022). "U.S. Military Funding to Israel Map." US Campaign for Palestinian Rights. https://uscpr.org/militaryfunding

Waldman, Peter, and Hugh Pope. "'Crusade' Reference Reinforces Fears War on Terrorism Is Against Muslims." *Wall Street Journal.* September 21, 2001. https://www.wsj.com/articles/SB1001020294332922160

Weiss, Phillip. "US watched ISIS rise in Syria and hoped to 'manage' it — Kerry on leaked tape." *Mondoweiss*. January 11, 2017. https://mondoweiss.net/2017/01/watched-manage-leaked/

Wells, Christopher. "Pope: Middle East a crossroads of suffering." *Vatican News*. June 22, 2018. https://www.vaticannews.va/en/pope/news/2018-06/pope-francis-audience-roaco-middle-east.html

Wilgenburg, Wladimir van. "Tensions soar between Syrian Kurds and Christians." *Middle East Eye*. January 14, 2016. https://www.middleeasteye.net/news/tensions-soar-between-syrian-kurds-and-christians

Wingert, Zachary, and Brad Hoff. *Syria Crucified: Stories of Modern Martyrdom in an Ancient Christian Land*. Chesterton, IN: Ancient Faith Publishing, 2021.

Zaman, Amberin. "Amnesty International Accuses Kurdish YPG of War Crimes." *Al-Monitor*. October 13, 2015. https://www.al-monitor.com/originals/2015/10/syria-turkey-right-groups-accused-kurds-rojava-of-war-crimes.html

9. The Betrayal of Yemen

Rally in Sanaa showing Ansarallah slogans. Source: Ansarallah

The one successful revolution of the so called Arab Spring of 2011 has been ruthlessly suppressed and misrepresented, not only by the interventionist Western powers, but also by the UN Security Council (UNSC). First those who claimed to support democratic revolutions declared war on revolutionary Yemen, then the international community imposed a genocidal blockade on the little country. While crocodile tears are sometimes shed, poor understandings of the roots of the humanitarian catastrophe in Yemen hide those responsible for the war and siege.

Since early 2015 an Ansarallah-led revolutionary coalition government (often disparagingly called 'the Houthis,' as though Yemen had family rule, like the Saudis) has controlled the Yemeni capital, Sanaa, and most of the country's population. In late 2016 this coalition, including the former president of a reunified Yemen, Ali Abdullah

Saleh, and his General Peoples' Congress (GPC), formed a National Salvation Government (NSG) (Rezeg 2016). This was led by Abdul Aziz Habtoor, a figure in the GPC and a defector from the transitional regime of Saudi-supported Mansour Hadi (CNN 2016).

By 2022, well informed commentators recognised that "Ansarallah, defined as 'the de facto authorities' in some U.N. documents, are organising the structures of daily life for a large majority of Yemenis" (Bell 2022). The North American Brookings think tank also recognises that "the Houthis have won in Yemen" (Riedel 2022). However, that recognition and its consequences are not yet widely understood, and ignorance has helped fuel mass participation in the war and siege. The result is that, while crocodile tears are shed over the bombed and besieged millions of Yemeni citizens, as at early 2023 a U.S.-Saudi-UAE-Israeli war coalition continued its bloody war and the UNSC continued to impose punishing sanctions on the de facto government and therefore also on the majority of the population. Perhaps the 2023 Irani-Saudi reconciliation will help change this.

Washington's line is that "the Houthis—officially known as AnsarAllah (Partisans of God)—are an Iranian-backed, Shiite Muslim military and political movement in Yemen ... [which] has waged a series of bloody insurgencies against the Yemeni government since 2004, overthrowing them and seizing power in Sanaa in 2015" (CEP 2022). The final version of the 'Yemeni government' referred to here is the transitional regime led by Mansour Hadi, which filled the gap after the ousting of long-term President Ali Abdullah Saleh in 2011 and the Ansarallah led takeover in 2014-2015. Hadi left the country for Saudi Arabia in early 2015 and has been in exile ever since (Amos 2015). Nevertheless, UNSC resolutions still designate Hadi as the 'President' of Yemen and maintain 'Houthi rebels' as a sanctioned entity.

U.S. aligned writers present Yemen as an inherently "tribal democracy" (al-Qarawi 2011) and naturally fragmented by "religious and cultural divisions" (Robinson 2021). However, this ignores both the role of imperial intervention in fragmenting Yemen and the decades long construction of a genuine national and "social revolution" (Zabarah 1984). Issaev (2018) explains in some detail why the Ansarallah led revolution of 2014 is best seen as a continuation of the 'unfinished' Republican revolution of the early 1960s.

The Western claim that Ansarallah/Houthis are an "Iranian-backed, Shiite Muslim" movement is also false. In a religious sense they are a Zaidi revivalist movement, quite distinct from Shiism, except that their religion, like that of the Shiia, urges rebellion against unjust rule, "drawing inspiration from the prophet Muhammad who revolted against the unjust rule of the Qurayshi elites of Mecca" (Tharappel 2019). Unlike the Shiia however, Zaidis do not believe in the infallibility or hereditary transmission of Imams. They are said to be closer in jurisprudence to the Hanafi school of Sunni Islam (Khan 2016). Nevertheless, Yemen's salafist sheikhs denounce Zaidism, especially over the "duty to rebel" against unjust rulers (Issaev 2018: 9). It was mainly after Ansarallah rose to power in 2014 that it began to enjoy at least moral support from Iran.

A popular political process led the Houthis to form Ansarallah in 2011–2012 and subsequently to create a coalition which would control the capital and most of the country. The process has involved alliances with other groups. They joined with the Baath Party (Arab nationalists), the GPC and socialists (Hizb al Ishtiraki) while creating the Steadfast Youth movement (Shabab al Sumud) (Wells 2012).

The Western line remains broadly that the 'revolution' of 2011 was just the ousting of Saleh, after which the Arab monarchies intervened. Even more independent sources present the revolution as the 2011 uprising which unseated Saleh, while the "Houthi' "takeover" is something separate (MEMO 2017). A better perspective is that the Ansarallah coalition is central to the continuation of a real, indigenous Yemeni revolution (al-Fasly 2015). The revolutionary government speaks of "The Revolution" as defined by their takeover of the capital on 21 September 2014, to demonstrate their pride in "embedding themselves in Yemeni history and a notion of Yemeni traditional culture" (Mohammad 2020).

A series of foreign interventions followed the Gulf Cooperation Council (the Arab monarchies of the Persian Gulf, led by Saudi Arabia) 'peace initiative,' which attempted to re-divide the country and block the revolution. From 2015 onwards attacks relied on Saudi-led air raids and the use of large mercenary ground forces.

U.S. troops directly intervened in Yemen several times since 2015, under the pretext of anti-terrorist operations. Of course, this is the same pretext used for the simultaneous proxy wars against

Syria and Iraq. In fact, the chief U.S. target, the Ansarallah led revolutionary government, is the most established anti-al Qaeda force in the Arabian Peninsula. Ansarallah has been "staunchly opposed to al-Qaida and Sunni Salafist movements." Indeed the Saudi support for sectarian salafism in Yemen's north is cited as "one of the key factors in the emergence of the Houthi movement" (Popp 2015). From 2015 Ansarallah forces have fought against (and also carried out prisoner exchanges with) the Saudi and Emirati backed al Qaeda groups (Sanaa Centre 2021).

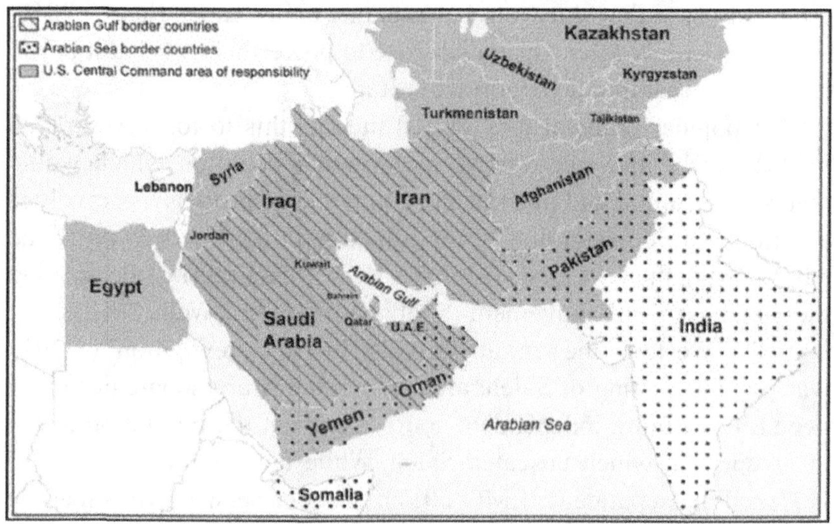

Strategic position of Yemen in U.S. military plans, U.S. "Central Command Area of Responsibility." Source: U.S. GAO

Contrary to so many of the arrogant foreign commentaries, Yemen is not a marginal, naturally divided, backward country but an educated nation held down by big power machinations, over many decades. As a country at the entrance of the Red Sea and opposite the Horn of Africa, Yemen remains at the centre of U.S. CENTCOM ambitions. It is also a key location in China's Belt and Road Initiative. The U.S. New Middle East project (Anderson 2019: Ch.1) is one of military-led imperial style domination, while China's new trade route infrastructure (the BRI) has no such coercive features. These two projects are quite different in character.

The U.S.-led blockade divides Yemen into three parts: (1) the more populated North and West, controlled by the revolutionary Ansarallah-led Government, (2) parts of Marib and the eastern desert, still controlled by the Saudi-based regime and al Qaeda groups, and (3) large parts of the South, controlled by a UAE/Emirati backed Southern Transitional Council (STC), which also controls the port city of Aden (ICG 2021). As at 2023, Israel and the UAE/STC still occupy Yemen's UNESCO listed Socotra island (Werleman 2021).

Washington-based analysts speak of twin wars against the Ansarallah led de facto government based in Sanaa and against Al Qaeda in the Arabian Peninsula (AQAP) (Green 2019), even though the al Qaeda groups were largely sustained by Saudi Arabia. The Trump administration designated Ansarallah (and some of its leaders) as a terrorist group in January 2021, but this was reversed just weeks later by the Biden administration (Blinken 2021).

Let's look in a little more depth at the history of the revolution, post 2011, then at the role and responsibility of the 'international community' and the impact of foreign interventions.

Yemen's unfinished revolution

This section will demonstrate that the Ansarallah led National Salvation Government (NSG) springs from a genuine, indigenous Yemeni revolution. Attempts to designate the uprising of 2011 as the 'revolution' and dismiss the subsequent 'Houthi rebel takeover' as something else are disingenuous. The foreign intervention by the USA, the Saudis, the UAE, Israel and others aimed at overthrowing this revolution and keeping the nation weak and divided, as it was before unification in 1990.

The Ansarallah party was created by the Houthi clan-led group, originally from the northern province of Saadah, at the start of the revolutionary process in 2011. Its slogan remains "God is Great, Death to America, Death to Israel, a Curse on the Jews, Victory to Islam." 'Death to America' has been explained to various Western writers as a rejection of the U.S. government and its practices, rather than aimed at the North American people. 'Death to Israel' is a demand for an end to the colonial regime. While Westerners more often distinguish between zionists and Jewish people, most Arab references to "the

Jews" are typically to the Western colonisers of Palestine, who call themselves "the Jews." The Israelis, who regard their colonial state as one belonging to "the Jews" (Wells 2012), now also occupy parts of south Yemen. So this Ansarallah 'curse' is for the colonisers.

Ansarallah made common cause from 2011 onwards with a range of other Yemeni factions and began an outreach in the Arab and Muslim world to independent states and parties, especially Iran, Hezbollah and Syria (Wells 2012). By 2023 it seemed that Iran and Syria were the only states which recognised the NSG government in Sanaa. But these relations were not fundamentally based on religion. Zaidi revivalism in Yemen "cannot be reduced to just a religious sect, it is [more broadly] the legacy of the Zaidi Hashemite Imams," a governance tradition which informs Yemeni social values today (Mohammad 2020).

Badr al-Din Houthi and his son Hussein launched the 'Faithful Youth' initiative in 1995, borrowing some ideas from the Salafis but opposing their vicious sectarianism. This more inclusive movement stressed "the patriotic education of the young generation" by studying Yemeni Zaydi doctrine (Issaev 2018: 12).

A wider range of Yemeni Youth did participate in the 2011 uprising, but many were already politically committed. A poll showed 77% as "politically active prior to 2011." Chair of the Muwatana Organisation for Human Rights Radhya Almutawakel concurred: "there were many independent youth in the square [in 2011], but the majority of them were Islah, Houthi or something else first" (Toska 2018).

Then there was the doctrinal fracture. The 'Faithful Youth' responded to Saudi-backed salafi/wahhabis by calling them "true terrorists" who wanted "to sow enmity and hatred and to impose their ideas on young Muslims" (Issaev 2018: 12). From this ideological split the movement led by Hussein al Houthi—and after his death in 2004, by his younger brother Abdul Malik al Houthi—gained support from Houthi clan allied groups and from those alienated by the sectarian Islah movement and its associated al Ahmar clan (Issaev 2018: 13).

Salafism and wahhabism in Yemen have older, traditional roots but they were reinforced by the Saudis. The Salafi centre at Dar al-Hadith "acted as a breeding ground for extremism in Yemen" often based on foreign funding (Issaev 2018: 15). Nevertheless, several currents of salafism had developed in Yemen, currents which have been variously described as 'traditional,' 'new' and 'jihadi' salafism, the latter "represented by al Qaeda in the Arabian Peninsula (AQAP) (Khoshafah 2021). After Ali Saleh resigned as president the Islah group backed the creation of another salafist movement, al Nusra, "led by Sheikh al Zindani and the Yemeni cell of the Muslim Brotherhood" (Issaev 2018: 14). It has been said that the Ansarallah idea is to "resurrect Zaydi leadership" so as to counter "encroaching Sunni ideologies" (Nagi 2019); but this really means countering sectarian ideologies, in particularly the Salafism sponsored by the Saudis and—until the 2017 split between Riyadh and Doha—the allied sectarian Muslim Brotherhood network promoted by Qatar.

By late 2011 the ouster of Saleh was followed by a Gulf Council Cooperation (GCC) proposal, headed by the Saudis. Mansour Hadi, a weak figure, was to be a transitional president (2012-2014) while a National Dialogue Conference (NDC) took place. From a European perspective, sympathetic to Saudi tutelage, it was said that this GCC initiative, to which Saleh had agreed, was a transition process which prevented a likely civil war. Saleh ceded power to Hadi, who appeared as the only candidate on the ballot and won more than 99 per cent of votes cast in February 2012 (Popp 2015).

Meanwhile Ansarallah pursued the revolution, taking over several provinces around the capital and removing the sectarian Salafi presence in the north. That included controlling clans loyal to the Muslim Brotherhood-aligned Islah Party in Saadah and Amran provinces. The slogans used included those of anti-extremism and anti-sectarianism (Nagi 2019).

Several analysts agree that there is little basis for "the accusation that the Houthis are controlled from Iran and just a tool of Tehran's expansion policy," in part because "the Iranians supplied only very moderate assistance and had even tried to dissuade the Houthis from making a bid for power" (Popp 2015). A Yemeni journalist in Sanaa says that Iran's subsequent support is unlikely to have a decisive role in AnsarAllah's "ultimate success or failure" (Abdulla Mohammed 2020). Iran certainly now provides at least "moral support" for the Ansarallah government. Yet that relationship is reinforced by the fact that the NSG opposes Riyadh and its sectarian, anti-Shia, Wahhabi mission. It might be the case that Hezbollah has assisted in an advisory role for similar reasons (Khan 2016). Even those analysts who place emphasis on sectarian political divides say that "Tehran's influence is likely limited, especially since Iranians and Houthis adhere to different schools of Shiite Islam" (Robinson 2021). Ansarallah-led Yemen has made common cause with Palestine, Iran and Syria for strategic and not sectarian reasons.

In any event, debates at the NDC lasted from March 2013 to January 2014; but Ansarallah rejected the NDC/GCC proposal for federal partition of the country into six regions. Instead, they allied with Saleh's GPC and, in September 2014, took over the capital. It has been recognised that the exclusion of "important political forces from the negotiations … cast doubt upon the legitimacy of the GCC initiative" (Popp 2015). Support for the NDC and the Hadi transitional regime evaporated. Hadi was a weak figure who had also alienated the sectarian groups: the Islah Party, the Yemeni Muslim Brotherhood and salafist groups. His interim mandate of two years was extended for one year by the House of Representatives (Issaev 2018: 16, 21). But the Ansarallah-led revolution of 2014-2015 changed everything.

The Saudi-UAE group intervened in March 2015 to prevent the Ansarallah coalition taking Aden (Nagi 2019). With this Saudi-led war the broader youth movement and the al Watan nationalist party fractured. Al Watan, established in 2011, had enjoyed 8 of the 40 youth representatives at the NDC and some al Watan figures participated in Hadi's transitional regime (Toska 2018). With the decline in support for Saudi-styled Wahhabism, and while Islah denounced all other groups (including the southerners) as 'atheists,' the al Ahmar clan resorted to collaboration with the mercenaries brought in to fight the Ansarallah coalition. That became the core force of the Saudi operation, 'Decisive Storm' (Issaev 2018: 14).

The Saudis and Emiratis hired these mercenaries and supplied them with Western weapons. What the Sanaa government called a "coalition of aggression" came to include the USA, the Saudis, Jordan, France, UK, Morocco, Pakistan, UAE, Sudan, Egypt, Eritrea and even Colombia (Stevenson 2019). Its breadth has a lot to do with successful U.S.-led moves at the United Nations to falsely designate the exile Hadi regime as the perpetual "government" and the de facto Ansarallah government in Sanaa as perpetual "Houthi rebels."

Thousands of foreign mercenaries were deployed by the UAE in South Yemen, to prop up the Southern Transitional Council (STC). This has included U.S. and German militia using contracted Western, Saudi, Eritrean, Sudanese, even Colombian and poor Yemeni foot soldiers. It is said that "up to 15,000 Sudanese mercenaries"—just from that one country—have been fighting on behalf of the foreign occupation powers in Yemen (Issa 2022).

Nevertheless, in July 2016 Ansarallah and the GPC formed a revolutionary government, the Supreme Political Council, which soon after was called the National Salvation Government (NSG) (Rezeg 2016; Nagi 2019). This political alliance in the capital arose because of the convergence of interests. After the Ansarallah coalition took Sanaa the General People's Congress Party, by itself, had "suffered from marginalization" (Al Hadaa 2017).

In December 2017, fearing Saleh would betray them to the Saudis, Ansarallah assassinated the former president as he tried to leave the country. The NSG interior ministry reported the "killing" of "Saleh and his supporters … after he and his men blockaded the roads and killed civilians in a clear collaboration with the enemy countries of the coalition" (Al Jazeera 2017b).

The Security Council betrays the Yemeni people

The appalling war against Yemen, leading to what has been called the world's 'worst humanitarian crisis' (WFP 2022) has been promoted, rather than resolved, by the United Nations Security Council (UNSC). The UN-sanctioned, genocidal siege takes advantage of the poor recognition of Yemen's revolution, many years on.

A serious revision of UNSC Resolutions is necessary, in particular Resolution 2216, which artificially pits the "legitimate power" of the exiled puppet regime against the "Houthi rebels" who are said to have carried out a "coup" (Issaev 2018: 5, 28). In reality, the UNSC sanctions imposed on Yemen's de facto government are inflicted on most of the Yemeni population, even as it is openly acknowleged that the country suffers a humanitarian crisis (Bell 2022).

Set up with a supposed primary purpose of preventing war, the UNSC over the past decade has effectively and repeatedly backed the U.S.-Saudi led military repression of the only genuine revolution arising from the so called Arab Spring (Ahmed 2021). Washington got its way at the UN from the beginning, as destroying the Ansarallah-led revolutionary coalition was part of its broader aim to remove all independent regimes and create a 'New Middle East' under U.S. tutelage (Bransten 2006).

The Pentagon delegated the task of destroying the new Ansarallah-led Yemeni coalition ('the Houthis') to the Saudis while Washington convinced the Security Council to rubber stamp Saudi attacks on those parts of central Yemen (including the capital) controlled by the new government. This repression has been carried out under Chapter VII powers of the UN Charter and in the name of fighting al Qaeda terrorism and defeating a supposed threat to 'international peace and security.' The war and siege involve direct UN intervention in the sovereign affairs of the Yemeni people, while siding with the Saudis, key sponsor of all the regional al Qaeda groups.

A recent study by the Yemen Centre for Human Rights (YCHR 2022) exposed the links between the systematic violence imposed on the Yemeni people and successive UNSC resolutions from 2011 to 2021 (CCHS 2022). In summary, the UNSC sought to defend an interim regime which arose during the democracy struggles between 2011 and 2012. It then demonised and sanctioned the emerging revolutionary government while consistently backing a GCC (i.e. Saudi) 'initiative' to divide the country and present a Saudi puppet to the world as president.

We might understand the involvement of three of the five permanent members of the UNSC (NATO members USA, UK and France), as they have initiated at least eight wars against the independent states and peoples of the region. But what of Russia and China? Those two counter-weights backed the use of Chapter VII powers against Libya in 2011 (under a Medvedev presidency in Russia) (UN 2011) but when NATO abused the 'no fly zone' pretext to destroy the little African country, they seemed to have learned a lesson. Russia and China opposed a similar UN- authorised intervention against Syria the following year, in 2012 (Reuters 2012).

So, what was different about Yemen in 2014? Syria was a recognised state under NATO attack, whereas Yemen was a society undergoing a revolutionary transition (Tharappel 2021). In any case, as with Libya, Russia and China were simply not paying attention.

Only in April 2015 did Russia abstain from the sixth UNSC resolution (2216), which enhanced sanctions against certain parties in Yemen (UN 2015).

That abstention was too little, too late. The Yemen Centre for Human Rights study (CCHS 2022) shows that UNSC resolutions #2014 of 2011 (UNSC 2014b) and #2051 of 2012 (UNSC 2012) "paved the way" for misleading the international community by claiming that the upheaval in Yemen was a "threat to international peace and security." That broader threat was the means— later in Resolution #2140 of February 2014 (UNSC 2014a)—to invoke Chapter VII coercive powers.

In successive resolutions (2014, 2051, 2140, 2201, 2204, 2216 and even 2564 of 2021) this alleged "threat to international peace and security" was linked to citations of al Qaeda groups in the Arabian Peninsula (AQAP), gangs notoriously backed by the Saudis (WION 2020) and some other GCC members. Even U.S. sources recognise that al Qaeda and ISIS in Yemen oppose the Ansarallah-led Coalition (Robinson 2022). In other words, properly understood, any wider threat to peace from international terrorism clearly did not come from the new Yemeni revolutionary government, but from what the Yemenis call the U.S.-Saudi led 'coalition of aggression' (Civil Conglomerate 2021).

The Yemen Centre for Human Rights says resolution 2216 of April 2015 "shocked the world" by turning "a blind eye" to the atrocities committed by the U.S.-Saudi coalition. From 2014 onwards the UNSC maintained the fiction that Abd Rabbo Mansour Hadi, the interim president in 2012, remained the legitimate president of the country (Press TV 2021). On the other hand, those in Yemen's National Salvation Government (Jonkers 2021), under Resolution 2216 of April 2015, were sanctioned and subject to travel bans and arms embargoes for supposedly engaging in "acts that threaten the peace security or stability of Yemen."

In successive resolutions (2014, 2140, 2201, 2216 and 2564) the UNSC promoted an 'initiative' by the Saudi dominated Gulf Cooperation Council (GCC) and its linked (and now defunct) 'National Dialogue Conference' while paying lip service to 'all parties' in Yemen.

Never mind what the Yemeni people had said and done since 2012. Never mind that from early 2015 Hadi was in exile and under effective 'hotel arrest' in Riyadh (al Jazeera 2017a). This extreme partisanship by the UNSC sought to freeze Yemen's political processes in time. Even the Western media recognised that UN backing of the war was futile and disastrous, with a 2016 *Time* magazine headline crying: 'The U.N. failed Yemen's Children' (Offenheiser 2016).

No UN. agency could function properly under this hopeless, interventionist regime. The UN's Human Rights Council wrung its hands, crying "we have failed Yemen," while impotently trying to blame both sides for violations (Reuters in Geneva 2021). In late 2021 UN Special Envoy Hans Grundberg filed a near useless report, speaking of his "frustration and despair" and urging an end to the fighting (Grundberg 2021).

The *New York Times*, which had backed every U.S.-led war in the region for decades, also resorted to moral equivalence arguments, claiming that war crimes were committed by "both sides" (Cumming-Bruce 2019). But where was mention of the UN Charter principles of sovereignty and non-intervention?

The defeat of Saudi-led, U.S.-backed forces in Yemen had become obvious by 2017 (Najjar and Al-Karimi 2017), even though the war media complained that this was all the fault of "the rebels" (Al-Mouallimi 2017).

With several years of defeat and humanitarian crisis the UNSC was left carrying the can for this failed war and still backing a 'government' with an exiled 'president' who has barely seen Yemeni soil since early 2015. This was a great betrayal of the Yemeni people on the part of the UN Security Council.

Futile foreign intervention

As with Washington's dirty war on Syria, the war and siege imposed on the people of Yemen has been futile. The foreign intervention certainly kills thousands and imposes starvation and suffering on millions, but there is little likelihood of any outcome favourable to the war coalition.

The large-scale foreign intervention, beginning in early 2015, is best understood in terms of the threat an independent Yemen poses to Washington's regional ambitions. The Saudis certainly have their own ambition to dominate the Arabian Peninsula, but for a century they have served as loyal agents of the British and then the USA. The war on Yemen is carried on principally because an independent Yemen—like an independent Syria and an independent Iran—pose a threat to Washington's New Middle East plan. That imperial strategy is reinforced by Pentagon doctrines of eliminating 'disconnectedness' from its rule and achieving full spectrum dominance in this designated CENTCOM zone, by which Washington arrogates to itself much of the Middle East as its "area of responsibility" (Anderson 2019: Ch.1; CENTCOM 2022).

Yemen sits on a key sea route between Washington's two principal agents in the region: the Israelis and the Saudis, and between the U.S.-designated CENTCOM zone and its Africom zone. Created in 2007, AFRICOM purports to supervise all the African states except Egypt, which remains within CENTCOM (AFRICOM 2022). The sea route past Yemen will also become important for China's Belt and Road Initiative (BRI), at the right time.

During the war Washington has relied on Saudi-led regional forces, only directly intervening from time to time. Their main target since the revolution has been the Ansarallah-led coalition. In May 2017 a U.S. group entered the desert area of Marib and claimed to have killed "seven al Qaeda" operatives (Cronk 2017). That claim is highly suspect as Washington, at this time, was consistently supporting al Qaeda groups in Iraq and Syria (Anderson 2016: Ch.12). More likely the U.S. groups were trying to reinforce the Saudi grip on Marib city.

The British have also played a role in suporting the war on Yemen, as they did in Afghanistan, Iraq and Syria. Both the U.S. and Britain point out that they have 'given' several billion dollars in aid to Yemen, but this mostly goes to foreign contractors linked to the exile regime and some small groups inside Yemen. None of it gets to the majority of the population in NSG-controlled areas. While Yemen's economy is crippled by sanctions, secret British operations assist in destabilisation as billions in arms are pumped into the Saudi regime (Bell 2022). Tehran says, correctly, that the British government "as a U.N. pen-holder on Yemen, has absolutely failed to progress peace … [and] has happily followed U.S foreign policy, while selling over £22 billion of military equipment to the [U.S.-Saudi led] Coalition" (IRNA 2022).

The Saudi regime itself "successfully lobbied for its removal from the UN's list of violators of children's rights," despite its atrocties against Yemeni children (Bell 2022). Yet the Saudi attacks on Yemen have revived "long standing territorial disputes" over three provinces, Jizan, Najran and Asir, which the Yemenis "consider to be occupied territories." If the war persists, it is possible that Yemen may seek to reclaim these territories. Failure of the Saudi intervention in Yemen may undermine the Saudi role in the Arabian Peninsula (Issaev 2018: 28). After many years the power play has moved against the Hadi regime and its successors in Riyadh. Time, it has been said, "plays in favour" of the Ansarallah-led government in Sanaa (Issaev 2018: 5, 21).

What proportion of the population is under NSG control? To assess this, we have to look at the population of each of the 21 governorates and put that together with best estimates of governorate control. As at 2023, the last census of the Yemeni population by governorate was in 2013 (CSO 2015). Most sources indicate that the NSG government controls the highly populated north and western provinces. In early 2022 Qatar's Al Jazeera recognised that "the bulk of Yemen's northern highlands, as well as Sanaa, remain under the control of Houthi rebels." They indicated that all or most of the following provinces were "under the control of Houthi rebels": Saadah, al Jawf, Amran, Sanaa, Hajjah, Mahwit, Hodeideh, Dhamar, Raymah, Ibb, al Bayda; and parts of Taiz and Dhale (Haddad 2022). Much of this is accepted by other media which are mostly hostile to Ansarallah (Glenn, Nada and Rowan 2022).

There are no accurate, independent measurements of control of the contested areas, which are almost 40% of the country. However, in December 2022, sources in Sanaa (MS 2022) gave the following estimates of governorates which are entirely, majority or partially under NSG control. This broadly fits the Al Jazeera estimates. Detail is in Table 1 below and includes assessments that the NSG controls 75% of Marib, except for the capital city and 2 districts, more than 50% of Taiz and 45% of Dhalea (MS 2022). If we assume 'majority' control means 50% to 80% that would mean from 16.9 to 20.5 million (of 28.2

million) or from 60% to 73% of the population is under NSG control. Population numbers are based on the 2013 census (CSO 2015).

Table 1: Control of Yemeni Governorates, Dec 2022	
Total population: 28.174m (2013)	**Yemen Governorates (Popn in 2013)**
Entirely under (National Salvation Government, Ansarallah-led) NSG control [11.079 million]	Sanaa (2.279), Dhamar (1.697), Mahweet (0.732), Amran (1.123), Raymah (0.502), Baydha (0.835), Ibb (3.911), Saadah (0.987)
Majority under NSG control [10.878 million] if NSG 50%/80%: 5.44/8.7 million	Hajjah (1.887), Jawf (0.663), Hodeidah (3.774), Taiz (4.554) [50-80%]
Minority under NSG control [1.757 million] if NSG 20-40%: 0.35-0.7 million	Mareb (Riyadh: 0.504), Dhalea (STC/UAE:0.602), Shabwah (Riyadh 0.651)
Control by foreign backed groups: STC / UAE and Riyadh [4.46 million]	Aden (STC/UAE: 1.087); Abyan (STC/UAE: 0.658), Al Mahrah (Riyadh: 0.400), Hadramaut (Riyadh: 1.329), Lahij (STC/UAE: 0.926), Socotra (STC/UAE: 0.060)
Sources: MS 2022; Haddad 2022; CSO 2015	

There is therefore little sign that foreign intervention has advanced Saudi hegemony or displaced the Ansarallah-led government. The intervention just maintains the killing and mass suffering through a UNSC backed siege. On the other hand, the U.S.-Saudi war has reinforced the Ansarallah slogan ‘Death to America,’ ensuring that the effective government in Sanaa links itself more closely to Iran, Syria and the other independent states of the region.

When the situation stabilises it is highly likely that Yemen, like post-Washington Afghanistan, will seek to engage with the Chinese BRI initiatives. China has a long history of supporting infrastructure development in Yemen, going back to the 1950s Chinese construction of a 266km road between Sanaa and the port city of Hodeidah. Over 2012–2013 China agreed to build three gas powered power plants and to expand container terminals in Aden and Mokha (Tekingunduz 2019). Like most of the world, China has maintained links with the exile Hadi regime, but has also had “routine meetings” with “all parties.” Aden remains particularly important for them (Tekingunduz 2019). Chinese pragmatism will eventually lead it to engage with the real government of Yemen.

References

Africom (2022). "About the Command." United States Africa Command. https://www.africom.mil/about-the-command

Ahmed, Omar. "Why Yemen's was the only real revolution, post-Arab Spring." *Middle East Monitor.* November 12, 2021. https://www.middleeastmonitor.com/20211112-why-yemens-was-the-only-real-revolution-post-arab-spring/

al-Fasly, Mahmoud Sagheer. "Witnessing the Yemeni Revolution." In Assad Alsaleh (Editor). *Voices of the Arab Spring: Personal Stories from the Arab Revolutions.* Columbia University Press, 2015. https://www.degruyter.com/document/doi/10.7312/alsa16318-037/html

Al Hadaa, Karima (2017) "The Dynamics of the Houthi-GPC alliance." The Yemen Peace Project. June 2, 2017. https://www.yemenpeaceproject.org/blog-x/houthi-gpc-alliance

Al Jazeera (2017a). "Yemeni President Hadi 'under house arrest' in Riyadh." November 7, 2017. https://www.aljazeera.com/news/2017/11/7/yemeni-president-hadi-under-house-arrest-in-riyadh

——— (2017b). "Yemen: Ex-President Ali Abdullah Saleh killed." December 10, 2017. https://www.aljazeera.com/news/2017/12/10/yemen-ex-president-ali-abdullah-saleh-killed

al-Qarawi, Hisham. *The Yemeni Revolution: replacing Ali Abdullah Saleh, or replacing obsolete institutions?* Arab Center for Research & Policy Studies, Doha Institute, 2011. online: https://www.dohainstitute.org/en/lists/ACRPS-PDFDocumentLibrary/Yemeni_Revolution.pdf

Al-Mouallimi, Abdallah Y. "It's Up to the Rebels to Stop Yemen's War." *New York Times.* October 3, 2017. https://www.nytimes.com/2017/10/03/opinion/yemen-war-houthis.html

Amos, Deborah. "For Yemen's Ousted President, A Five-Star Exile With No End In Sight." *NPR.* June 14, 2015. https://www.npr.org/sections/parallels/2015/06/14/413913530/for-yemens-ex-president-a-five-star-exile-with-no-end-in-sight

Anderson, Tim. *The Dirty War on Syria.* Montreal: Global Research, 2016.

———. *Axis of Resistance.* Atlanta: Clarity Press, 2019.

Bell, Steve. "Time to end, not escalate, the war on Yemen." Stop the War Coalition UK. January 24, 2022. https://www.stopwar.org.uk/article/time-to-end-not-escalate-the-war-on-yemen/

Blinken, Antony. "Revocation of the Terrorist Designations of Ansarallah." U.S. Department of State. February 12, 2021. https://www.state.gov/revocation-of-the-terrorist-designations-of-ansarallah/

Bransten, Jeremy. "Middle East: Rice Calls For A 'New Middle East." RFERL. July 25, 2006. https://www.rferl.org/a/1070088.html

CCHS. "The UN Security Council has betrayed the Yemeni people." Centre for Counter Hegemonic Studies. January 21, 2022. https://counter-hegemonic-studies.site/unsc-yemen-1/

CENTCOM (2022). "Map of the U.S. Central Command area of responsibility." U.S. Central Command. https://www.centcom.mil/MEDIA/igphoto/2002844889/

CEP (2022). "Houthis." Counter Extremism Project [U.S. Govt led]. https://www.counterextremism.com/threat/houthis

Civil Conglomerate. "Ministry of Human Rights Denounces Recent UN Security Council Statement On Yemen." Civil Conglomerate for Development and Freedom. October 24, 2021. http://www.ccdf-ye.org/en/2021/10/24/ministry-of-human-rights-denounces-recent-un-security-council-statement-on-yemen/

CNN. "Yemen's Houthis form surprise new government." *CNN.* November 29, 2016. https://edition.cnn.com/2016/11/29/middleeast/yemen-houthis-new-government/index.html

Cronk, Terri Moon. "Pentagon spokesman describes U.S. raid in Yemen." U.S. Central Command. May 23, 2017. https://www.centcom.mil/MEDIA/NEWS-ARTICLES/News-Article-View/Article/1191797/pentagon-spokesman-describes-us-raid-in-yemen/

CSO (2015). *Yemen: National Health and Demographic Survey, 2013.* Central Statistical Organisation, Republic of Yemen. July 2015. https://dhsprogram.com/pubs/pdf/fr296/fr296.pdf

Cumming-Bruce, Nick. "War Crimes Committed by Both Sides in Yemen, U.N. Panel Says." *New York Times.* September 3, 2019. https://www.nytimes.com/2019/09/03/world/middleeast/war-crimes-yemen.html

Glenn, Cameron, Garrett Nada, and Mattisan Rowan. "Who are Yemen's Houthis?" Wilson Centre. July 7, 2022. https://www.wilsoncenter.org/article/who-are-yemens-houthis

Green, Daniel R. (2019). "Defeating al Qaeda Shadow Government in Yemen." Washington Institute for Near East Policy. https://www.washingtoninstitute.org/media/950

Grundberg, Hans. “Briefing to United Nations Security Council by the Special Envoy for Yemen—Hans Grundberg, 14 December 2021.” Reliefweb. December 14, 2021. https://reliefweb.int/report/yemen/briefing-united-nations-security-council-special-envoy-yemen-hans-grundberg-14-december

Haddad, Mohammed. “Infographic: Yemen’s war explained in maps and charts.” *Al Jazeera.* February 9, 2022. https://www.aljazeera.com/news/2022/2/9/yemens-war-explained-in-maps-and-charts-interactive

ICG. “Yemen’s Southern Transitional Council: A Delicate Balancing Act.” International Crisis Group. March 30, 2021. https://www.crisisgroup.org/middle-east-north-africa/gulf-and-arabian-peninsula/yemen/yemens-southern-transitional-council-delicate-balancing-act

IRNA. “British analyst stresses Ansarallah’s role in Yemen peace process.” Islamic Republic News Agency. June 22, 2022. https://en.irna.ir/news/84798662/British-analyst-stresses-Ansarallah-s-role-in-Yemen-peace-process

Issa, Mona. “Mercenaries in Yemen: Nationalities, numbers & horrors.” *Al Mayadeen.* March 29, 2022. https://english.almayadeen.net/news/politics/mercenaries-in-yemen:-nationalities-numbers-horrors

Issaev, Leonid M. *Yemen: Unfinished Revolution.* Istanbul, Al Sharq Forum Paper Series, 2018. https://www.hse.ru/mirror/pubs/share/224915854

Jonkers, Brecht. “Defying Odds, Yemen’s Revolutionary Forces Score Stunning Victories.” *The Crescent.* January 1, 2021. [Jumada’ al-Ula’ 17, 1442]. https://crescent.icit-digital.org/articles/defying-odds-yemen-s-revolutionary-forces-score-stunning-victories

Khan, Sabahat. “The ideological affinities of the Houthis with Iran.” *The Arab Weekly.* October 30, 2016. https://thearabweekly.com/ideological-affinities-houthis-iran

Khoshafah, Amjad. “Houthi-Salafi Coexistence Agreements: Motives and Future Prospects.” Sana’a Center for Strategic Studies. December 3, 2021. https://sanaacenter.org/publications/analysis/15839

MEMO. “Remembering the September 21 Revolution in Yemen.” *Middle East Monitor.* September 21, 2017. https://www.middleeastmonitor.com/20170921-remembering-the-september-21-revolution-in-yemen/

Mohammed, Mohammed Abdulla. “The Houthi Movement from a Local Perspective: A Resurgence of Political Zaidism.” Sana’a Center for Strategic Studies. November 18, 2020. https://sanaacenter.org/publications/analysis/11925

MS (confidential source in Sanaa). Personal communication with this author. December 18, 2022.

Nagi, Ahmed. "Yemen's Houthis Used Multiple Identities to Advance." Carnegie Middle East Centre. March 19, 2019. https://carnegie-mec.org/2019/03/19/yemen-s-houthis-used-multiple-identities-to-advance-pub-78623

Najjar, Farah, and Khalid Al-Karimi. "Saudi Arabia's war in Yemen 'a strategic failure.'" *Al Jazeera.* August 23, 2017. https://www.aljazeera.com/features/2017/8/23/saudi-arabias-war-in-yemen-a-strategic-failure

Offenheiser, Ray. "The U.N. Failed Yemen's Children." *Time.* June 15, 2016. https://time.com/4370208/the-u-n-failed-yemens-children/

Popp, Roland. "War in Yemen: Revolution and Saudi Intervention." *CSS Analyses in Security Policy* 175 (June 2015). https://www.research-collection.ethz.ch/bitstream/handle/20.500.11850/118212/eth-49383-01.pdf

Press TV. "Yemenis Rally on Sept. 21 revolution anniversary, condemn foreign aggression." September 21, 2021. https://www.presstv.ir/Detail/2021/09/21/666972/Yemen-September-21-Revolution-Ansarallah-Movement-Rally-Saudi-Arabia-Foreign-Aggression

Reuters. "Russia against no-fly zone over Syria – Sky News Arabia." August 18, 2012. https://www.reuters.com/article/us-syria-russia-lavrov-idUSBRE87H02U20120818

Reuters in Geneva. "'We have failed Yemen': UN human rights council ends war crime probe." *The Guardian.* October 7, 2021. https://www.theguardian.com/world/2021/oct/07/un-human-rights-council-votes-to-end-yemen-war-crimes-investigation

Rezeg, Ali Abdo. "Houthis announce 'national salvation' govt in Yemen." AA. November 28, 2016. https://www.aa.com.tr/en/middle-east/houthis-announce-national-salvation-govt-in-yemen/695048

Riedel, Bruce. "The Houthis have won in Yemen: What next?" Brookings. Feb. 1, 2022. https://www.brookings.edu/blog/order-from-chaos/2022/02/01/the-houthis-have-won-in-yemen-what-next/

Robinson, Kali. "Yemen's Tragedy: War, Stalemate, and Suffering." Council on Foreign Relations. October 21, 2022. https://www.cfr.org/backgrounder/yemen-crisis

Sana'a Center. "The Curious Tale of Houthi-AQAP Prisoner Exchanges in Yemen." Sana'a Center For Strategic Studies. December 17, 2021. https://sanaacenter.org/publications/analysis/16002

Stevenson, Tom. "Saudi's coalition in Yemen: Militias and mercenaries backed by western firepower." *Middle East Eye.* March 28, 2019. https://www.middleeasteye.net/news/saudis-coalition-yemen-militias-and-mercenaries-backed-western-firepower

Tekingunduz, Alican. "What is China doing in Yemen?" *TRT News.* December 13, 2019. https://www.trtworld.com/middle-east/what-is-china-doing-in-yemen-32183

Tharappel, Jay. "Yemen: understanding the Zaydi Revival." *Oriental Despot.* January 20, 2019. https://theorientaldespot.com/2019/01/20/salafismvszaydism/

Tharappel, Jay. "Who is really fighting whom in Yemen?" *The Communists.* February 20, 2021. https://thecommunists.org/2021/02/20/news/who-really-fighting-whom-yemen-jay-tharappel-wpb-antiwar/

Toska, Silvana. "The rise and fall and necessity of Yemen's youth movements." Middle East Political Science, Elliot School of International Affairs, 2018. https://pomeps.org/the-rise-and-fall-and-necessity-of-yemens-youth-movements

UN (2011). "Security Council Approves 'No-Fly Zone' over Libya, Authorizing 'All Necessary Measures' to Protect Civilians, by Vote of 10 in Favour with 5 Abstentions." United Nations. March 17, 2011. https://www.un.org/press/en/2011/sc10200.doc.htm

——— (2015). "Security Council Demands End to Yemen Violence, Adopting Resolution 2216 (2015), with Russian Federation Abstaining, Also Imposes Sanctions on Key Figures in Militia Operations." United Nations. April 14, 2015. https://www.un.org/press/en/2015/sc11859.doc.htm

UNSC (2012). "Resolution 2051 (2012) Adopted by the Security Council at its 6784th meeting, on 12 June 2012." United Nations Security Council. June 12, 2012. online: http://unscr.com/en/resolutions/doc/2051

——— (2014a). "Resolution 2140 (2014) Adopted by the Security Council at its 7119th meeting, on 26 February 2014." United Nations Security Council. February 26, 2014. http://unscr.com/en/resolutions/doc/2140

——— (2014b). "Resolution 2014 (2011) Adopted by the Security Council at its 6634th meeting, on 21 October 2011." United Nations Security Council, 21 October 21, 2014. http://unscr.com/en/resolutions/doc/2014

Wells, Madeleine. "Yemen's Houthi movement and the revolution." *Foreign Policy.* February 27, 2012. https://foreignpolicy.com/2012/02/27/yemens-houthi-movement-and-the-revolution/

Werleman, C. J. "UAE-Israeli Annexation of Socotra is Most Significant ME Occupation Since 1967." *Inside Arabia.* October 5, 2021. https://insidearabia.com/uae-israeli-annexation-of-socotra-is-most-significant-me-occupation-since-1967/

WFP (2022). "The world's worst humanitarian crisis." World Food Programme. https://www.wfp.org/yemen-crisis

WION. "Epicenter' of al-Qaeda financing: How Saudi Arabia's terror policy backfired." November 13, 2020. https://www.wionews.com/world/epicenter-of-al-qaeda-financing-how-saudi-arabias-terror-policy-backfired-343023

YCHR (2022). Yemen Center for Human Rights. https://ychr.org

Zabarah, Mohammed A. (1984) "The Yemeni Revolution of 1962 Seen as a Social Revolution." In B. R. Pridham (Editor). *Contemporary Yemen: Politics and Historical Background.* Routledge, 2016.

PART 2

Recreating the Future

10. Washington's Strategic Retreat

Withdrawal from the 20-year occupation of Afghanistan marked a turning point for Washington. Source: Associated Press

Failure of the dirty war on Syria, peace talks in Yemen and the chaotic withdrawal from Afghanistan are clear signs that Washington has begun a partial strategic retreat from the region. The more astute U.S. officials have already begun the relevant rationales just as the move strikes fear in regional collaborators. The continuity between the Trump and Biden administrations is visible not just in the sustained angry rhetoric against Iran, declarations of undying support for Apartheid Israel and ongoing economic siege of the peoples of region; it can also be seen in U.S. adaptation to a series of regional defeats.

U.S. thinking on this move is reminiscent of the Guam Doctrine, later called the Nixon Doctrine, developed in 1969 as it became clear that the U.S. was failing in its military objectives in Vietnam. Although the U.S. would continue to slaughter millions across Indochina for several more years, this doctrine called for a 'Vietnamization' of the war and a pull-back of U.S. forces while supporting its 'regional allies.'

The rhetoric was not of withdrawal but of "staying in and continuing to play a responsible role in helping the non-Communist nations and neutrals as well as our Asian allies to defend their independence." In practice it was a strategic withdrawal and a call to "not make any more commitments unless they were required by our own vital interests" (Nixon Foundation 2008).

Washington now faces a similar trajectory in West Asia. The most articulate recent U.S. voice for strategic retreat has been former colonel and military historian Douglas McGregor, appointed by U.S. President Trump as a special advisor in late 2020 (Perry 2020). Earlier, in January 2020, McGregor had told Fox News: despite some counter-arguments, the U.S. had "no vital strategic interest" to stay in Syria and Iraq: "that war is over and we lost it; Iran is a winner, for the moment." McGregor said that Turkey and 'Sunni Islamists' could be left to compete with Iran for control of Syria and Iraq, but that U.S. interests "begin with a line that runs across the top of Israel, Jordan, Saudi Arabia, around Kuwait and down to the middle of the Persian Gulf" (Fox News 2020). No doubt McGregor represents a realist faction within the U.S. 'deep state' that is contemplating a similar 'repositioning.'

Importantly, the prospect of this strategic withdrawal has opened up differences between Washington and Israel. Both want to disempower Iran, leader of the emerging, independent resistance bloc. Yet the U.S. may eventually accept pulling back from its direct occupations in several countries, relying on occasional missile attacks and economic warfare, while delegating destabilisation to the Saudis, Turkey and proxies like ISIS, the MEK and HTS.

The multiple failures and their costs, leading to the idea of a strategic partial withdrawal, was argued strongly by Trump as a presidential candidate in 2016 (Chulov 2016). Though he was unable to act as he had argued, this was not just one man's idea. That pragmatism returned in the Biden administration's 2020-2021 withdrawal from Afghanistan. At the same time the Saudis, after a series of losses, showed they were keen for a ceasefire with Yemen (Riedel 2020).

The failing Syrian and Iraqi occupations are closely linked and will collapse together, sooner or later. While the Biden administration has sent mixed messages on Syria (MEE 2021) it seemed to back away from the Trump position of punishing regional allies such as the

UAE, and Bahrain (Quilliam 2021) or blocking NGOs which seek to reopen relations with Damascus (IO 2021). The UAE, in particular, has anticipated normalisation with Damascus, since at least 2018.

So why would Washington retreat? The U.S. is quite capable of persisting in losing wars to punish and weaken its adversaries. It demonstrated that by prolonging its war in Vietnam seven years after the first Paris peace talks (Schultz 2013). Yet it did retreat from Vietnam, as it had from Korea in the 1950s, after slaughtering millions but without achieving its military objectives.

Nevertheless, this notoriously cold-blooded bad loser remains capable of calculating the costs of losing wars, both in material and prestige terms; even when they hide facts and falsify histories.

U.S. economic and global decline is not unrelated to these losing wars, despite the offset achievement of making subordinate 'allies' pay for many of these wars. The losing war in Afghanistan reputedly cost the USA more than two trillion dollars (CNBC 2021); and this in a declining, would be empire with no real public health system at home (Reich 2020).

In late 2018 Trump adviser Stephen Miller argued his President's decision to pull troops out of Syria (Kelly 2018), a decision quickly countermanded by other forces in the deep state. Yet some U.S. troops in Syria were redeployed. An interim rationale, given by Trump to placate the dogs of war, was a partial ongoing occupation to 'protect' Syria's oil. According to Defence Secretary Mark Esper this 'protection' was from ISIS (Baldor 2019). In practice the remnants of ISIS remained a tool of Washington and the oil was shipped to Iraq with funds eventually allocated to the SDF proxy (AJ 2020).

In August 2021 Biden finalised the Afghan withdrawal. Partial withdrawals from Iraq are flagged and when the Iraqi operation ends the occupation in Syria (denounced by Turkey, Russia and Iran) will be over. This series of defeats catalysed a debate within the U.S. deep state over future strategy, one side of which was reflected in Trump's over-arching criticism of pointless, seemingly endless and unwinnable wars and the need for a strategic retreat (Mead 2019).

Until fairly recently, the U.S.-NATO occupation of Afghanistan was described as a hedge against China's westward expansion, in particular of its BRI infrastructure, keeping Uyghur Islamists as an al Qaeda style destabilisation tool to be used in the region (Sidiq

2018), just as thousands had been used in Syria's Idlib (Al-Ghadhawi 2020). But those considerations were countermanded. Furthermore, the resurgent Taliban asserted that they will not be used against either Iran or China (Goldkorn 2021). It is a credible claim, because productive relations with these big neighbours are squarely in the Taliban's interests.

Regional realignment has serious consequences for the Israelis, who suffer great anxiety about any sort of U.S. retreat. The idea frightens them, and this is why they constantly seek assurance from Washington that they will not be abandoned if and when Iran actually responds to their constant provocations. The 2021 visit by zionist leader Naftali Bennett to Washington, proposing 'death by a thousand cuts' for Iran, as a 'Plan B' for the virtually defunct JCPOA nuclear agreement (Khalid 2021), was surely to seek renewed protection guarantees.

But as Lebanon's resistance leader Sayyed Hassan Nasrallah has pointed out, Israel does not control the USA (Nasrallah 2021); the zionist tail does not wag the imperial dog. In the past U.S. leaders have told subordinate 'allies' (e.g. Britain, France, Georgia) that they will not be taken for granted and will not be drawn into a war without their explicit consent. Israelis and all other collaborators fear a changing U.S. role in the region. They saw images of desperate, abandoned collaborators left behind at Kabul airport.

References

AJ. "Syria slams US firm's oil deal with SDF as 'null and void.'" *Al Jazeera.* August 2, 2020. https://www.aljazeera.com/news/2020/8/2/syria-slams-us-firms-oil-deal-with-sdf-as-null-and-void

Al-Ghadhawi, Abdullah. "Uighur Jihadists in Syria." New Lines Institute. March 18, 2020. https://newlinesinstitute.org/uyghurs/uighur-jihadists-in-syria/

Baldor, Lolita (2019). "US may now keep some troops in Syria to guard oil fields." *AP News.* October 22, 2019. https://apnews.com/article/donald-trump-syria-ap-top-news-mark-esper-afghanistan-a66bf441fdfb43ca80d200dcbfb5d09d

Chulov, Martin. "Syrian opposition left with nowhere to turn after Trump's victory." *The Guardian.* Nov. 11, 2016. https://www.theguardian.com/world/2016/nov/11/syrian-opposition-left-with-nowhere-to-turn-after-trumps-victory

CNBC. "The Fall of Afghanistan: How America's $2 trillion, Two-Decade War Ended In Chaos." *CNBC.* August 28, 2021. Video, 10:14. https://www.youtube.com/watch?v=DjhOGlUQNcw

Fox News. "War in Iraq, Syria 'is over, we lost it': Retired Army Colonel." *Fox News.* January 8, 2020. Video, 3:22. https://www.youtube.com/watch?v=_2Ut5Yyx_K8

Goldkorn, Jeremy. "China makes a deal with the Taliban." The China Project. July 28, 2021. https://thechinaproject.com/2021/07/28/china-makes-a-deal-with-the-taliban/

IO. "Caesar Act amendments make life easier for pro-Damas NGOs." Intelligence Online. April 27, 2021. https://www.intelligenceonline.com/government-intelligence/2021/04/27/caesar-act-amendments-make-life-easier-for-pro-damas-ngos,109660888-art

Kelly, Caroline. "Stephen Miller defends Trump's Syria withdrawal: 'Are we supposed to stay in Syria for generation after generation spilling American blood?'" *CNN.* December 21, 2018. https://edition.cnn.com/2018/12/20/politics/miller-syria-mattis-cnntv/index.html

Khalid, Tuqa. "Israel's PM presents Biden with 'death by a thousand cuts' Iran strategy." *Al Arabiya.* August 28, 2021. https://english.alarabiya.net/News/middle-east/2021/08/28/Israel-s-PM-presented-Biden-with-death-by-a-thousand-cuts-Iran-strategy-Reports

Mead, Walter Russell. "Trump's Jacksonian Syria Withdrawal." *Wall Street Journal.* October 7, 2019. https://www.wsj.com/articles/trumps-jacksonian-syria-withdrawal-11570487847

MEE. "Biden administration warns allies against restoring ties with Syria." *Middle East Eye.* June 25, 2021. https://www.middleeasteye.net/news/syria-biden-team-warns-countries-against-restoring-ties-assad

Nasrallah, Hassan. "Israel does not control America: Hassan Nasrallah, 2018." July 6, 2021. Centre for Counter Hegemonic Studies. https://counter-hegemonic-studies.site/nasrallah-israel-usa/

Nixon Foundation. "25 July 1969: The Nixon Doctrine." July 24, 2008. https://www.nixonfoundation.org/2008/07/25-july-1969-the-nixon-doctrine/

Perry, Mark. "The revenge of Col. Douglas Macgregor." Responsible Statecraft. November 12, 2020. https://responsiblestatecraft.org/2020/11/12/the-revenge-of-col-douglas-macgregor/

Quilliam, Neil. "The Middle East Is Preparing for the United States' Exit From Syria." *Foreign Policy.* August 25, 2021. https://foreignpolicy.com/2021/08/25/assad-middle-east-preparing-united-states-exit-syria/

Reich, Robert. "America has no real public health system—coronavirus has a clear run." *The Guardian.* March 15, 2020. https://www.theguardian.com/commentisfree/2020/mar/15/america-public-health-system-coronavirus-trump

Schultz, Colin. "Nixon Prolonged Vietnam War for Political Gain—And Johnson Knew About It, Newly Unclassified Tapes Suggest." *Smithsonian.* March 18, 2013. https://www.smithsonianmag.com/smart-news/nixon-prolonged-vietnam-war-for-political-gainand-johnson-knew-about-it-newly-unclassified-tapes-suggest-3595441/

Sidiq, Erkin. "Retired Army Colonel Lawrence B. Wilkerson on Uyghurs (2018)." January 7, 2021. Speech video clip, 1:41. https://www.youtube.com/watch?v=tVmliB0rVIo

11. Soleimani's ghost

Washington saw Soleimani as an enemy because he did what the Pentagon falsely claimed to be doing: fighting and destroying ISIS, Source: *Press TV*

The Trump regime imagined that its January 2020 murder of Qassem Soleimani would help divide and weaken the independent peoples of the region. It did indeed cause grief and pain, but the killing also generated unprecedented resolve and coherence amongst resistance forces. The legend of Soleimani is now a force driving liberation of the region from Washington's plan for a New Middle East.

Washington may have dreamed that, by removing Soleimani, the unique regional commander, the regional coalition would despair and lose direction. But Soleimani was not just a commander, he was a trainer, leaving his 40-year creation of hundreds of commanders across the region in his wake. Even at the start of Saddam's U.S.-backed war against Iran he had been a trainer.

The decision to murder Soleimani and Abu Mahdi al-Muhandis, the Iraqi-Iranian commander of the Popular Mobilisation

Forces, followed a mafia style logic: kill the leader and you may decapitate your rivals. Yet neither Iran nor the regional resistance were rival mafia gangs. Between them, Soleimani and Muhandis were almost universally credited with leading the destruction of ISIS (Daesh).

Destroying ISIS was never Washington's main concern. Properly understood, ISIS was created by the U.S. through the Saudis (with later help from Erdogan, the Israelis and some others), precisely to inflame sectarian divisions and so divide the peoples of Iraq and Syria, while Soleimani and Muhandis represented the brotherly bonds between Iraq and Iran and were the true heroes of the anti-terrorist struggle.

In any case this U.S. act of terrorism backfired and created a legend. It helped bring Palestinian and Iraqi factions together, thus building a much stronger sense of regional resistance.

The legend

Soleimani played a critical role in defeating the U.S. plot to use mass terrorism in a series of proxy wars to subjugate the entire region and create a New Middle East, dominated regionally by the Israeli colony and the Saudi regime. The Iranian general did not simply defend Iran. As Quds Force leader he helped arm all the Palestinian resistance factions, worked closely with the resistance in Lebanon, helped the Syrian Arab Army defeat the proxy wars across Syria and worked closely with the Popular Mobilisation Forces in Iraq. In November 2017 he was able to report to his leader, Sayyed Ali Khamenei, that the regional resistance had defeated ISIS in all the major towns and cities of the region (Iran Primer 2017). That regional victory was important in exposing to the world the multiple dirty wars launched by Washington, dressed up as 'smart power.'

The great fear of Washington and Tel Aviv has been that the resistance forces would rally together after the defeat of the NATO-backed proxies in Syria and Iraq. Their nightmare is to see a battle hardened coalition of Hezbollah, the Syrian Arab Army, Iraqi PMUs and Iran's Quds Force at the border of Occupied Palestine, ready to liberate the Syrian Golan and dismantle the colonial regime.

This is why Washington—after the invasions of Afghanistan, Iraq and Lebanon—seized the opportunity in 2011 to back Muslim Brotherhood and Wahhabi terrorism in Libya and Syria, culminating in the destruction of the Libyan state and the declaration by ISIS of an Islamic State in eastern Syria. A weak and divided Syria would have removed a central independent anti-zionist state from the picture and so helped protect the zionist colony.

The leaked U.S. intel memo of August 2012 indicated that the U.S. foresaw and welcomed the ISIS 'caliphate,' saying that the "possibility of establishing a declared or undeclared Salafist principality … [was] exactly what the supporting powers to the opposition want, in order to isolate the Syrian regime" (DIA 2012). That is, the ISIS caliphate would weaken and divide Syria, just as its predecessor in Iraq (ISI) had been designed to weaken Baghdad and create divisions with Tehran. Only Western countries called ISIS an 'Islamic State'; the terror group was never recognised as a state by the independent nations of the region—nor indeed, as operating according to the principles of Islam, despite the Islamist rhetoric.

In late 2014, the head of the U.S. military General Martin Dempsey and U.S. Vice President Joe Biden separately admitted that their key allies— notably Turkey, the Saudis, Qatar and the UAE—were funding and arming all the sectarian terrorist groups in Syria, so as to overthrow the Syrian Government (Anderson 2019a: Ch.7). The *raison d'etre* for backing these terrorist groups remained the practice of divide and rule.

In face of this proxy war Qassem Soleimani facilitated the September 2015 entry of Russia into a more direct defence of Syria, as he led ground wars against Jabhat al Nusra and ISIS in both Syria and Iraq. This unification of resistance forces was a central and necessary condition for survival of the independent peoples of the region.

Soleimani had played a key role in the defence of Gaza from murderous zionist attacks, and in the defence of Lebanon, especially during the 2006 zionist invasion. The Hamas representative in Lebanon, Ahmad Abdul Hadi, revealed that Hezbollah commander Imad Mughniyeh and Iran's Qassem Soleimani had visited Gaza repeatedly, leading plans to construct hundreds of kilometres of tunnels, as a defence against the zionist siege and bombing (Al Manar 2020).

As a regional resistance commander Soleimani assumed a leading role in counter-terrorist operations across Syria and in Iraq, leading up to his November 2017 announcement of victory over ISIS. Ever humble, the Quds Force leader thanked Ayatollah Khamenei's wise leadership and the sacrifices of the Iraqi and Syrian people and their governments for their courageous fight against the terrorist group. He also thanked Lebanon's Hezbollah and Iraq's Popular Mobilization Units, for their "decisive role" in the fight against ISIS (Iran Primer 2017).

ISIS had committed horrific crimes, he said, "including beheading children, skinning men alive before their families, enslaving innocent girls and women and raping them, burning people alive and killing hundreds of young people en masse" (*Tehran Times* 2019) The U.S.-backed, Saudi-funded terror group also displaced millions and inflicted enormous property damage, including on mosques and World Heritage sites. In all these atrocities, ISIS served as a tool of Washington.

U.S. occupation forces were by this time well entrenched in both Iraq and Syria under the pretext of fighting ISIS. Were their stated aims genuine, they should have hailed Soleimani as a hero. However since those forces themselves were tools of a deceptive regime, they saw him as a key rival.

The peoples of the region knew better. Soleimani and his colleagues, like Iraq's Abu Mahdi Muhandis, Syrian Army leaders including General Suheil al Hassan and General Issam Zahreddine (pictured below) and the leaders of Lebanon's Hezbollah, in particular Sayyed Hassan Nasrallah, alongside the leaders of Palestine's resistance movement, had emerged in the Arab and Muslim world as the genuine anti-terror, anti-zionist and anti-imperial heroes of the region.

Soleimani's key companion in Iraq, Abu Mahdi al Muhandis, had a remarkable history as a resistance fighter, first against the regime of Saddam Hussein, then against U.S. occupation forces, after the 2003 invasion, and then again against Washington's vicious, sectarian proxies. He developed relations with resistance commanders in Lebanon, in particular Imad Mughniyeh and Mustapha Badreddine, as well as with Soleimani (Daoud 2017). Prior to the Iraq invasion Muhandis opposed Saddam through the Islamic Dawa Party. After the U.S. and Saudis unleashed mass terrorism to divide and weaken Iran, Iraq and Syria, he became effective leader of the Popular Mobilisation Forces (Majidyar 2018; MEE 2020) which led the victory over ISIS in Iraq.

Qassem Soleimani (left) with Syrian General Issam Zahreddine (centre) in Deir Ezzor, October 2017, days before Zahreddine was killed on Sakr Island. Source: SANA

In that context President Trump, enraged and frustrated, suddenly decided to murder both Soleimani and Muhandis, the leading anti-terrorist heroes of Iraq and Iran, and the leading symbols of fraternity and cooperation between those two neighbouring countries.

The hero's daughter, Zeinab Soleimani, would later say that her father "did his job so well" he upset Washington. Her father "saved people … not just in his own country ... he did this for all countries … he destroyed ISIS because he doesn't want innocent people in Europe to get killed by such a dangerous virus … he fought for everyone" (Z. Soleimani 2020).

The Western media reflected the schizoid view of their governments. Many recognised that Soleimani was indeed the region's leading anti-ISIS commander, but they also observed that Washington was angered by his precedence in that role.

So while Trump's political cronies and Tel Aviv spoke of the murders as "self-defence," British state media (BBC 2020a) reported the killing of Qassem Soleimani as "good news for IS [DAESH] jihadists," while the American PBS channel spoke of "Soleimani's Complex Legacy in Iraq" (PBS 2020). Meanwhile India's *Economic Times* recognised that "Soleimani was the face of armed resistance against ISIS in Iraq and Syria and contributed in a big way in defeating ISIS" (Chaudhury 2020).

A number of analysts concluded that Trump's murder of Soleimani backfired. Far from dividing the resistance, the assassinations helped them unify. With U.S. media stressing the increased potential for direct U.S.-Iran conflict (which both sides want to avoid), more thoughtful analysts pointed to the further frustration of U.S. ambitions in the Middle East.

British-Syrian analyst Danny Makki said that Soleimani's legacy in Syria would endure, as "there are still tens of thousands of fighters and any number of commanders in Syria who he helped train that may yet carry on his work to expand Iran's influence and hegemony across the Middle East" (Makki 2021). Similarly, Iranian-Australian Mohsen Solhdoost (2020) wrote that, with the rise of new resistance groups attacking U.S. forces in Iraq, the killing of Soleimani "has strengthened Iran's hand" in the region.

The mourning for Muhandis and Soleimani and their Iraqi colleagues was tremendous. President Trump may have wanted to hurt the Iranian and Iraqi people, but instead he succeeded in galvanizing them. Huge rallies began in Baghdad and spread throughout Iraq and Iran. Both countries declared national days of mourning. The public grief was plain to the world. The U.S. colonial media tried to downplay the numbers, but even foreign channels (BBC 2020; ABC 2020) recognised that millions came out to mourn.

In subsequent political analysis, some Western sources pointed out that the murder of Soleimani was "a huge blow to Hezbollah," as the Lebanese Resistance group (branded as terrorist by Washington and Tel Aviv) openly relies on support from Iran. Other U.S. media were concerned about likely Iranian retaliation against U.S. occupation forces in the region.

However, reaction within the region was striking, especially in Iraq. Warring factions came together for the first time in many years. Iraqi Prime Minister Adil Abdul-Mahdi said that: "the assassination of an Iraqi military commander who holds an official position is considered aggression on Iraq ... and the liquidation of leading Iraqi figures or those from a brotherly country on Iraqi soil is a massive breach of sovereignty" (Reuters 2020).

Within days Iraq's Parliament voted to expel all U.S. forces from the country (DW 2020). Important figures in Iraqi politics also called for closure of the U.S. Embassy, as the Iranian Revolution had done back in 1979. Some U.S. political commentators called this "Iran's True Victory," albeit orchestrated by Washington (Connable 2020). All the effort made over decades to divide Iraq from Iran had been placed at risk. Resistance groups called for revenge and repeated the Iraqi call, demanding expulsion of U.S. forces from the entire region (MNA 2020). This sparked a new level of public debate.

On 8 January in 'Operation Martyr Soleimani' Iran's military launched a missile strike on the U.S. airbase at Ayn al Assad airbase, in Iraq. This was the first direct Iranian attack on U.S. forces. Warning had been given and there were no deaths, but 110 U.S. servicemen were later reported as having received concussive traumatic brain injuries. Pentagon General Kenneth McKenzie estimated the U.S. was close to losing between 100 and 150 personnel and up to 30 aircraft (Harkins 2021). Presumably because of the controlled and accurate nature of the strike and the low level of casualties, the Trump administration did not launch a counter strike.

In the wake of its failing wars in Afghanistan, Syria, and Yemen, and having united Iraq against it, Washington under the Trump administration sought to maintain its "maximum pressure" campaign against Iran. That had grown to include an economic siege against much of the region and reneging on the JCPOA, the nuclear agreement finalised by the Obama administration back in 2015 designed to forestall Iran's purported intent to produce nuclear weapons. That withdrawal alienated Washington from its European allies, even as they showed themselves incapable of acting independently from the U.S. and of standing up to its anti-Iran sanctions regime in order to keep Iran engaged in the deal.

Russia and China, formerly allies in the U.S. nuclear campaign against Iran, were now themselves subject to Washington's unilateral coercive measures. The progressive failure of Washington's New Middle East wars had helped expand the role of both countries in the region. In December 2019, just prior to the murder of Soleimani and Muhandis, Russia, China and Iran held joint naval exercises in the Persian Gulf (Westcott and Alkhshali 2019). This was a response to false U.S. claims about Iranian threats to shipping. In mid-2020 China and Iran revealed a $400 billion 25-year economic agreement focussed on energy, infrastructure and manufacturing (Telesur 2021).

China and Russia were developing parallel economic agreements with Syria. This was not what Washington wanted.

Iran's revenge, which began with a strike on the U.S. airbase at Ayn al Asad (Harkins 2021), was followed by the Iranian indictment of Trump and dozens of others (Al Taher, Kiley and John 2020), then the apparent execution of at least two army officers. U.S. Lt. Col. James C. Willis and Israeli Col. Sharon Asman are said to have been killed in Erbil, Iraq, in retaliation for their roles in the assassinations, though the causes of their deaths were officially hidden (The Cradle 2021). Three years on, Iran's revenge is said to have become "a strategy" which will only be fulfilled with the expulsion of the U.S. occupation from the region and the dismantling of its regional proxies (Fereydounabadi 2023).

Soleimani in the Levant

Qassem Soleimani with Iranian leader Sayyed Ali Khomenei and Hezbollah Secretary General Sayyed Hassan Nasrallah. Source: Khameini.IR

This chapter cannot begin to do justice to the history of Soleimani in the Levant or Iraq; that would require the combined efforts of Palestinian, Lebanese, Syrian, Iraqi and Iranian historians. However, two brief accounts of his activities in Lebanon and Syria are possible here.

In an extended interview just months before his death Soleimani (2019) spoke about his role during the 2006 Israeli invasion of Lebanon. He was in Lebanon most of this time as an advisor, relaying messages from Tehran and serving as a unique witness to that remarkable war. In quite a short time the Lebanese resistance inflicted a second defeat (after expulsion of the occupiers in 2000) on what most had assumed were superior Israeli armed forces.

As to the context of the invasion, Soleimani drew attention to the massive presence of the U.S. military in the region at that time, following the invasions of Afghanistan and Iraq. Those "200,000 troops, hundreds of planes and helicopters, as well as thousands of armoured vehicles" encouraged the Israelis to think that they had the advantage. Additionally, Zionist leader Ehud Olmert spoke of support the Israelis enjoyed from most of the Arab regimes, by which he meant "the countries of the Persian Gulf, with the Saud regime leading them" (Soleimani 2019).

On the one hand the zionists wanted revenge for their expulsion in 2000 and, more than that, they wanted to destroy Hezbollah and expel the mainly Shia population which supported them. They had even prepared camps and ships for this purpose. Soleimani said that the zionist goal was "to get rid of Hezbollah forever, and the prerequisite was to get rid of a big part of the Lebanese people who lived in a significant part of the country—not only in the south but also in Beqaa Valley and the north of Lebanon" (Soleimani 2019). The war had been planned for some time and had been waiting on the right moment. It was certainly urged on by the 25 July declaration of U.S. Secretary of State Condoleezza Rice while in Jerusalem, that the U.S. would be creating a "New Middle East" (Bransten 2006).

On the other hand, Hezbollah, the only group with the capacity to free prisoners held in Israeli jails, knew that the only diplomacy that worked on the Israelis was prisoner exchange. "The Lebanese people, including the Druze, Muslim, and Christian prisoners, had no hope or haven apart from Hezbollah; as they do today" (Soleimani 2019). Hezbollah had promised to liberate the prisoners and set out a complex operation to do this, led by Commander Imad Mughniyeh, by capturing some Israeli soldiers who could be exchanged. The capture of those two soldiers was used by the zionists as a pretext to launch the war.

The Israelis often denied that they held Lebanese prisoners but at different times, prisoner exchanges were carried out. They had held many hundreds in the notorious Khiam prison (now a museum in south Lebanon) prior to 2000. In an early 2004 agreement the zionists agreed to release "35 prisoners from Arab countries, including 23 Lebanese, as well as 400 Palestinian prisoners" (AP 2004). During the July-August 2006 war "Hezbollah demanded the release of the hundreds of Lebanese prisoners held in Israeli jails who in some cases have remained in prison for over 20 years" (Christoff 2006). After the war there was "a drawn-out prisoner exchange" (Salem 2006) which stretched into late 2007, when the bodies of "two Lebanese fighters [were exchanged] for the corpse of a drowned Israeli civilian" (AP 2007).

Soleimani came to Lebanon the day the war began, crossing from Syria through a back road. But the damage from Israeli bombing was catastrophic and he returned to Iran after a week, to report to the Iranian leader. "My report was a sad, bitter one," he said. He saw no hope for a resistance victory. "12-story buildings [in Beirut] were knocked down by a bomb." Yet Ayatollah Khamenei, after absorbing all the details, saw it differently. While the battle was very difficult, the leader compared it to the Quranic "Battle of the Trench," suggesting Hezbollah would win. He pointed out that "Israel had prepared this project in advance, and wanted to conduct a raid to destroy Hezbollah by launching a surprise attack. The action of Hezbollah—capturing two Zionist soldiers—disturbed the surprise plan" (Soleimani 2019).

Soleimani returned to Lebanon and conveyed this more hopeful message to Hassan Nasrallah. "Nothing could raise [Nasrallah's] morale like these words ... he strongly believed in the statements of the Supreme Leader and regards them as divine and oracular." The morale boosting message was passed on to "all the combatants" that "the outcome of this war will be like the victory of the Battle of the Trench, and even though it involves severe hardships, a major victory will be gained" (Soleimani 2019).

The Iranian general stayed in Lebanon for the remainder of the 33-day war, holding discussions with Nasrallah and Mughniyeh in south Beirut. They had to move around because of Israeli bombing but never left that area. Soleimani noted how "Hezbollah surprised and confused the enemy at every stage with a new tool, or a new action. That is, they would not reveal all their cards at once." Further, Hezbollah forces did not defend a single "stronghold" but rather "every location" had its surprises for the invader. "One could imagine the tactics of Hezbollah as a vast minefield, a vast intelligent minefield with no empty or secure place within its bounds … the enemy was unable to enter through villages, even those villages right at the border" (Soleimani 2019).

The Quds Force commander spoke of the famous incident when an Israeli warship off the Lebanese coast was smashed by a missile, just as Nasrallah was speaking live on Lebanese television. Because there had been rumours that Nasrallah was injured, he made this public appearance. As he approached his closing words, the supersonic missile was launched "and it hit the frigate at once." Nasrallah said, "you can see now in front of you the Israeli frigate burning" (Soleimani 2019), a dramatic gesture which certainly enhanced the sense of resistance power.

The second half of the war was also very difficult but marked by resistance initiatives and morale boosting moves. It seems that Commander Mughniyeh organised a letter from the fighters to their Secretary General (Moqawama 2006), in which they said, amongst other things:

We are steadfast here along the borders of Palestine and in every part of the south with pride, dignity and fulfilment. We are still the promise that was made like thunder over the heads of the Zionists ... We are the freedom of Samir Kuntar ... of Nasim Nisr, Yahya Skaf, Muhammad Farran and all the detainees. We are the liberation of the Shebaa Farms, the hills of Kafar Shuba, and every inch of our dear Lebanon (Moqawama 2006).

The Hezbollah leader replied in a letter that was later turned into the famous song 'Ahi Bhaii' (My Dear Ones) by the Lebanese Christian singer Julia Boutros:

> I received your message and heard your words … you are the true promise of the victory that will come, God willing. You are the freedom for the detainees, liberation for the land, and protection for the homeland, for honour, and for faith. My brothers, you are the essence of the history of this nation and the epitome of its spirit ... its culture, values, love and gratitude, you are the epitome of its manhood, the eternity of the cedar in our mountain peaks and the humility of the ears of wheat … lofty like the majestic mountains of

> Lebanon, towering over the mighty … after God Almighty you are the hope and our promise is on you, you were and still are and will remain the hope and the promise, I kiss your heads that have raised high every head (Nasrallah 2006).

Soleimani remarked that those letters were "so important" for all on the battlefield. Of the letter from the fighters, he said "I didn't see anyone listening to this letter and not cry." For its part, Nasrallah's letter "in praise of his warriors was like Imam Hussain's speech in praise of his own companions on the eve of Ashura." Together Soleimani saw the letters as "very influential, and divine," having a great impact on the battle (Soleimani 2019).

Soon after this an Israeli helicopter was downed and seven Merkava tanks were destroyed in one day. The sponsors in Washington, through the then Qatari Prime Minister, sued for a ceasefire. Although the Israelis had killed many more people than the resistance, the colonists could not tolerate their own casualties, through repeated humiliating and damaging blows. This was not a war of attrition. The resistance was, after all, defending its own land, its towns, and villages. After the war the game changed. Soleimani (2019) says "the Zionist regime's strategy changed from the Ben-Gurion strategy of a pre-emptive and offensive strike and gradually gave way to a defensive strategy."

Something should be said here about Soleimani's role in Syria, combating the U.S.-led dirty war from 2011 onwards. His impact was both pervasive and profound. U.S. sources trace the role of Soleimani in Syria through the initial move of Hezbollah to team up with the Syrian Arab Army, including training Syrian's National Defence Forces, to help defeat the U.S. and GCC backed sectarian proxies in the Qalamoun mountains along the Syria-Lebanon border (Sullivan 2014). Of course, Jabhat al Nusra (the initial al Qaeda affiliate, later rebadged as HTS) posed a serious threat to Lebanon, as well as to Syria, and Nusra had wealthy sponsors in Lebanon.

After Soleimani's death many U.S. sources, and in particular U.S. state media Voice of America, tried to stress a sectarian Shia motivation; they portrayed the Hezbollah connection as extending some insidious Iranian religious mission (Kajjo, Mohammad, Jedinia,

Sahinkaya, Ahmado and Orokzai 2020). Such misleading discussions typically omit these key counterpoints: (i) Iran supports every resistance faction in Palestine, where there are very few Shia Muslims, (ii) Syria is a committed secular-pluralist state which bans all political parties based on religion. Strategic cooperation in the region cannot be understood by the rampant sectarian 'Shia crescent' theories.

Nonetheless, Soleimani's advisory and training role in Damascus and western Syria over 2021–2013 is properly linked to Hezbollah, especially through the battles in the border areas, such as at Yabrud and al Qusayr (Sullivan 2014). Israeli sources (e.g. Debka 2015) were very conscious of this.

Multiple sources confirm that Soleimani played a central role in brokering the September 2015 entry of Russian air power to support Syria, after renewed ISIS and al Qaeda assaults on Syria from Turkey, Occupied Iraq and Israel. He is said to have gone to Moscow and argued for a decisive air power intervention, which could also help Russia's role in the region, adding that, after four years, "we haven't lost all the cards" (*Indian Express* 2015; Baranova 2016).

In late 2016 Western media paid attention to Soleimani's activities in Aleppo, leading up to the liberation of the eastern part of that city in late December 2016 (Weiss 2015; AA 2016). In the photo below he is shown with Syrian Colonel Eyad Salloum who, with a group of

Qassem Soleimani and Syrian Colonel Eyad Salloum in Aleppo, December 2016. Source SANA

200 Syrian soldiers, had been trapped under siege for more than three years inside Aleppo's citadel. The soldiers were cut off by terrorist occupation of large parts of the city. Supplies were dropped in by air. This writer met Colonel Salloum in Aleppo after the city's liberation, and heard directly about the 'war of tunnels' between the Syrian Arab Army and the various armed group factions. Most of the soldiers with him were from Aleppo city and some of them were married under siege, living inside the castle until liberation day.

Soleimani's role in eastern Syria was also crucial. This writer was one of several foreign observers in Deir Ezzor, October 2017, as the Syrian Arab Army (SAA) was driving ISIS out of that city and down the Euphrates River through Al Maydeen to AbuKamal. Soleimani and the militia under his command played a large part in this decision, finally destroying ISIS control of cities and towns and securing the Iraq-Syria border crossing at the Euphrates (Majidyar 2017a).

Regional resistance coordination was evident during this operation. It was reported that "video footages … showed militiamen from Lebanese Hezbollah and two Iraqi Shiite groups—Kata'ib Hezbollah and Harakat al-Nujaba—linking up with the Syrian Army ... Iranian-sponsored Iraqi militia groups that had helped liberate the Iraqi border town of al-Qaim entered Syria to take part in the Abu Kamal operation" (Majidyar 2017b). That was an important strategic move, which placed the Abu Kamal crossing in the hands of regional Resistance forces. That base has been attacked by the U.S. and its collaborators ever since. The U.S. military secured most other Iraq-Syria border crossings.

The danger of ongoing media manipulation can be seen from reports of the 2019 U.S. air force attack very close to Abu Kamal, near the village of al Baghouz. The *New York Times* in late 2021 uncovered this attack, which had killed dozens of Syrian villagers. Under media pressure, the U.S. military admitted to this massacre; but the *NYT* accepted and promoted the Pentagon's false cover story: that this happened as a result of the U.S. military claiming to fight ISIS (Phillipps and Schmitt 2021). However it was Soleimani who had driven out all ISIS forces from this area. By early 2019 Al-Baghouz was a town dominated by the U.S.-backed SDF (Kurdish separatists), but with SAA posts on the outskirts of the town, as occurs in much of eastern Syria. A Syrian general with experience in the Deir Ezzor region told this writer that there were no ISIS at al Baghouz at that time; the U.S. attack was on Syrian forces, in an attempt to deliver full control to its SDF proxy (Anderson 2021).

I never got to see General Soleimani in Deir Ezzor and his Syrian colleague, the legendary General Issam Zahreddine, was killed on Sakr Island the day we arrived. However, I did speak with another senior Syrian general in that city. He pointed out that ISIS in Syria's eastern desert had located some very recent SAA positions, indicating ISIS had access to U.S. satellite intelligence. I said to him, "You must feel you are fighting a U.S. command?" "100%!" he responded. That is what Soleimani faced, from the Levant to Afghanistan.

Having defeated the terrorist group in Iraq's Mosul and Syria's Deir Ezzor, in November 2017 Soleimani made his report to Iran's leader that ISIS had been removed from all the main cities and towns of the region (Iran Primer 2017). Iran's leader Khamenei said the U.S. had created ISIS and Iran had destroyed it (FARDA 2017). Yet, while recognising the role of Soleimani and of Iraq's Popular Mobilisation Forces (PMF) in the defeat of ISIS, the U.S. media also repeated Washington's demand for the PMF to be disbanded (PBS 2017). The U.S. could not tolerate either Iraqi or Iranian national heroes.

Dangerous in death

After murdering the Iranian hero, Washington designated Soleimani, even in death, as "a dangerous person" so as to eliminate sympathetic references across a wide range of media. This mass censorship took place by destroying hundreds of supposedly Iranian backed websites, systematically blocking or obscuring Iranian media posts and banning thousands of Soleimani sympathisers on U.S. social media.

The initial problem for this campaign was the online video of huge funerals for Muhandis and Soleimani in both Iraq and Iran. While Euronews (Jamieson 2020) said "thousands" had attended Soleimani's funeral, the *Washington Post* wrote of "tens of thousands" (Sly and Dadouch 2020) but Iranian media and even British and Australian state media (BBC 2020: ABC 2020) and Britain's *Daily Mirror* (Hafezi and Bazaraa 2020) wrote of "millions" in public mourning.

The largest social media company, Facebook, immediately began a campaign of taking down or restricting accounts which posted sympathy for Soleimani. Posts on the Soleimani and Muhandis funerals by this writer (5, 7, 11 and 20 January 2020) were taken down and tagged as "against our standards on dangerous individuals and organisations." They were said to have been removed "to prevent and disrupt offline harm" (screenshots below).

Facebook takes down the author's posts (5 & 7 Jan. 2020) on the funerals of Trump regime murder victims, Soleimani and Muhandis

Facebook announced its rationale, which reinforced previous practice. The media giant's claim ran this way: as we are a U.S. company we must comply with U.S. law. Facebook stated that "to comply with these [U.S.] sanctions, we remove accounts maintained by or on behalf of a sanctioned party as well as content posted by others that supports or represents the sanctioned group or individual" (Zimmerman 2020; Chamas 2020).

This censorship intensified after the murders; it did not begin with them. In 2019 Instagram (also owned by the Facebook mother company, Meta Platforms) had banned all sites linked to the Iranian IRGC military (Esfandiari 2019). Prior to that, all posts on Hezbollah leader Hassan Nasrallah (designated a terrorist by the Israeli regime and its supporters) had been widely banned, even though Nasrallah's words were virtually compulsory reading within the Israeli colony itself (Anderson 2019). 'Know your enemy' is a wise phase.

On 13 October 2019 Facebook deleted one of my posts which noted 'Syrian Arab Army gains, since September 2013.' This was simply said to be "against our community standards." Earlier Facebook had suggested I "relive" my prominent posts of 2018, which began with a "Tribute to fallen soldiers defending Syria." When I did as invited, it was blocked as the post was said to be "against our community standards" (screenshots below). Something was changing.

Two of the author's blocked Facebook posts, 2019

Later in 2020 Washington began to "seize" (i.e. destroy) dozens of websites it claimed were funded or controlled "by Iran's Islamic Revolutionary Guard Corps (IRGC) [so as] to engage in a global disinformation campaign" (DOJ 2020). It was not clear before this that the U.S. government had any legitimate power to close down such websites.

By mid-2020 the United Nations expert on extrajudicial killings, Ms Agnes Callamard, confirmed that the drone strike on Soleimani and Muhandis was an "unlawful" killing, i.e. murder (Al Jazeera 2020). Subsequently the Iraqi judiciary (a judge in Baghdad's investigative court) issued an arrest warrant for Donald Trump over the killing of Qassem Soleimani (ABS 2021).

The import of this mass censorship, coordinated with the White House and U.S. Congress, was to assist Washington in presenting its own version of events over any matters to do with Iran, or any other country with which it was in conflict. In the same way that the U.S.

Government and its embedded media tried to recast the murder of Soleimani and hide the outpouring of sympathy at his funeral, many other matters could and would be distorted.

For example, in late 2022 the young Iranian woman, Mahsa Amini, died in police custody. Washington and its agents immediately initiated an anti-Iran campaign, falsely claiming she had been beaten to death for not wearing a head scarf. In fact, the coroners' report and CCTV footage showed she had not been beaten and had died from an "underlying disease" (Reuters 2022; Halawi 2022; HRCI 2022). Regardless of these facts, a 'colour revolution' styled disinformation campaign swung into action. The campaign was aided by mass censorship. Iranian perspectives were heavily suppressed and replaced by those of expat U.S.-Iranians, such as Masih Alinejad and Nazanin Boniadi, who were elevated by Western governments and western media (e.g. AFP 2022). The U.S. social media played along. The purpose, of course, was 'regime change,' an attempt to overthrow a government of which Washington did not approve, by repeated use of false propaganda.

An artificial bubble was created by this media manipulation. Analyst Marc Owen Jones showed that, on Twitter alone in a few weeks, there were more than 400 million 'Mahsa Amini' linked tweets (in English and Farsi), 32% of those were from Twitter accounts created just in September and October 2022. By contrast the Black Lives Matter campaign in the USA, involving a number of public police killings only gathered 63 million tweets over several years (Jones 2022). In the USA more than 1,000 civilians are "shot to death" by police each year (Statista 2023); but Washington has powerful media tools at its disposal, both to cover up its own crimes and to carry out propaganda attacks on others.

The censorship over Soleimani aimed to smear the man most prominently responsible for the defeat of ISIS terrorism, a role Washington had claimed for itself, despite the 2014 admissions that its 'major allies' had armed and funded ISIS. Nevertheless, evidence kept emerging that the U.S. military "did not participate in any operation to liberate Iraq from ISIS." In 2022, for example, an Iraqi fighter revealed that, in the March 2015 battle of Tikrit, the Popular Mobilisation Forces had done all the work while U.S. forces obstructed them (The Cradle 2023).

In yet another blocked Facebook post in late 2020 this writer quoted Soleimani's daughter Zeinab, who said that her father was murdered because he "did his job so well" and upset Washington. Facebook again claimed that these comments were against "our community standards." The video remains posted in many places; it cannot be fully covered up (Z. Soleimani 2020).

U.S. propaganda is pervasive but shallow. Scratch the surface and it is not hard to see a distinct but divergent reality. The independent opinion polls carried out in Iran gave little comfort to the 'regime change' crowd. In 2018, after another Western-promoted 'protest movement,' the UNDP reported that 71% of Iranians trusted their national government, compared to 39% in the USA (UNDP 2018: Table 14). Another poll, carried out by the University of Maryland (USA) and its Canadian-based partner Iranpoll, on Iran's social and political opinion showed that 81% saw the country's top problem as economic (unemployment, inflation, and low income), while 77% did not agree that 'Iran's political system needs … fundamental change' (only 15% agreed). On regional security matters, represented by Soleimani, there was overwhelming support (95%) for the country's defence missile program and for its nuclear program (86%). A strong majority (86%) supported Iran's regional campaigns against terrorism and 55% wanted to increase them. Of the 2018 protests, 66% thought the police handled them well (24% said 'badly') but 65% felt the arrested protestors should be released. Most thought that those who had burned the flag (63%) or damaged public property (60%) should be 'punished harshly' (Gallagher, Mohseni and Ramsay 2018). That is the nation Soleimani defended, but it is not the image Washington wants others to see.

Dangerous even in death, Qassem Soleimani remains a powerful symbol of the regional resistance to imperial interventions and a ghost which haunts Washington across all of West Asia.

References

AA. "Photos show Iranian general in Aleppo during evacuation." December 17, 2016. https://www.aa.com.tr/en/middle-east/photos-show-iranian-general-in-aleppo-during-evacuation/708335

ABC (2020). "Iran minister goads Donald Trump as millions attend funeral for top general Qassem Soleimani." *ABC News.* January 7, 2020. https://www.abc.net.au/news/2020-01-07/millions-attend-quassem-soleimani-funeral-in-iran/11845580

ABC (2021). "Iraq issues arrest warrant for Donald Trump over killing of Qassim Soleimani." January 8, 2021. https://www.abc.net.au/news/2021-01-08/iraq-issues-arrest-warrant-for-us-trump-soleimani-killing/13040752

AFP. "Exiled Iran Opposition Figures Release United 'Victory' Message." *Voice of America News.* January 2, 2023. https://www.voanews.com/a/exiled-iran-opposition-figures-release-united-victory-message-/6901460.html

Al Jazeera. "US killing of Iran's Qassem Soleimani 'unlawful': UN expert." July 7, 2020. https://www.aljazeera.com/news/2020/7/7/us-killing-of-irans-qassem-soleimani-unlawful-un-expert

Al Manar. "Imad Mughniyeh, Qassem Suleimani Masterminded Gaza Tunnels." January 9, 2020. https://english.almanar.com.lb/911000

Al Taher, Nada, Sam Kiley, and Tara John. "Iran issues arrest warrant for Trump over drone strike that killed Qasem Soleimani." *CNN.* June 29, 2020. https://edition.cnn.com/2020/06/29/middleeast/iran-arrest-warrant-donald-trump-intl/index.html

Anderson, Tim (2019). "Nasrallah: Banned in the West but Mandatory Viewing in Israel." Tajammo3. July 22, 2019. https://www.tajammo3.org/24388/nasrallah-banned-in-the-west-but-mandatory-viewing-in-israel.html

——— (2019a). Axis of Resistance. Atlanta: Clarity Press, 2019.

——— (2021) "Syria: Why the US massacre at Al-Baghouz?" *Al Mayadeen,* December 28, 2021. https://english.almayadeen.net/articles/analysis/syria:-why-the-us-massacre-at-al-baghouz

AP (2004). "Israel, Hezbollah prisoner exchange Thursday." *NBC News.* January 26, 2004. https://www.nbcnews.com/id/wbna4054582

AP (2007). "Israel, Hezbollah swap prisoner and dead." CTV News. October 15, 2007. https://www.ctvnews.ca/israel-hezbollah-swap-prisoner-and-dead-1.260361?cache=lcf

Baranova, Maria. "Qasem Soleimani: Iran's 'architect' of Russian operations in Syria." Russia Beyond. October 5, 2016. https://www.rbth.com/international/2016/10/05/qasem-soleimani-irans-architect-of-russian-operations-in-syria_636137

BBC (2020). "Millions turn out in Iran for General Soleimani's funeral – BBC News." January 6, 2020. News video, 8:18. https://www.youtube.com/watch?v=1ndfa37Y4-0

BBC (2020a). "Qasem Soleimani: Why his killing is good news for IS jihadists." *BBC News*. January 10, 2020. https://www.bbc.co.uk/news/world-middle-east-51021861

Bransten, Jeremy. "Middle East: Rice Calls For A 'New Middle East.'" *Radio Free Europe Radio Liberty*. July 25, 2006. https://www.rferl.org/a/1070088.html

Caleb Weiss. "Iran's covert mastermind was just spotted near one of the most important battlefronts in Syria." Business Insider. October 20, 2015. https://www.businessinsider.com/irans-covert-mastermind-was-just-spotted-near-one-of-the-most-important-battlefronts-in-syria-2015-10

Chamas, Zena. "Facebook admits censoring posts supporting slain Iranian General Qassem Soleimani." *ABC News*. January 15, 2020. https://www.abc.net.au/news/2020-01-15/instagram-bans-iranians-from-posting-about-soleimani/11864410

Chaudhury, Dipanjan Roy. "Soleimani, face of fight against ISIS, Taliban." *The Economic Times*. January 4, 2020. https://economictimes.indiatimes.com/news/politics-and-nation/soleimani-face-of-fight-against-isis-taliban/articleshow/73093126.cms

Christoff, Stefan. "Bombs over Beirut." Electronic Intifada. July 20, 2006. https://electronicintifada.net/content/bombs-over-beirut/6171

Connable, Ben. "Iraq's Vote to Expel U.S. Troops Is Iran's True Victory." The Rand Blog. January 6, 2020. https://www.rand.org/blog/2020/01/iraqs-vote-to-expel-us-troops-is-irans-true-victory.html

Cradle, The (2021). "Resistance Axis killed two US and Israeli operatives involved in Soleimani/Muhandes assassinations." September 20, 2021. https://thecradle.co/article-view/2066/exclusive-resistance-axis-killed-two-us-and-israeli-operatives-involved-in-soleimanimuhandes-assassinations

Cradle, The (2023). "Exclusive interview with Hezbollah commander in Iraq: 'The Americans did not fight ISIS.'" January 4, 2023. https://thecradle.co/Article/Interviews/19989

Daoud, David. "PMF deputy commander Muhandis details Hezbollah ops in Iraq." *Long War Journal.* January 9, 2017. https://www.longwarjournal.org/archives/2017/01/pmf-deputy-commander-muhandis-details-hezbollah-ops-in-iraq.php

Debka. "Qalamoun battle is do-or-die for Bashar Assad, Hassan Nasrallah and Iran's Gen. Soleimani." May 9, 2015. https://www.debka.com/qalamoun-battle-is-do-or-die-for-bashar-assad-hassan-nasrallah-and-irans-gen-soleimani/

DW (2020). "Iraqi parliament votes to expel US troops." *Deutsche Welle.* January 5, 2020. https://www.dw.com/en/iraqi-parliament-votes-to-expel-us-troops-awaits-government-approval/a-51892888

DIA (2012). "Department of Defence Information Report, Not Finally Evaluated Intelligence, Country: Iraq." Defence Intelligence Agency, August 2012. 14-L-0552/DIA/297-293. Also see: Hoff, Brad. "2012 Defense Intelligence Agency document: West will facilitate rise of Islamic State 'in order to isolate the Syrian regime.'" Levant Report. May 19, 2015. http://levantreport.com/2015/05/19/2012-defense-intelligence-agency-document-west-will-facilitate-rise-of-islamic-state-in-order-to-isolate-the-syrian-regime/

DOJ (2020). "United States Seizes Domain Names Used by Iran's Islamic Revolutionary Guard Corps, Seizure Documents Describe Iranian Government's Efforts to Use Domains as Part of Global Disinformation Campaign." U.S. Department of Justice. October 7, 2020. online: https://www.justice.gov/opa/pr/united-states-seizes-domain-names-used-iran-s-islamic-revolutionary-guard-corps

Esfandiari, Golnaz (2019) "Instant Ban For Iran's IRGC On Instagram: Social-Media Giant Blocks Commanders' Sites,' 17 April, online: https://www.rferl.org/a/instant-ban-for-iran-s-irgc-on-instagram-social-media-giant-blocks-commanders-sites/29886908.html

FARDA. "Khamenei Says U.S. Created ISIS and Iran Defeated It." *Radio Farda.* November 22, 2017. https://en.radiofarda.com/a/iran-khamenei-isis-is-syria-soleimani/28869633.html

Fereydounabadi, Sadegh. "The strategy of revenge." *Tehran Times.* January 3, 2023. https://www.tehrantimes.com/news/480413/The-strategy-of-revenge

FNA – Fars News Agency (@EnglishFars). "Zeinab Soleimani Says Her Father Was A Big Monster for US, But A Savior for Nations in Region." *Twitter,* December 16, 2020. https://twitter.com/englishfars/status/1338850903575576578

Gallagher, Nancy, Ebrahim Mohseni, and Ray Ramsay. *Iranian Public Opinion after the Protests: A public opinion study.* School of Public Policy, Center for International Security Studies at Maryland, July 2018. https://www.jstor.org/stable/resrep20428#metadata_info_tab_contents

Hafezi, Parisa, and Danya Bazaraa. "Qassem Soleimani funeral: Millions line streets as new general vows revenge." *Daily Mirror.* January 6, 2020. https://www.mirror.co.uk/news/world-news/millions-soleimanis-funeral-replacement-vows-21224203

Halawi, Bahia. "Disinformation campaign targeting Iran over Mahsa Amini's death." *Al Mayadeen.* October 3, 2022. https://english.almayadeen.net/articles/analysis/disinformation-campaign-targeting-iran-over-mahsa-aminis-dea

Harkins, Gina. "Al Asad Missile Attack Nearly Killed 150 US Troops, Destroyed 30 Aircraft: Report." *Military News.* March 1, 2021. https://www.military.com/daily-news/2021/03/01/al-asad-missile-attack-nearly-killed-150-us-troops-destroyed-30-aircraft-report.html

HRCI. "CCTV and Report on the Death of Mahsa Amini & Ensuing Events, by Human Rights Council of Iran." Human Rights Council of Iran. Centre for Counter Hegemonic Studies. October 11, 2022. https://counter-hegemonic-studies.site/mahsa-amini-report-2/

Indian Express. "Qassem Soleimani: He plotted the Syrian assault in Moscow." October 12, 2015. https://indianexpress.com/article/world/middle-east-africa/qassem-soleimani-he-plotted-the-syrian-assault-in-moscow/

Iran Primer. "Iran Declares End of ISIS." November 22, 2017. https://iranprimer.usip.org/blog/2017/nov/21/iran-declares-end-isis

Jamieson, Alastair. "Thousands mourn Iranian general Qassem Soleimani at funeral in Baghdad." *Euronews.* January 6, 2020. https://www.euronews.com/2020/01/04/thousands-mourn-iranian-general-qassem-soleimani-at-funeral-in-baghdad

Jones, Marc Owen (@marcowenjones). "This is a thread on the #MahsaAmini hashtag…" *Twitter,* October 27, 2022. https://twitter.com/marcowenjones/status/1585704740067086337?lang=en

Kajjo, Sirwan, Niala Mohammad, Mehdi Jedinia, Ezel Sahinkaya, Nisan Ahmado, and Nawid Orokzai. "How Qassem Soleimani Managed Iran's Proxies in the Middle East." *VOA News.* January 7, 2020. https://www.voanews.com/a/extremism-watch_how-qassem-soleimani-managed-irans-proxies-middle-east/6182243.html

Majidyar, Ahmad (2017a). "Fatemiyoun: We'll Capture Al-Mayadin and Abu Kamal to Fulfill Soleimani's Promise." Middle East Institute. October 5,

2017. https://www.mei.edu/publications/fatemiyoun-well-capture-al-mayadin-and-abu-kamal-fulfill-soleimanis-promise

——— (2017b). "Syrian, Iranian-Led Forces Capture Abu Kamal, Threaten to Confront U.S. and S.D.F." Middle East Institute. November 8, 2017. https://www.mei.edu/publications/syrian-iranian-led-forces-capture-abu-kamal-threaten-confront-us-and-sdf

——— (2018). "Iran-backed groups seeking to consolidate gains in post-ISIS Iraq." Middle East Institute. January 26, 2018. https://www.mei.edu/publications/iran-backed-groups-seeking-consolidate-gains-post-isis-iraq

Makki, Danny. "Qassem Soleimani's reign may be over, but his legacy in Syria will endure." Middle East Institute. January 22, 2020. https://www.mei.edu/publications/qassem-soleimanis-reign-may-be-over-his-legacy-syria-will-endure

MEE. "Who was Abu Mahdi al-Muhandis?" *Middle East Eye.* January 3, 2020. https://www.middleeasteye.net/news/who-abu-mahdi-al-muhandis-qassem-soleimani-iran-iraq

MNA. "'Hard Revenge' to continue until expulsion of US forces from region." The Iran Project. February 14, 2020. https://theiranproject.com/blog/2020/02/14/hard-revenge-to-continue-until-expulsion-of-us-forces-from-region/

Moqawama (2006). "Message from the Mujahideen of the Islamic Resistance to the Secretary-General, Sayyed Hassan Nasrallah." https://www.moqawama.org/essaydetails.php?eid=7813&cid=319

Nasrallah, Hassan (2006) "Sayyed Nasrallah's 2006 Letter to the Resistance Men and Their Response." *Alahed News.* Video, 6:25. https://english.alahednews.com.lb/34189/370

PBS (2017). "This Iran-backed militia helped save Iraq from ISIS. Now Washington wants them to disband." *PBS News Hour.* December 7, 2017. https://www.pbs.org/newshour/show/this-iran-backed-militia-helped-save-iraq-from-isis-now-washington-wants-them-to-disband

PBS (2020). "Qassem Soleimani's Complex Legacy in Iraq." *PBS Frontline.* January 5, 2020. https://www.pbs.org/wgbh/frontline/article/qassem-soleimani-killed-airstrike-iran-iraq-legacy/

Phillipps, David, and Eric Schmitt. "How the U.S. Hid an Airstrike That Killed Dozens of Civilians in Syria." *New York Times.* November 15, 2021. https://www.nytimes.com/2021/11/13/us/us-airstrikes-civilian-deaths.html

Reuters (2020). "Iraqi PM says US killing of Iranian commander will 'light the fuse' of war." January 3, 2020. https://news.abs-cbn.com/overseas/01/03/20/iraqi-pm-says-us-killing-of-iranian-commander-will-light-the-fuse-of-war

Reuters (2022). "Iranian coroner says Mahsa Amini did not die from blows to body." *National Post.* October 7, 2022. https://nationalpost.com/pmn/news-pmn/iranian-coroner-says-mahsa-amini-did-not-die-from-blows-to-body

Salem, Paul. "The Future of Lebanon." *Foreign Affairs.* November 1, 2006. https://www.foreignaffairs.com/articles/israel/2006-11-01/future-lebanon

Sly, Liz, and Sarah Dadouch. "Hezbollah says retribution for Soleimani's death must target U.S. military, not civilians." *Washington Post.* January 5, 2020. https://www.washingtonpost.com/world/middle_east/hezbollah-says-retribution-for-soleimanis-death-must-target-us-military-not-civilians/2020/01/05/50869828-2e62-11ea-bffe-020c88b3f120_story.html

Solhdoost, Mohsen. "Has killing Soleimani backfired on the US?" ASPI Strategist. July 20, 2020. https://www.aspistrategist.org.au/has-killing-soleimani-backfired-on-the-us/

Soleimani, Qassem (2019) "Untold facts on Israel-Hezbollah war in an interview with Major General Qassem Soleimani." *Khamenei.ir.* October 1, 2019. https://english.khamenei.ir/news/7074/Untold-facts-on-Israel-Hezbollah-war-in-an-interview-with-Major

Soleimani, Z. (2020). "Exclusive interview with Zeinab Soleimani; Daughter of the Late General Qasem Soleimani." Mrs Bret X TV. Dec. 16, 2020. RT video, 14:01. https://www.youtube.com/watch?v=USBqif2_XBk

Statista (2023). "Number of people shot to death by the police in the United States from 2017 to 2022, by race." https://www.statista.com/statistics/585152/people-shot-to-death-by-us-police-by-race/

Sullivan, Marisa. *Hezbollah in Syria.* Middle East Security Report 19. Institute for the Study of War. April 1, 2014. https://www.jstor.org/stable/resrep07896

Tehran Times. "Iran foils assassination plot against General Soleimani." October 3, 2019. https://www.tehrantimes.com/news/440760/Iran-foils-assassination-plot-against-General-Soleimani

Telesur. "Iran and China Sign 25-Year $400 Billion Cooperation Agreement." Transcend. March 29, 2021. online: https://www.transcend.org/tms/2021/03/iran-and-china-sign-25-year-400-billion-cooperation-agreement/

UNDP. "Human Development Indices and Indicators, 2018 Statistical Update." United Nations Development Programme. https://hdr.undp.org/content/statistical-update-2018

Westcott, Ben, and Hamdi Alkhshali. "China, Russia and Iran hold joint naval drills in Gulf of Oman." *CNN*. December 27, 2019. https://edition.cnn.com/2019/12/27/asia/china-russia-iran-military-drills-intl-hnk/index.html

Ya Ali. "Christian Singer Honors Hezbollah at 2013 Concert. (English Subtitles)." February 4, 2014. Performance video, 8:13. https://www.youtube.com/watch?v=5tFhDc5SO3c

Zimmerman, Max. "Facebook to Remove Pro-Soleimani Posts on Instagram, CNN Reports." Bloomberg. January 10, 2020. https://www.bloomberg.com/news/articles/2020-01-11/facebook-to-remove-pro-soleimani-posts-on-instagram-cnn-reports

12. Dismantling Israeli Apartheid

Israeli checkpoint in Jerusalem restricting access to the Al Aqsa Mosque

The future of the Israeli regime in Palestine is often seen as either (1) maintenance of the racist state, with more than half the population excluded and brutally repressed or (2) complete collapse of the regime and Palestinian liberation—a simple dichotomy. However, tensions amongst zionist elites and the historic unravelling of previous racist regimes suggest that the dismantling of Apartheid Israel may come sooner than expected but in a more complicated manner. Racist states have often been dismantled, albeit with serious compromises.

Cracks in the colony are showing. Israel is losing badly in the international legitimacy stakes, with the apartheid brand now firmly attached to its rump. Since the murder of Iranian Commander Qassem Soleimani, relative unity in the resistance forces has grown while division on the Israeli side has widened; for example, the large liberal zionist faction in the USA has begun to play a role in destabilising the Tel Aviv regime.

The Israeli regime is built on a fictional 'racial' privilege with a thoroughgoing apartheid system which includes more than 65 systematic racially discriminatory laws (Adalah 2017). A huge dilemma for 'liberal' Zionists, is the naked reality of apartheid, now recognised by six independent reports (CCHS 2022). A 2009 South African report and the 2017 report of U.S. international law experts Richard Falk and Virginia Tilly were joined by two 2021 Israeli-Palestinian reports (Al Haq and Btselem) and two others in 2022 from the U.S.-based Human Rights Watch and the British-based Amnesty International. All confirmed the status of the Israeli regime as one of Apartheid and therefore a crime against humanity. These reports have contributed to the collapse of the regime's legitimacy worldwide and have also spurred a response from some influential liberal zionists.

Two former Israeli leaders, both of the liberal faction, had earlier warned of the existential threat the apartheid brand poses for their dream of a Jewish state. In 2007 Ehud Olmert warned that Israel faces an "apartheid like struggle" if the two-state myth collapses (McCarthy 2007). Similarly in 2017 Ehud Barak warned that his state was "on a slippery slope" towards apartheid (Kaplan 2017).

This matter is of less concern for the more openly fascist zionists, who dominate the regime these days. However liberal zionists, with greater influence in the USA, have not been sitting on their hands. They are alarmed at the damage to the reputation of their 'Jewish state,' after it having been labelled an apartheid regime and therefore, by the 1973 U.N. Convention, a crime against humanity (UN 1973) which must be dismantled.

At this point it seems useful to distinguish between the Israeli factions to appreciate the tensions. We can almost interchangeably speak of Israeli and Jewish factions, as the colony describes itself as "the nation state of the Jewish people." First there is an openly fascist group, most often led by Benjamin Netanyahu, which has controlled the Tel Aviv regime in recent years. They have always wanted the entirety of historic Palestine and do not care much about international criticism. Then there is a large liberal zionist grouping, which still shares illusions about 'two states' and, most importantly, values the moral standing of Jewish Israelis. They hate the Netanyahus of the world and are desperate to escape the apartheid brand. Third is a group of communists, Arabs, and others, which has some representation in the colonial parliament, which are nominally anti-zionist but also embedded in the system. Finally, we have a genuinely anti-zionist group which rejects Jewish privilege, does not identify with Israel, and will publicly support the Palestinian right to resist.

Table 1: Zionist / Jewish factions		
1	Open fascists	Prosecute the ethnic cleansing of entire historic Palestine, calling openly for the ethnic cleansing of the indigenous Arab population.
2	Liberal Zionists	Those who want colonisation of most Arab land while maintaining the fig-leaf of 'two states', very concerned at their international image. Critical of Israeli fascism but reject resistance.
3	Embedded 'anti-zionists'	Internal critics which, nevertheless, remain embedded in the colonial Israeli system (e.g. Haaretz style critics, minority Knesset groups)
4	Genuine anti-zionists	Those who reject Jewish colonial privilege and support the Palestinian and regional resistance (e.g. Israeli historian Ilan Pappe, some religious groups like Neturei Karta, disaffected youth)

The second group, the liberal zionists, have already begun agitation against the Netanyahu-led fascists and would love to rid the colony of its apartheid tag. In this respect they follow in the tradition of famous Jewish liberals like Albert Einstein and Hannah Arendt, who campaigned against Menachem Begin, Yitzhak Shamir and their Likud Party in the late 1940s, considering the latter "closely akin to the Nazi and Fascist parties." Einstein in 1946 wrote that he was "firmly convinced" that demands for a "Jewish state" would have "only undesirable results for us." However, in the end he reluctantly agreed, from a distance, to support the idea of a "national home" for the Jewish people, so long as there was no "undue encroachment upon the Arab population" (Jerome 2009). That naïve hope was betrayed long ago.

Some liberal zionists, unhappy with the fascist brand, have already addressed a post-apartheid regime. They are not prepared to live with that "shame" (Herbst 2022) and are looking for their own version of restructuring. For example, former Israeli negotiator Daniel Levy, now President of the U.S.-based Middle East Project, told the United Nations Security Council that the notion of an 'Arab state' was dead and that apartheid in Palestine was a reality (Weiss 2022). Similarly Peter Beinart, an editor at Jewish Currents and contributor to *The Atlantic* and CNN, *wrote in the New York Times* about the many fake zionist claims of anti-semitism. He said that zionist groups were "abandoning a traditional commitment to human rights out of blind support for Israel" (Beinart 2022).

Then in early 2023, 170 "significant American-Jewish leaders" released a joint statement harshly criticising the policy and practices of the Tel Aviv regime. Signatories include "former heads of four major rabbinical seminaries, two former policymakers, three retired ambassadors and senior past leaders of Jewish Federations, the United Jewish Appeal, AIPAC, and the Obama administration." They called their criticisms part of a "critical and necessary debate" which "emanate from a love for Israel and a steadfast support for its security and well-being" (Samuels 2023). But the stakes are high for the apartheid regime, which has in the past demanded Jewish unity in the face of international condemnation.

In the event that influential liberal zionists find a way to broker serious reform, they will likely be joined by the third and fourth groups. It is significant that young Jewish North Americans have a steadily diminishing attachment to the colony. In a 2020 poll only 48% of U.S. Jewish people aged 18-29 felt "very or somewhat" attached to Israel (c.f. average 58%) while only 35% of this young group saw "caring about Israel as essential to being Jewish" (c.f. average 45%) (PRC 2021). This erosion of support is in many ways a reaction to the open fascism of recent Tel Aviv administrations, including the systematic racist violence and limitless colonisation.

In contrast to this colonial fractiousness, there has been some reconciliation of the Palestinian resistance factions as well as of the regional resistance. Particularly after the death of Soleimani, when Iranian sponsorship of all the resistance factions was openly acknowledged (Subeiti 2022), the resistance has presented a more unified front. Evidence for this can be seen in the joint operation Saif al Quds (Sword of Jerusalem) to defend the Al Aqsa Mosque and eventually to liberate the holy city from Israeli occupation (QINA 2021). Driven by the shared Iranian-Syria policy of supporting every faction of the Palestinian resistance, there was even a 2022 reconciliation between Hamas and Damascus (AFP 2022; Palestine Chronicle 2022).

Relations had been shattered in 2012 when Hamas sided with the Muslim Brotherhood, taking shelter in Qatar, breaking with Iran and Damascus and helping Jabhat al Nusra terrorists against Syria.

So given concerted resistance efforts, collapsing international legitimacy and a liberal zionist 'fifth column' at work, regime change seems a closer reality. But what sort of dismantling? Two of the three modes most cited on the Palestinian side—creating an Arab state (the 'two-state solution') and expelling all Jewish colonists—seem impractical. The two-state idea has been killed by the massive colonisation of the West Bank. As for mass expulsions, there are now several generations of colonists native to Israel, even if they do not outnumber indigenous Palestinians. For some years the Jewish Israeli and the Palestinian Arab populations—those between the Jordan Valley and the Mediterranean—have been roughly equal, at about 6.5 million each (Cohen and Scheer 2015; Heller 2018). That is not counting the large Palestinian diaspora. So, while the Palestinian population is not going away, expelling all the colonists would also face huge difficulties. The third mode, a South African style transition to a single democratic state, seems more plausible, but that too contains a number of uncertainties. As UN expert Francesca Albanese (2022) reminds us, even dismantling apartheid would not address three important issues: war crimes, land theft and the refugees. Apartheid is not the only Israeli crime.

Then there are myths about 'dismantling.' For years defenders of the colony have claimed that their regional enemies want to 'drive them into the sea,' raising echoes of past German crimes against the European Jews. That might well be a sentiment amongst parts of the aggrieved Palestinian population. However, it is neither a political agenda nor a practical reality. Though former U.S. President Barack Obama had even claimed at the UN that former Iranian President Mahmoud Ahmadinejad said Israel should be 'wiped off the map,' this was a distortion. The more serious U.S. media debunked this claim, noting that Ahmadinejad was quoting Ayatollah Ruhollah Khomeini, who said Israel would collapse and disappear from the 'pages of time' (Kessler 2011).

As the major supporter of Palestinian armed resistance, the Iranian position remains important. It has been clarified by Leader Ayatollah Ali Khamenei in this way:

> We do not suggest launching a classic war by the armies of Muslim countries, or throwing immigrant Jews into the sea, or mediation by the U.N. and other international organizations. We propose holding a referendum with [the participation of] the Palestinian nation. The Palestinian nation, like any other nation, has the right to determine their own destiny and elect the governing system of the country" (Khamenei 2011).

This is a version of the 'one democratic state' solution. Of course, such a process does not negate the real possibility of armed conflict, leading up to such a transition.

Further, the zionist colony is not autonomous; it also serves as the key forward base for Anglo-American hegemonic power in the Middle East. U.S. President Joe Biden said, back in the 1980s and has repeated ever since, that "if there were not an Israel we'd have to invent one" (Biden 2021). Washington's ambitions remain important, including its need to engage in strategic withdrawal and maintain its own global image.

But sustained resistance and plummeting illegitimacy dictate that there will indeed be a transition. Further, as should be clear from the South African experience, neither of the major sponsors, Britain and the USA, can save the Israeli regime. Apartheid South Africa, too, was nuclear armed and with powerful allies, and was once thought invincible. The Reagan administration, for example, "demonized opponents of apartheid … as dangerous and pro-communist"; but in the end the U.S. Congress voted for sanctions and change (Elliot 2011). British PM Margaret Thatcher also claimed sanctions on South Africa were "irrelevant" and would be ignored (Mellor 2020). She even argued for a return to a pre-WW1 racially partitioned South Africa (Wright 2018). Yet in the end even Thatcher, albeit at the last moment, "still played a role in the dismantling of South Africa's apartheid regime" (Onslow 2013). Yet while neither Britain nor the USA can save the Israeli regime, there is a high likelihood that they will position themselves to have a say in the compromises of transition.

The combined forces of steadfast Palestinian resistance and the rising international illegitimacy of Israel remain the most powerful forces working towards a democratic Palestine (Anderson 2018). Yet the disunity of Palestinian factions (Abdou 2013)—actively encouraged by the zionist regime—can still undermine their bargaining position. Amongst the elements of disunity, sectarian Islamism combined with the Muslim Brotherhood (*Ikhwani*) strategy remain the most serious. Palestinian public opinion had always strongly favoured national unity and opposed the *Ikhwani* idea of first defeating the enemy at home (i.e. nationalist, socialist or secular Palestinians) before turning to the external enemy (Shadid 1988).

The Palestinian population remains at odds with all the current elites. In a 2013 poll only minorities saw as 'legitimate' the Mahmoud Abas-led Palestinian Authority (31%) and the Haniyeh-Hamas–led Gaza administration (25%). Most wanted Palestinian national unification but were pessimistic about the chances; 53% supported the two-state solution and 46% opposed but 56% believed that two states were no longer practical due to the expansion of the zionist colonies (PCPSR 2013). A subsequent 2019 poll showed strong support for national legislative and presidential elections (83-87%) and for national reconciliation (89%), but little faith in current parties and leaders. Fatah had 35% support, Hamas 12% and the PFLP 3%. Of all presidential candidates, long term prisoner Marwan Barghouti had the highest support at 12.6%. A large majority of 78% rejected any peace deal which involved 'land swaps' (JMCC 2019). By 2021 trust in the parties remained low, with 36% for Fatah and 7.3% for Hamas; 39% did not trust anyone and 23.5% said they would not vote. The largest group of 39.3% still believed a 'two-state solution' was preferable, while 21.4% said a binational state was the best solution (JMCC 2021). This failure in trust and institutions and serious disunity leaves the door open for dirty deals. On the other hand, the more recent unity talks between Fatah and Hamas (Al Jazeera 2022) do offer some hope.

Nevertheless, the enemy is intelligent. Liberal zionists are well aware that Palestinians will increasingly "frame demands for citizenship and sovereignty in the clearest possible manner" while, on the other hand, "Israelis are increasingly aware that the possibility of maintaining the state's Jewish character alongside its democratic identity is strained as never before" (Anziska 2017). This raises a challenge to seek a "more expansive definition of citizenship that would accommodate non-Jews in line with a civic Israeli identity," including by "emerging forms of Jewish-Muslim solidarity," which "speak to more profound changes ahead." All this has political implications for the USA as well as for the ongoing colonisation ('settlements') in the occupied Palestinian territories. What new possibilities might come out of these new contradictions "remains to be seen." While reluctant to give up the two-state myth, this liberal zionist reasoning recognises that "the question of how to direct the Palestinian national struggle remains as relevant as ever" (Anziska 2017). That aim of redirecting (or co-opting or subverting) the Palestinian struggle has long been an ambition of liberal zionists and other false friends, who pretend to support the Palestinian cause.

Combined with the weight of Israel's key sponsors, the notion of redirecting the Palestinian cause presupposes also controlling transition compromises. Let's remember that the abolition of mass slavery in the USA was followed by another century of brutal Jim Crow racial discrimination (CRF 2022), a system which has been called 'slavery by another name' (PBS 2021). This next stage racist system was given legal blessing by the 'separate but equal' Supreme Court decision in *Plessy v. Ferguson* (1896), a decision not overturned until Brown v. Board of Education of Topeka decision (1954). Abolition of slavery in the USA did not mean emancipation.

Correctly pointing to parallels with the dismantling of apartheid in South Africa, Omar Barghouti calls for an increase in boycott and sanction initiatives against Israel (Barghouti 2021). Yet he does not refer to the compromises involved in the South African transitional process, which led to extreme economic injustice and post-apartheid South Africa becoming one of the most unequal countries on earth (SA-TIED 2020).

Perhaps even more relevant are the compromises made when the racial regime in Zimbabwe (formerly 'Rhodesia') was dismantled at the end of the 1970s. Talks hosted in Britain led to the 'Lancaster House Accords' (SRCC 1979) with the following features. First, 'equal citizenship' was created but it was accompanied by several protective provisions. A 'white roll' was created to maintain ten (of 40) 'white' senators and 20 (of 100) 'white' reps in the Assembly. There were then requirements for 70% parliamentary agreement for constitutional changes. A unanimous requirement to change "the separate representation of the white minority in parliament" gave that group veto power. Second, under the "freedom from deprivation of property" provisions, the compulsory expropriation of property was banned, and consensual compensation provisions were required. Protective provisions to privilege white minority representation and ban state acquisition of land could, for a period of ten years, only be carried out "by the unanimous vote of the House of Assembly." That 'froze' white colonist control of most of the country's arable land. Nevertheless, the Lancaster House agreement went on to claim that "the question of majority rule … has been resolved." Britain promised to provide capital for land buyouts but failed to do so. Twenty years after independence, as the Mugabe government attempted to finally implement land reform, Britain and the USA imposed unilateral coercive sanctions on the country (BTN 2022).

The land question is particularly important in Palestine, where steady land grabs, house thefts and demolitions have economically marginalised the indigenous population and, in the process, exposed the seven-decade myth of 'two states' (Ferris 2020).

The parallel histories warn us of some important lessons for dismantling the zionist regime. Liberal zionists will use their influence with Washington and London to help cut a deal with the more compliant, property owning elements of the Palestinian community. Almost certainly the emerging deal will involve specific protection of 'settler rights,' limits to war crimes prosecutions, entrenchment of Zionist privileges and a freeze on land relations. The 'right to return,' which affects millions, will also be subject to a deal.

How will the resistance address this challenge? The likely Palestinian collaborators for a 'New Israel' will be those linked to the Arab monarchies, with property and embedded interests in the Palestinian Authority, which has long functioned as a municipality of the Apartheid regime. Religion will be no barrier, as secular collaborators will be joined by those who threw in their hand with the Muslim Brotherhood players, notably Qatar and Turkey—leading false friends of the Palestinian cause.

There is a real risk that a coalition of Anglo-American powerbrokers, liberal zionists and Palestinian collaborators will begin to cut a deal behind closed doors, betraying the legacy of Palestinian sacrifice and resistance. Such betrayals often occur at the last moment. If deep divisions persist amongst Palestinian resistance factions, that deal will be easier to sell to an unsuspecting Palestinian and world audience.

The dismantling of the 'Old Israel' will be so dramatic that few will pay attention to key details of the 'New Israel.' But such details will be crucially important for the long-suffering Palestinian people.

References

Abdou, Mahmoud. "Disunity in Palestine: Its history and implications for the peace process." Ideas for Peace. April 18, 2013. https://www.ideasforpeace.org/content/disunity-in-palestine-its-history-and-implications-for-the-peace-process/

Adalah (2017). The Discriminatory Laws Database. September 25, 2017. https://www.adalah.org/en/content/view/7771

AFP. "Hamas resumes Syria ties in Damascus visit." *Al-Monitor.* October 19, 2022. https://www.al-monitor.com/originals/2022/10/hamas-resumes-syria-ties-damascus-visit

Albanese, Francesca. "Situation of human rights in the Palestinian territories occupied since 1967." UN General Assembly. September 21, 2022. https://www.un.org/unispal/wp-content/uploads/2022/10/A.77.356_210922.pdf

Al Jazeera. "Palestinian groups Fatah, Hamas meet in Algeria to heal rift." October 11, 2022. https://www.aljazeera.com/news/2022/10/11/palestinian-groups-fatah-hamas-meet-in-algeria-to-heal-rift

Anderson, Tim. "The Future of Palestine." Centre for Counter Hegemonic Studies. August 7, 2018. https://counter-hegemonic-studies.site/future-palestine-1/

Anziska, Seth. "Neither Two States nor One: The Palestine Question in the Age of Trump." *Journal of Palestine Studies* XLVI, no. 3 (Spring 2017). https://www.usmep.us/media/filer_public/ca/93/ca932e8a-6a3c-4a02-b671-eebbd189251b/neither_two_states_nor_one_anziska.pdf

Barghouti, Omar. "Let's Dismantle Apartheid!" BDS. November 23, 2021. https://bdsmovement.net/Lets-Dismantle-Apartheid

Beinart, Peter. "Has the Fight Against Antisemitism Lost Its Way?" *New York Times.* August 26, 2022. https://www.nytimes.com/2022/08/26/opinion/antisemitism-israel-uae-saudi.html

Biden, Joe (2021). "Joe Biden's long history of pro-Israel statements." Middle East Eye. May 22, 2021. Video clips, 2:19. https://www.youtube.com/watch?v=86Nrv5izaTs

BTN (2022). "Zimbabwe: 21 Years of Sanctions for Repossessing Land and Defying Western Powers." Break Through News. November 7, 2022. Video, 18:13. https://www.youtube.com/watch?v=DkDFtM4Blr4

CCHS. "SIX (6) important reports on Israeli Apartheid." Centre for Counter Hegemonic Studies. Centre for Counter Hegemonic Studies. February 24, 2022. https://counter-hegemonic-studies.site/israeli-apartheid-6/

Cohen, Tova, and Steven Scheer. "Israel's soaring population: Promised Land running out of room?" Reuters. September 25, 2015. https://www.reuters.com/article/uk-israel-demographics-idUKKCN0RP0ZG20150925

CPI. "Fast Track Land Reform in Zimbabwe." Centre for Public Impact. August 30, 2017. https://www.centreforpublicimpact.org/case-study/fast-track-land-reform-zimbabwe/

CRF (2022). "A Brief History of Jim Crow." Constitutional Rights Foundation. https://www.crf-usa.org/black-history-month/a-brief-history-of-jim-crow

Elliot, Justin. "Reagan's embrace of apartheid South Africa: His foreign policy legacy includes an alliance with a racist government." *Salon.* February 5, 2011. https://www.salon.com/2011/02/05/ronald_reagan_apartheid_south_africa/

Ferris, Seth. "Great Land Grab: Two-State Solution or a Two-State Problem?" New Eastern Outlook. January 30, 2020. https://journal-neo.org/2020/01/30/great-land-grab-two-state-solution-in-palestine-israel-really-a-two-state-problem/

Heller, Jeffrey. "Jews, Arabs nearing population parity in Holy Land: Israeli officials." Reuters. March 27, 2018. https://www.reuters.com/article/us-israel-palestinians-population/jews-arabs-nearing-population-parity-in-holy-land-israeli-officials-idUSKBN1H222T

Herbst, Robert. "Israeli Apartheid: The power of the frame, the shame of the name." *Mondoweiss.* July 4, 2022. https://mondoweiss.net/2022/07/israeli-apartheid-the-power-of-the-frame-the-shame-of-the-name/

Jerome, Fred. *Einstein on Israel and Zionism: His Provocative Ideas About the Middle East.* New York: St. Martin's Press, 2009.

JMCC (2019). Poll No. 94 – Shtayeh Government & Elections. April 9, 2019. http://www.jmcc.org/documentsandmaps.aspx?id=884

——— (2021). Poll No. 97 – Palestine Before the Elections. April 20, 2021. online: http://www.jmcc.org/documentsandmaps.aspx?id=892

Kaplan, Allison. "Ehud Barak Warns: Israel Faces 'Slippery Slope' Toward Apartheid." *Haaretz.* June 21, 2017. https://www.haaretz.com/

israel-news/2017-06-21/ty-article/ehud-barak-warns-israel-on-slippery-slope-to-apartheid/0000017f-ef8b-d0f7-a9ff-efcf52ce0000

Kessler, Glenn. "Did Ahmadinejad really say Israel should be 'wiped off the map'?" *Washington Post.* October 5, 2011. https://www.washingtonpost.com/blogs/fact-checker/post/did-ahmadinejad-really-say-israel-should-be-wiped-off-the-map/2011/10/04/gIQABJIKML_blog.html

Khamenei, Ayatollah Ali. "Two-state solution rejected outright: Leader." *Mehr News.* October 1, 2011. https://en.mehrnews.com/amp/48277/

McCarthy, Rory. "Israel risks apartheid-like struggle if two-state solution fails, says Olmert." *The Guardian.* November 30, 2007. https://www.theguardian.com/world/2007/nov/30/israel

Mellor, Joe. "Newly revealed documents show Margaret Thatcher's support for apartheid South Africa." *The London Economic.* December 27, 2020. https://www.thelondoneconomic.com/news/newly-revealed-documents-show-margaret-thatchers-support-for-apartheid-south-africa/27/12/

Onslow, Sue. "Thatcher, the Commonwealth and apartheid South Africa." LSE. April 9, 2013. https://blogs.lse.ac.uk/africaatlse/2013/04/09/thatcher-the-commonwealth-and-apartheid-south-africa/

Palestine Chronicle. "Hamas Declares a 'Glorious Day' from Damascus after Meeting Assad." October 19, 2022. https://www.palestinechronicle.com/hamas-declares-a-glorious-day-from-damascus-after-meeting-assad/

PBS. "Slavery by Another Name: Jim Crow and Plessy v. Ferguson." Public Broadcasting Service, 2021. https://www.pbs.org/tpt/slavery-by-another-name/themes/jim-crow/

PCPSR. "Palestinian Public Opinion Poll No (50)." Palestinian Centre for Policy and Survey Research. December 19, 2013. https://www.pcpsr.org/en/node/189

PRC. "Jewish Americans in 2020." Pew Research Centre. May 11, 2021. https://www.pewresearch.org/religion/2021/05/11/jewish-americans-in-2020/

QINA. "Palestinian resistance launches Operation al-Quds Sword as Israeli airstrikes kill 27 in Gaza." *Qods International News Agency.* November 5, 2021. http://qodsna.com/en/355807/Palestinian-resistance-launches-Operation-al-Quds-Sword-as-Israeli-airstrikes-kill-27-in-Gaza

Samuels, Ben. "Nearly 170 Leading U.S. Jews Call for 'Critical and Necessary Debate' on Israel's Far-right Gov't." *Haaretz.* February 1, 2023. https://www.haaretz.com/israel-news/2023-02-01/ty-article/.

premium/170-leading-u-s-jews-call-for-critical-and-necessary-debate-on-israels-far-right-govt/00000186-0df8-d0a3-adc6-4df9c8830000

SA-TIED (2020). "Extreme inequalities: The distribution of household wealth in South Africa." Southern Africa – Towards Inclusive Economic Development. December 2020. https://sa-tied.wider.unu.edu/article/extreme-inequalities-distribution-household-wealth-south-africa

Shadid, Mohammed K. "The Muslim Brotherhood Movement in the West Bank and Gaza." *Third World Quarterly* 10, no. 2 (April 1988): 658–682

Sherwood, Harriet. "Palestinian collaborator: 'I am a traitor. I sold my people. But for what?'" *The Guardian.* May 17, 2011. https://www.theguardian.com/world/view-from-jerusalem-with-harriet-sherwood/2011/may/17/israel-palestinian-territories

SRCC. "Report: Lancaster House Agreement." Southern Rhodesia: Constitutional Conference held at Lancaster House, London, September–December 1979. December 21, 1979. https://sas-space.sas.ac.uk/5847/5/1979_Lancaster_House_Agreement.pdf

Subeiti, Batool. "Soleimani's effective role in Palestine, from resistance to liberation." *Al Mayadeen.* January 12, 2022. https://english.almayadeen.net/articles/blog/soleimanis-effective-role-in-palestine-from-resistance-to-li

UN. "1973 UN Convention on Apartheid as a Crime Against Humanity." United Nations. May 15, 2018. PoliticsWeb. https://www.politicsweb.co.za/documents/1973-un-convention-on-apartheid-as-a-crime-against

Weiss, Phillip. "'NYT' and UN Security Council platform apartheid charge against Israel." *Mondoweiss.* August 28, 2022. https://mondoweiss.net/2022/08/nyt-and-un-security-council-platform-apartheid-charge-against-israel/

Wright, Patrick. "Margaret Thatcher believed South Africa should be a 'whites-only state,' says UK's former chief diplomat." *The Independent.* January 22, 2018. https://www.independent.co.uk/news/uk/politics/margaret-thatcher-south-africa-whites-only-state-patrick-wright-a8171356.html

13. Syria: Siege and Recovery

Syrian soldier passes a Russian coffee shop, Hama city

Having defeated a decade of U.S.-led proxy war, Syria still faced a vicious economic blockade, which aims to starve and 'punish' the people of the independent nation. Syrian diplomat Dr Bashar al Jaafari speaks of "unprecedented" military interventions and occupations which accompany this economic war (Al Jaafari 2022). The two largest NATO armies, those of the USA and Turkey, occupy huge swathes of Syrian land in the north and east and an Israeli occupation remains in the south. Each one provides a safe haven for proxy terrorist groups.

While UN officials acknowledge that 90% of the Syrian population is living in poverty, they pay most attention to the minority living in occupied areas. With astonishing cynicism, UN official Martin Griffiths cites ongoing terrorist violence in areas occupied by the USA and Turkey as a reason for ongoing international intervention in these areas in the name of selective "humanitarian assistance" and "recovery," while failing to call for an end to the occupations (OCHA 2022).

The propaganda war was heavy, intended to dehumanise the country, its leaders and army. Repeated chemical weapons of mass destruction scams, false flag massacres, fake claims of 'freedom and democracy,' 'moderate armed opposition' slogans and the demonising of President Assad were all part of a war to destroy, not just the Syrian government but the Syrian state (Anderson 2016: Ch.3). There were successive U.S. plans to partition Syria into sectarian or 'autonomous' enclaves (e.g. Mackler 2018).

UN Security Council resolutions from 2012 onwards (e.g. UNSC 2015 and UNSC 2021) have tried to sustain a role for the NATO states and exiled 'opposition' groups in a political reconstruction of the Syrian state and its constitution. However, since 2015 that state, with its allies, has liberated virtually all the terrorist-held areas except those above-mentioned, which are now under direct foreign occupation.

But the economic blockade remains, and the NATO states and their collaborators blame Syria for its economic depression (MEMO 2022). Those same Western regimes which drove the dirty war blame the Syrian government and army for the devastation—despite the fact that Vice President Biden (corroborated by head of the U.S. Army General Martin Dempsey and Senator Lindsey Graham) admitted that U.S. allies had financed and armed all the terrorist groups in Syria, in an effort to overthrow the government in Damascus (HOS 2020; Anderson 2016: Ch.12).

Yet life goes on in Syria with greater normality than in NATO-devastated Libya, war torn Afghanistan or fragmented Lebanon. The schools are open, the hospitals, while desperately short of resources, still function, basic infrastructure is being repaired, the streets are clean and there is subsidised fuel, bread and some other essential items. But there is also hunger and deprivation as, in wake of the failure of Washington's New Middle East wars (Anderson 2019: Ch.1), the U.S.-led siege has spread to seven contiguous Middle East nations.

Washington does not even bother to deny that it is stealing Syrian oil and wheat (al Jaafari 2022). While the U.S. signs UN declarations supporting the "sovereignty and territorial integrity" of Syria, U.S. troops and their proxies occupy Syrian land, seemingly out of spite, to punish and divide both Syria and the peoples of the region.

Yet Syria has held together and focused on local production while building an economic future with eastern blocs. Recovery will be through gradual liberation of the occupied lands and populations, then finding new financial relations, then through integration into a new regional infrastructure. This chapter sets out the elements of the siege imposed on the peoples of West Asia, before turning to the character of Syrian resistance and its strategy for recovery and reconstruction.

The siege of West Asia

With multiple failing wars, Washington, its NATO partners and regional collaborators (in particular Israel, Qatar, Turkey and Saudi Arabia) imposed a genocidal economic siege on a contiguous bloc of seven West Asian countries, between the Mediterranean and the Himalayas. The physical blockades on Palestine and Yemen are joined by partial or full coercive measures on Lebanon, Syria, Iraq, Iran, and Afghanistan. Among other things, this brutal regional siege has led to 90% of the Syrian population living in poverty (OCHA 2022) while the blockaded people of Yemen suffer what has been called "the world's worst humanitarian crisis" (WFP 2022).

The aim in all cases has been 'to starve and cause desperation' amongst the entire population—as was said about Washington's blockades on Cuba and on Iran (OTH 1960; Cole 2018). The explicit aim is imposing 'deliberate harm' in the hope of coercing political change. That is why these coercive measures should never be called 'sanctions,' which suggest just punishment for wrongdoing in accord with international law (Anderson 2019: Ch.3). A key associated aim is to help the zionist colony persist in its theft of Palestinian, Syrian, and Lebanese land, and so destabilise and cripple the development of the entire region.

While much of this siege is imposed in the name of democracy, human rights and anti-terrorism, none of the NATO affiliated states of the region—like the Saudis and Qataris, who actually financed and armed mass sectarian terrorism (Al Jazeera 2019; Norfolk 2021)—face such sanctions.

The pretexts for this siege are buried in pseudo-legal inventions. The U.S. Treasury's OFAC database has lists of dozens of sanctioned entities and individuals in Palestine, Lebanon, Syria, Iraq, Iran and Yemen (OFAC 2022). There are not many sanctions against Afghanistan, after 20 years of U.S. and NATO military occupation. However Washington notoriously seized several billion dollars belonging to Afghanistan's Central Bank (Byrd 2022), simply because the U.S. is dissatisfied with the current Afghan government. That theft will likely add to the looming mass starvation of millions of Afghan people (Lee 2021).

So what are sanctions and when can they be justified? In international law two principles are said to limit a state's retaliation against others: that the response should be 'in proportion' to alleged wrongful action by the other; and that any reprisal only comes after attempts at negotiation (Anderson 2021).

However, retaliation is unlawful when (1) the aim is to damage the economy of another nation, or (2) there is an attempt at political coercion or (3) the measures imposed also damage the rights of third parties. All these illegal elements are at work in Washington's current regional siege. Such unilateral sanctions are now termed 'unilateral coercive measures' (UCMs) and are subject to special scrutiny at the United Nations (OHCHR 2020).

For some time, international agencies have reported on the catastrophic impact of this siege, for example in Syria and Yemen. Despite the theoretical 'humanitarian' exemptions in both U.S. and European coercive measures, the U.S. stranglehold on finance means there is a severe impact on essentials such as food, medicine, and energy.

UCM regimes, now so popular with the USA and the European Union, have been condemned by independent UN experts for violating international law and impeding the UN's Sustainable Development Goals (CGTN 2022). While UCMs are "imposed mostly in the name of human rights, democracy and the rule of law," Rapporteur Alena Douhan concludes they actually "undermine those very principles, values and norms" while inflicting humanitarian damage (OHCHR 2021).

The WHO has reported that unilateral U.S.-EU sanctions damage children's cancer treatment in Syria (Nehme 2017). Medical studies have condemned Europe's coercive sanctions for their damage to COVID-19 prevention and treatment in Syria (Hussain and Sen 2020), while the UN rapporteur on the impact of Unilateral Coercive Measures, Alena Douhan, has called for an end to Washington's UCMs, which inhibit the rebuilding of Syria's civilian infrastructure destroyed by the conflict (OHCHR 2020).

"The sanctions violate the human rights of the Syrian people, whose country has been destroyed by almost 10 years of ongoing conflict," said Ms Douhan. She also condemned Washington's anti-Syrian 'Caesar Law' as it attempts to block third party support for the Syrian population.

> "I am concerned that sanctions imposed under the Caesar Act may exacerbate the already dire humanitarian situation in Syria, especially in the course of COVID-19 pandemic, and put the Syrian people at even greater risk of human rights violations," she said.

In a November 2022 report, after a 12-day visit to Syria, Ms Douhan added:

> I am struck by the pervasiveness of the human rights and humanitarian impact of the unilateral coercive measures imposed on Syria and the total economic and financial isolation of a country whose people are struggling to rebuild a life with dignity, following the decade-long war ... as 12 million Syrians grapple with food insecurity, I urge the immediate lifting of all unilateral sanctions that severely harm human rights and prevent any efforts for early recovery, rebuilding and reconstruction. No reference to good objectives of unilateral sanctions justifies the violation of fundamental human rights. The international community has an obligation of solidarity and assistance to the Syrian people (OHCHR 2022).

Siege measures on North African countries have come under similar criticism. In 2015 the United Nations Special Rapporteur on the impact of sanctions on human rights, Idriss Jazairy, urged States which had imposed UCMs on Sudan to review their policies. "Sudan has been under unilateral coercive measures for two decades without any adaptation ... The signal given by compulsory measures is in contradiction with their proclaimed objectives," he said, referring to the financial restrictions imposed on all business transactions with Sudan (OHCHR 2015).

In Yemen the rationale is a little different. The U.S.-EU sanctions which sustain the humanitarian crisis are carried out with direct approval by the UN Security Council, under the misguided idea that Mansour Hadi, an interim president for 2021-2014 but after that an exile, is still the legitimate president of the country. The actual revolutionary government led by Ansarallah is under UNSC sanctions. So the siege on Yemen is authorised under international law, unlike the UCMs against Lebanon, Syria, Iraq and Iran.

Nevertheless, the UN's Office of the High Commissioner for Human Rights has said that the Western powers and their Persian Gulf allies (especially the Saudis and the UAE) waging war on Yemen should be held responsible for war crimes (BBC 2019). That 2019 report detailed a range of war crimes over the previous five years, including airstrikes, indiscriminate shelling, snipers, landmines, as well as arbitrary killings and detention, torture, sexual violence, and impeding access to humanitarian aid (OHCHR 2019).

Syria and Lebanon

Ordinary basic Syrian salaries in late 2022 ranged between 80,000 and 160,000 Syrian pounds (about US$20 to $40) per month. Many had no employment. Syrians rely heavily on family support and government subsidies on basic commodities such as fuel, bread, rice, and sugar. There was still free education and free health care in the crowded public hospitals, but much else had become very expensive.

The rise in fuel prices is passed on to transport and food costs. Rents are high and two bags of supermarket groceries can easily cost one month's wages. How people survive is a mystery which has much to do with state support, informal economies, and sharing.

There is little controversy about the poverty which most Syrians now experience. The distorted information comes in explanations of who is responsible. Despite their crocodile tears, NATO-dominated United Nations officials often do not help.

Citing UN Security Council Resolution 2254 (2015) Secretary-General António Guterres (2021) effectively blamed the Syrian Government for the situation while letting Washington off the hook. Demanding "a negotiated political settlement" he insists that his representatives preside over the "Syrian-led" creation of a new constitution and a "transitional government" in which NATO-backed exiled Syrians would have similar status to the elected Syrian government. Instead, in the seven years after UNSC 2254, Syria and its allies had militarily resolved most of the terrorism, liberating Palmyra, Aleppo city, East Ghouta, Deir Ezzor city and the southern region around Daraa.

The UN Secretary General correctly points out that millions of children are "out of school" and that "the COVID-19 pandemic has made it all even worse" (Guterres 2021). However, the school problem appears even worse in the Turkish- and U.S.-occupied areas.

Some UN agencies are helping Syria. The World Food Program is present in several parts of the country and UNICEF is assisting with the construction of Syrian state schools in Syria's northeast, especially after the U.S. proxy SDF militia closed most of the province's schools. In late 2021 this writer observed thousands of children coming to the severely overcrowded Syrian schools in the small 'security zones' of Hasaka and Qamishli cities, which are still controlled by the Syrian Arab Army (HOS 2021)

Most Western reports have focussed on poverty in the foreign occupied parts of Syria, and particularly in al Qaeda-controlled Idlib. However, civilian numbers in the Turkish occupied two-thirds of Idlib have been exaggerated—just as they were in occupied Aleppo up to 2016. This misinformation seems to be aimed at helping justify disregard of most Syrians living elsewhere. A 2021 Brookings report claimed there were "3.4 million civilians in Idlib—over 2 million of them displaced from elsewhere in Syria" (Karasapan 2021). Similarly, the UNHCR in February 2020 spoke of "over four million civilians in north-west Syria," without distinguishing between the Syrian government controlled and Turkish-al Qaeda occupied areas. By contrast, the Syrian government estimate of the total population of occupied Idlib in late 2021 was 1.3 million (al Jaafari 2021), about a quarter of whom are likely armed groups and their families.

The Turkish-occupied segment of north-west Syria has become a substitute for the humanitarian problems of all Syrians, according to many Western reports. The poverty and suffering of the other 18 million Syrians is routinely ignored. Like António Guterres, NATO-linked analyst Joumana Qaddour (2021) of the Atlantic Council draws attention to Syria's poverty while blaming Damascus. She claims "the sanctions imposed both by the United States and the Europeans [are] really tied to the activity of the Assad regime," because Damascus is committed to a "military solution" to the problems of terrorism and foreign occupation.

The pressure on Lebanon has been similar though the context is different. Syria has a strong, unified state with some socialist features, while Lebanon remains divided along sectarian grounds. Just as the British divided peoples in the former Ottoman territories it seized, installing monarchies and the zionist colony, so the French carved out what they hoped might remain a loyal Maronite-Christian dominated coastal enclave.

In Lebanon the Maronite majority has long gone, but the sectarian system remains, modified only slightly after a terrible civil war, and leaving a highly privatised system with little political will and few national institutions. The result is that Lebanon is dealing with the U.S. siege in a quite different way to Syria. Some Lebanese factions even refuse to accept that they are under siege.

Yet Washington has spread the series of coercive measures imposed on the resistance party Hezbollah (Reuters 2021) to its domestic allies (BBC 2020). Third party coercive measures imposed on Syria (Shatz 2021) and on Iran also constrain Lebanon. The U.S. is trying, without much success, to remove from the Lebanese government those who have resisted the Israelis.

Regional siege measures were a major factor in Lebanon's 2019 financial collapse, with Syria's currency devaluing to a sixth of its value over two years, while Lebanon's currency devalued to less than a tenth. The ongoing pace of devaluation of Lebanon's Lira is also greater. Lebanon has relied much more on the cash economy and imports, a liability in a crash.

With the financial crash average Lebanese GDP per capita fell from $8,000 pc in 2018 to $3,000 by the end of 2021. The Lebanese 'middle class' was virtually destroyed. Poverty rose from 30-35% in 2019 to 85-90% in 2021. That meant lack of medicines, fuel shortages, power cuts down to two hours of electricity per day and waves of emigration. By 2022 some boats fleeing Lebanon for Cyprus or Greece carried more Lebanese than Palestinians or Syrians (Snaije 2022).

Even with large parts of Syria's own oil supply blocked or stolen by U.S. occupation forces and their SDF proxies (*Tehran Times*

2021), Syria has been able to help its neighbour, in coordination with Lebanon's Hezbollah, by rehabilitating and using its Baniyas port and refinery to channel Iranian fuel into Lebanon (Chehayeb 2021). Despite Israel's sabotage war against Iranian ships (Lubold, Faucon and Schwartz 2021), after stern warnings from Hassan Nasrallah, the Israelis seemed reluctant to sabotage this particular operation.

Still, Lebanon's post-crash government led by billionaire Najib Mikati invited in IMF overseers (Reuters 2021a) to make sure that Lebanon imposes no new subsidies to help the Lebanese people. The IMF-led destruction of food subsidies has previously been linked to starvation and food riots in many countries (Palast 2001). However, unlike Syria, Lebanon has few subsidies left to destroy. Poverty-stricken Syrians at least enjoy some relief through state subsidies on basic items such as bread, fuel, rice. and sugar. Nevertheless, over 2021-2022, those subsidies were removed for higher income Syrians (MEMO 2021).

Lebanon's health services are highly privatised and remain mostly under 'user pays' regimes. Only in respect of pandemic measures was Lebanon ahead of Syria, due to higher levels of testing and vaccination. By late 2022 Lebanon had one hundred times the COVID testing rate of Syria: 709,923 tests per million compared to 7,915 (Worldometers 2022). Both countries have much the same policies, but Syria has lacked test kits and vaccines.

There are still many Syrian war refugees in Lebanon, but here there is a reciprocal history. In 2019 in the ancient Christian village of Maaloula a local priest proudly showed me a 2006 letter from Hezbollah's Hassan Nasrallah, thanking the town for taking in refugees from Lebanon's south. This was during the Israeli invasion of that year which displaced tens of thousands (Rehrl 2006). At the same time the priest acknowledged that, when in 2014 the town was threatened by the NATO-backed Jabhat al Nusra terrorists, it was young Muslim men from Lebanon who defended the town.

Although progress is slow, it is this broader Levantine cooperation which has been bringing the two neighbours together again, under common siege. The Biden administration had to waive its own third party "sanctions" on Syria, to allow "the first official visit" (MEO 2021) of a Lebanese government delegation to Syria in ten years. That was because the only energy alternative to Iranian fuel that Washington could think of was to port Egyptian or Jordanian gas through Syria to Lebanon (Martin 2021). As it happened the cheap Iranian fuel (to be paid for in the Lebanese currency) came through while the Egyptian-Jordanian gas idea still faced uncertainties and was eventually blocked by the Washington-based World Bank (Egypt Today 2022).

In the longer term, both countries need each other. Lebanon has been the highly commercialised coastal hub and Syria the stronger, productive hinterland. An important obstacle to deeper cooperation is Lebanon's sectarian, privatised system. That prevents the little country from asserting itself either at home or abroad—just what the U.S., French and British want.

Resistance and recovery

Despite being under extreme pressure, Syria has been stabilising. Against a massive proxy war followed by multiple foreign interventions it has reclaimed almost all its major cities and—unlike Lebanon—produces most of its own basic goods. Its relations with Iran, Russia and China are building the foundation for both a security strategy and a restructured external economy.

The country's capacity to recover comes from its resistant character; but that has also made it a target for big powers. Its centuries-old refusal to take orders from foreign powers and its resistance to repeated foreign interventions can be traced back to ancient times, when Queen Zenobia broke from Roman rule (Stoneman 1995). It was inflamed a century ago when Sultan Pasha al Atrash led the Great Arab Revolt of the 1920s against the French colonial power (Provence 2005). And it rose again with Syria's defeat of a massive, decade long proxy war driven by Washington, other NATO states and the Persian Gulf monarchies (Anderson 2016).

Syria as an Arab nation once included current day Iskenderun, Lebanon, Palestine and Jordan. Colonists tried to crush its Pan-Arab ideology, which rose against the French and the British, leading to the hard-fought renewal of independence in 1947. The Pan Arabism which forms the basis of the Syrian Arab Baath Party and other groups like the Nasserites and the Syrian Social National Party (SSNP), is a reflection of the region's Arab speaking peoples, with a shared history, aspiration and culture (Al Jaafari 2022).

Further, almost uniquely in the region, Syria has led the process of separating religion from politics, which supports its broader, inclusive Arab traditions and historic defence of multiple social communities. Syria's famous pluralism was attacked by the NATO sponsored terrorist groups, mainly Jabhat al Nusra and ISIS/DAESH, which abused minority communities contrary to Quranic injunction and historic Islamic practice, while slaughtering anyone who backed the Damascus government.

The U.S. strategy aimed to make Syria "a failed state." That meant undermining Syria's means of subsistence and strength: wheat, water, oil, the Tabaqa dam, irrigation for agriculture, health systems and energy sources. Without a state the foreign powers can do "whatever they want, because there is no state" (Al Jaafari 2022). But Syria, with its regional allies, had resisted for four years before Russia came to assist. After that the progress was consistent, if costly. The Syrian Arab Army bore most of the sacrifices in liberating Syria's cities and towns.

Syria's independent economic strategy in the subsequent period can be thought of in domestic and international terms. Domestically there has been a huge effort to maintain social unity, then to focus on production, self-reliance and social support or subsidies. Maintenance of a functioning state, army and the pluralist constitution have been fundamental to this. Internationally, the strategy has been to oppose the Western blockade while building new relations with the emerging eastern blocs.

In domestic terms President Bashar al-Assad, after his 2021 swearing in for a fourth term, emphasised the importance of production, investment and anti-corruption, in view of the difficult economic circumstances. Increasing production was "the key to improving livelihoods." Some investment was still possible, especially in the field of renewable energy (CGTN 2021). Social cohesion was maintained by a range of social subsidies for most people, even though they have been cut back for wealthier Syrians (MEMO 2021).

At the international level, while working against the propaganda used to sustain the Western economic blockade (perhaps fragmenting the Europeans, who often have a distinct view to that of the European Union) Syria has begun an engagement with eastern and southern institutions, themselves the product of widespread dissatisfaction with Western dominated institutions such as the IMF, the World Bank, the WTO, and the dollar-based SWIFT system. Syria has sound and developing bilateral relations with other states under blockade, such as Iran, Venezuela, Cuba and Russia. Iran in turn has 'strategic partnership' relations with both Russia and China (Carl, Fitzpatrick and Lawlor 2022; Hamrah and Eliasen 2021) and has recently joined the Shanghai Cooperation Organization (SCO) (Telesur 2022).

The rise of the BRICS and the SCO shows that a substantial "Asian part of the world" has given up on Western dominated organizations like the WTO, the IMF, and the World Bank. They don't believe in that anymore and they want to create alternatives"; that includes Syria, which has applied to join the SCO (al Jaafari 2022). That could bypass the U.S.-controlled SWIFT system and open up new financial mechanisms to restart trade and investment.

The first step in recovery must be the liberation of the territories occupied by Turkey, the USA and Israel. That will free human and natural resources. Second is opening access to a new financial architecture, a process most likely to be led by China and Russia. Third will be the development of regional infrastructure and integration, not least the road, rail, energy and communication channels between Tehran and the Mediterranean. Some elements of this have been tried before but were derailed by Western driven divisions and wars. Nevertheless, such integration remains key to the future of Syria and the region.

References

Al Jaafari, Bashar (2021). Interview with this writer. Damascus. November.

Al Jaafari, Bashar (2022). Interview with this writer. Damascus. September.

Al Jazeera. "Saudi Arabia, UAE gave US arms to al-Qaeda-linked groups: Report." February 5, 2019. https://www.aljazeera.com/news/2019/2/5/saudi-arabia-uae-gave-us-arms-to-al-qaeda-linked-groups-report

Anderson, Tim (2016). *The Dirty War on Syria.* Montreal: Global Research.

——— (2019). *Axis of Resistance.* Atlanta: Clarity Press.

——— (2021). "Sanctions as Siege Warfare." Centre for Counter Hegemonic Studies. June 14, 2021. https://counter-hegemonic-studies.site/sanctions-3/

BBC (2019). "Yemen: Western powers may be held responsible for war crimes—UN." September 4, 2019. https://www.bbc.co.uk/news/world-middle-east-49563073

BBC (2020). "Lebanon's Gebran Bassil hit by US sanctions 'for corruption.'" November 6, 2020. https://www.bbc.com/news/world-middle-east-54823667

Byrd, William. "Demands for Prompt Return of Afghan Central Bank Reserves Miss the Full Picture." US Institute of Peace. August 15, 2022. https://www.usip.org/publications/2022/08/demands-prompt-return-afghan-central-bank-reserves-miss-full-picture

Carl, Nicholas, Kitaneh Fitzpatrick, and Katherine Lawlor. "Russia and Iran double down on their strategic partnership." Institute for the Study of War. August, 11, 2022. https://www.understandingwar.org/backgrounder/russia-and-iran-double-down-their-strategic-partnership

CGTN (2021). "Assad highlights production, investment, anti-corruption as fourth term as Syrian president begins." July 17, 2021. https://news.cgtn.com/news/2021-07-17/Assad-sworn-in-as-Syrian-president-11YoKmIOG1G/index.html

CGTN (2022). "UN Human Rights official: Unilateral sanctions violate international law." July 30, 2022. https://news.cgtn.com/news/2022-07-30/UN-official-Unilateral-sanctions-violate-international-law-1c5CHprNcxa/index.html

Chehayeb, Kareem. "Hezbollah-brokered Iranian fuel arrives in crisis-hit Lebanon." *Al Jazeera.* September 16, 2021. https://www.aljazeera.com/news/2021/9/16/first-shipment-hezbollah-iranian-fuel-arrives-lebanon

Cole, Brendan. "Mike Pompeo Says Iran Must Listen to U.S. 'If They Want Their People to Eat.'" *Newsweek.* November 9, 2018. https://www.newsweek.com/mike-pompeo-says-iran-must-listen-us-if-they-want-their-people-eat-1208465

Egypt Today. "Gas deal between Egypt, Lebanon stalled because of WB new terms: Minister." September 19, 2022. https://www.egypttoday.com/Article/3/119305/Gas-deal-between-Egypt-Lebanon-stalled-because-of-WB-new

Guterres, António. "As Plight of Syrians Worsens, Hunger Reaches Record High, International Community Must Fully Commit to Ending Decade-Old War, Secretary-General Tells General Assembly." United Nations. March 30, 2021. https://press.un.org/en/2021/sgsm20664.doc.htm

Hamrah, Satgin, and Alexander Eliasen. "The China-Iran Strategic Partnership: 40 Years in the Making." December 4, 2021. https://thediplomat.com/2021/12/the-china-iran-strategic-partnership-40-years-in-the-making/

HOS (2020). "Syria by admissions – revisited." Hands Off Syria. November 13, 2020. Video, 5:33. https://www.youtube.com/watch?v=fjtdJX2gVmI

HOS (2021). "Syrian students flood Hasakeh's state schools, despite SDF/QSD repression." Hands Off Syria. October 28, 2021. Video, 1:48. https://www.youtube.com/watch?v=sifwoflSmr4

Hussain, Hamid Yahiya, and Kasturi Sen. "EU guidance impedes humanitarian action to prevent COVID-19 in Syria." *The Lancet.* July 2, 2020. https://www.thelancet.com/journals/langlo/article/PIIS2214-109X(20)30289-8/fulltext

Karasapan, Omar. "The coming crisis in Idlib." Brookings. May 13, 2021. https://www.brookings.edu/blog/future-development/2021/05/13/the-coming-crisis-in-idlib/

Lee, Michael. "Mass starvation looms in Afghanistan as half the country faces hunger under Taliban rule." *New York Post.* December 7, 2021. https://nypost.com/2021/12/07/mass-starvation-looms-in-afghanistan-as-half-the-country-faces-hunger-under-taliban-rule/

Lubold, Gordon, Benoit Faucon, and Felicia Schwartz. "Israeli Strikes Target Iranian Oil Bound for Syria." *Wall Street Journal.* March 11, 2021. https://www.wsj.com/articles/israel-strikes-target-iranian-oil-bound-for-syria-11615492789

Mackler, Jeff. "The US Plan to Partition Syria." *CounterPunch.* February 9, 2018. https://www.counterpunch.org/2018/02/09/the-us-plan-to-partition-syria/

Martin, Jose Maria. "Lebanon to reactivate Arab Gas Pipeline to import natural gas from Egypt." Atalayar. December 29, 2021. https://atalayar.com/en/content/lebanon-reactivate-arab-gas-pipeline-import-natural-gas-egypt

MEMO (2021). "Syria to lift subsidy system from richest citizens." *Middle East Monitor.* November 4, 2021. https://www.middleeastmonitor.com/20211104-syria-to-lift-subsidy-system-from-richest-citizens/

MEMO (2022). "Syria war has cost $650bn, poverty rate hits 90%." *Middle East Monitor.* October 4, 2022. https://www.middleeastmonitor.com/20221004-syria-war-has-cost-650bn-poverty-rate-hits-90/

MEO (2021). "TV report on major development in Syria-Lebanon ties." *Middle East Observer.* September 24, 2021. http://middleeastobserver.net/tv-report-on-major-development-in-syria-lebanon-ties/

Nehme, Dahlia (2017) 'Syria sanctions indirectly hit children's cancer treatment." Reuters. March 16, 2017. https://www.reuters.com/article/us-mideast-crisis-syria-sanctions-idUSKBN16M1UW

Norfolk, Andrew. "Qatar 'funnelled millions of dollars to Nusra Front terrorists in Syria.'" *The Sunday Times.* June 4, 2021. https://www.thetimes.co.uk/article/qatar-funnelled-millions-of-dollars-to-nusra-front-terrorists-in-syria-x5rnbsr3l

OCHA. "Under-Secretary-General for Humanitarian Affairs and Emergency Relief Coordinator, Mr. Martin Griffiths – Briefing to the Security Council on the humanitarian situation in Syria. June 20, 2022. https://reliefweb.int/report/syrian-arab-republic/under-secretary-general-humanitarian-affairs-and-emergency-relief-coordinator-mr-martin-griffiths-briefing-security-council-humanitarian-situation-syria-20-june-2022

OFAC (2022). "Specially Designated Nationals List – Data Formats & Data Schemas." U.S. Department of the Treasury. https://home.treasury.gov/policy-issues/financial-sanctions/specially-designated-nationals-list-data-formats-data-schemas

OHCHR (2015). "Sudan: Unilateral sanctions hit the innocent harder than the political elites, warns UN rights expert." Office of the High Commissioner for Human Rights. December 1, 2015. https://www.ohchr.org/en/press-releases/2015/12/sudan-unilateral-sanctions-hit-innocent-harder-political-elites-warns-un

——— (2019). "Yemen: Collective failure, collective responsibility—UN expert report,' Office of the High Commissioner for Human Rights." December 1, 2019. https://www.ohchr.org/en/press-releases/2019/09/yemen-collective-failure-collective-responsibility-un-expert-report?LangID=E&NewsID=24937

——— (2020). "US must remove sanctions and allow Syria to rebuild – UN expert." Office of the High Commissioner for Human Rights. December 29, 2020. https://www.ohchr.org/en/press-releases/2020/12/us-must-remove-sanctions-and-allow-syria-rebuild-un-expert

——— (2021). "A/HRC/48/59/Add.2: Visit to the Bolivarian Republic of Venezuela – Report of the Special Rapporteur on the negative impact of unilateral coercive measures on the enjoyment of human rights, Alena Douhan." https://www.ohchr.org/en/documents/country-reports/ahrc4859add2-visit-bolivarian-republic-venezuela-report-special

——— (2022). "UN expert calls for lifting of long-lasting unilateral sanctions 'suffocating' Syrian people." Office of the High Commissioner for Human Rights. November 10, 2022. https://www.ohchr.org/en/node/104160

OTH (1960) "499. Memorandum From the Deputy Assistant Secretary of State for Inter-American Affairs (Mallory) to the Assistant Secretary of State for Inter-American Affairs (Rubottom)." *Foreign Relations of the United States, 1958–1960, Cuba,* Vol. VI. Washington, D.C.: Office of the Historian, April 6, 1960. https://history.state.gov/historicaldocuments/frus1958-60v06/d499

Palast, Gregory. "IMF's four steps to damnation." *The Guardian.* April 29, 2001. https://www.theguardian.com/business/2001/apr/29/business.mbas

Provence, Michael. *The Great Syrian Revolt.* Austin: University of Texas Press, 2005.

Qaddour, Jomana. "Civil War Has Left Syria In Ruins And Its People In Poverty." NPR. March 18, 2021. https://www.npr.org/2021/03/18/978495982/civil-war-has-left-syria-in-ruins-and-its-people-in-poverty?t=1635858994268

Rehrl, Annette. "Syrian villagers open their doors to mass arrival of Lebanese refugees." UNHCR. August 8, 2006. https://www.unhcr.org/news/latest/2006/8/44d8ca652/syrian-villagers-open-doors-mass-arrival-lebanese-refugees.html

Reuters (2021). "U.S. issues sanctions tied to supporters of Hezbollah, Iran." September 18, 2021. https://www.reuters.com/world/middle-east/us-issues-sanctions-tied-supporters-hezbollah-iran-treasury-2021-09-17/

——— (2021a). "Lebanon's Mikati says IMF talks a necessity not a choice." September 20, 2021. https://www.reuters.com/world/middle-east/lebanons-mikati-says-imf-talks-necessity-not-choice-2021-09-20/

Shatz, Howard. "The Power and Limits of Threat: The Caesar Syrian Civilian Protection Act at One Year." Rand. July 8, 2021. https://www.rand.org/blog/2021/07/the-power-and-limits-of-threat-the-caesar-syrian-civilian.html

Snaije, Bassem. "Lebanon: Financial crisis or national collapse?" CIDOB. June 2022. https://www.cidob.org/es/publicaciones/serie_de_publicacion/notes_internacionals_cidob/275/lebanon_financial_crisis_or_national_collapse

Stoneman, Richard. *Palmyra and Its Empire: Zenobia's Revolt against Rome.* University of Michigan Press, 1995.

Tehran Times. "U.S.-backed SDF militants steal 140,000 barrels per day of Syrian oil in Hasakah." February 22, 2021. https://www.tehrantimes.com/news/458438/U-S-backed-SDF-militants-steal-140-000-barrels-per-day-of-Syrian

Telesur. "Iran to Become Full Member of Shanghai Cooperation Organization." September 15, 2022. https://www.telesurenglish.net/news/Iran-to-Become-Full-Member-of-Shanghai-Cooperation-Organization-20220915-0004.html

UNSC (2015). UNSC Resolution 2258 (2015). Adopted by the Security Council at its 7595th meeting, on 22 December 2015. https://documents-dds-ny.un.org/doc/UNDOC/GEN/N15/447/61/PDF/N1544761.pdf

UNSC (2021). UNSC Resolution 2585 (2021). Adopted by the Security Council at its 8817th meeting, on 9 July 2021. http://unscr.com/en/resolutions/doc/2585

WFP (2022). "The world's worst humanitarian crisis." World Food Programme. https://www.wfp.org/yemen-crisis

Worldometers. "COVID-19 CORONAVIRUS PANDEMIC." October 25, 2022. https://www.worldometers.info/coronavirus/

14. An Iranian Land Bridge to China

The West Asian alliance led by Iran has the best prospects of integration with Chinese infrastructure, including very fast trains. Source: CGTN

The idea of 'an Iranian land bridge' has excited the imagination of Washington, the Israelis and others committed to the Western destabilisation of West Asia. That group sees the construction of strong links between Iran and the Levant as resulting from U.S. failures in Iraq, Syria and Lebanon, and also as "the most serious long term existential threat to Israel" (Milburn 2017: 35). The notion has an even wider meaning: a large, independent Iran is pivotal to the U.S.-China competition, and U.S. efforts to obstruct China's creation of a 'new silk road' across the Eurasian supercontinent.

It should, at first glance, appear obvious that China, the East Asian giant, has both logistical and moral advantages over the North American giant which, from the other side of the world, has mostly waged war and tried to divide, dominate, and destabilise a series of West Asian nations. China, by contrast, proceeds for the most part slowly and steadily, developing its economic power with the logic of mutual benefit.

Yet that contrast is not always obvious, particularly insofar as North American expertise in double speak and its domination of cultural and media industries confuses the matter. The political and economic future of the West Asian region is thus clouded by imperial mythology, a construct which we must be address here before moving to the important questions of strategic realignment and economic integration. As the leading independent state of the region, Iran has become central to both the regional resistance and to the transmission to West Asian peoples of the political and economic benefits of global restructuring.

An "Iranian land bridge"?

In some earlier more reflective writing, there had been discussion of Iran as the 'pivot' of a north-south Eurasian corridor, creating a bridge between "two important energy zones of the Caspian and the Persian Gulf" (Homayoun 1997), or as a "land bridge between the Caspian Sea and the Persian Gulf," in relation to Iran's future orientation (Sciolino 2001). Yet an integrated Eurasia was already a spectre for U.S. strategists, a threat of which Zbigniew Brzezinski (1997a) warned. How could Washington sustain its predominance over both Asia and Europe if there were good relations across Eurasia and, in particular, between China, Russia and western Europe?

Eurasia's potential power would overshadow that of the USA, he said, urging efforts to block any new poles of power, especially those which would help integrate Asia with Europe (Brzezinski 1997b). To maintain global "supremacy" Washington had to develop "a comprehensive and integrated Eurasian geostrategy" (Brzezinski 1997a: xiv). This would mean creating an eastern European barrier to block Russian influence and a Central European barrier to contain the expansion of China.

With the second wave of 'New Middle East Wars' underway in September 2011, Secretary of State Hillary Clinton announced her ambition for an American "New Silk Road" which could "bind together a region too long torn apart by conflict and division" (Clinton 2011). The reference to opposing "conflict and division" was astonishingly cynical, coming on the heels of the U.S.-led invasions of Afghanistan and Iraq, a renewed Israel invasion of Lebanon, the NATO destruction of Libya and the regime change proxy war in Syria. But Clinton's idea of integration from U.S.-occupied Afghanistan to India and Pakistan had little of actual substance. A sympathetic commentator noted U.S. ideas for energy projects between Turkmenistan, Afghanistan and Pakistan, but observed that these were "hardly firm foundations" for an Afghan future and that it was "not clear that Afghanistan's neighbours will be interested," given the risks involved (Kucera 2011).

Afghanistan's large western neighbour, Iran, had long been the target of U.S. hostility since the 1979 revolution. The U.S. intel site, Stratfor, spoke of the Islamic Republic with a mixture of jealous confusion and acuity. On the one hand Iran was seen as a "land bridge for southern Asia" and a potential conqueror of the resource rich Iraqi plains to the west, on the other as a strong, centralised nation mainly concerned with "internal cohesion" and wary of its enemies' efforts to "foment ethnic dissent" and separatism at its borders. The paper added that Washington was doing just that using the Baloch, Arab and Kurd minorities (Stratfor 2011).

However, Iran was more significantly seen as a threat because of its potential to back regional forces opposed to U.S. interventions and occupations. A wider piece, sympathetic to the Obama-Clinton strategy, set out the differences between the Chinese and U.S. views of a "New Silk Road," while arguing—without much evidence and before Beijing's Belt and Road Initiative (BRI) had been unveiled—that China was pursuing a Japanese style imperial project (Lin 2011).

Yet Washington's talk of a 'New Silk Road' was mostly rhetorical, while China's moves were substantial and based in history. Indeed, it is impossible to speak of a 'Silk Road' without implicit reference to China, the point of origin of the silk traded to Europe—yet very easy to speak of one without the USA. Nevertheless, to reject a moral equivalence between Washington and Beijing, in terms of imperial motives, does not discount the fact that we are witnessing a new 'Great Game' between large powers (Chen and Fazilov 2018). Any expansion of Chinese influence is seen in North America as a 'threat' to U.S. hegemony.

The original Silk Road was a trading route from China to Europe, passing through central Asia and persisting from the 2nd century BC to the 16th century AD (Vaid 2016). Ideas of a revival seem to have come in the mid-20th century. In 1959 the UN's Social and Economic Commission for Asia and the Pacific (ESCAP) put up a proposal for a Trans-Asian Railway Network project (TAR), which would link Shanghai to Rotterdam in Europe, also opening up new trade possibilities for landlocked-Central Asian countries (Rousseau 2011).

Chinese Premier Li Peng, during a visit to central Asia in 1994, said that "it was important to open up a modern version of the Silk Road." Soon after India's prime minister endorsed the idea (Vaid 2016). It was at a UNESCAP conference in November 2006 that about 40 countries agreed to help with an 81,000-kilometer railway network, linking 28 countries by road and sea to European markets (Rousseau 2011).

Table 1: Which 'Iranian Landbridge'?	
A	Historical north-south conduit between the Caucasus, the Persian Gulf and South Asia
B	Threat to US-Israeli 'divide and rule' plans for the region
C	Potential regional fulcrum of eastern integration

Putting aide for a moment the first and oldest Eurasian line, the northern Trans-Siberian railway which crosses Russia (Liliopoulou, Roe and Pasukeviciute 2005), China has done the most in recent years to build the new Eurasian transport links (Lin 2011). In simple terms, the second corridor runs from Lianyungang in N.E. China through Mongolia and Russia to the port city of Rotterdam. *China Daily* in 2004 spoke of this second corridor as a "Eurasian continental bridge," in use since 1992, which will allow China "to develop its own western regions by cooperating with Central Asian and Western countries" (Fu 2004). The third corridor begins in China's industrial south-east and is set to run through many central and West Asian nations. Both these second and third corridors allow land passage of Chinese goods in much shorter times than the equivalent sea routes, while linking more than 40 Asian and Eurasian countries (Fu 2004; Lin 2011; Xu and Schramm 2020).

All this was precursor to President Xi Jinping's announcement during his 2013 visits to Kazakhstan and Indonesia of a 'Belt and Road Initiative' (BRI), a massive Chinese investment in infrastructure mainly aimed at Eurasian links, but also reaching into Africa and Latin America (Zhang 2019). The Washington- based World Bank estimates substantial benefits in reduced travel times, expanded trade and poverty reduction for the 70 BRI "corridor economies" (Ruta 2018). China itself speaks of enormous mutual benefits (CGTN 2022). The U.S. Council on Foreign Relations (CFR) recognises the BRI would "significantly" expand China's economic and political influence, while worrying that it could also be "a trojan horse for China-led regional development and military expansion" (Charsky and McBride 2020). The main evidence suggested for Chinese 'military expansion' was China's commitment to use its army to protect overseas infrastructure and investment (Lin 2011: 10). This is a long way from the hundreds of overseas bases maintained by Washington. Nor has China pursued any equivalent to Washington's multiple invasions, interventions, and uninvited military occupations in West Asia (Afghanistan, Iraq, Syria, Libya, Yemen) (Anderson 2019).

The key to reconciling the competing views is to remind ourselves that Washington regards expansion of Chinese influence in Eurasia as eroding its own hegemonic footholds on the Asian and European continents. Obstructing West Asia and Eurasian integration is precisely why there are such sustained efforts to divide Iran from Iraq, to fragment Iraq and Syria internally, to place occupation forces at the borders of Iraq and Syria, to divide Yemen and destabilise Xinjiang in western China.

Conversely, from China's perspective, the 'Eurasian land bridge' is central to a global restructuring which will advance Chinese politico-economic interests and attract willing participants. From the West Asian perspective this process has a focus on Iran and is more recently spoken of as an "Iranian land bridge" for two main reasons. The first is that Iran is the undisputed strategic leader of the West Asian bloc of independent nations: Palestine, Lebanon, Syria, Yemen, Iraq and Iran itself. The Israelis fear a strong Iran-led coalition at the 'borders' of occupied Palestine. That is why zionist strategists regard "a secure land bridge from Iran to Syria and Lebanon … [as] the most serious long term existential threat to Israel" (Milburn 2017: 1) and argue for ongoing direct attacks on Iran alongside support for Kurdish separatists in Iraq and Syria (Milburn 2017: 35, 46). U.S. military analysts, similarly, see an "Iranian Land Corridor to the Mediterranean" as a key element in "Iran's sustained campaign to pursue hegemonic influence in the Middle East, export its revolutionary ideology and threaten Israel and the West" (Adesnik McMaster and Taleblu 2019). As with China's economic expansion through a New Silk Road, Washington seeks to brand an indigenous player as some sort of rival adventurer.

The second reason for the focus on Iran and talk of an Iranian land bridge is that Iran's strategic relations with Russia and China have become key to transmission of the benefits of global restructuring to the other nations of West Asia. This is because of its political will, energy resources, technological and industrial capacity, and integration with the other members of this 'Axis of Resistance.' Iran's new strategic partnerships are therefore central to consideration of the political and economic future of West Asia, a region presently divided and besieged.

New strategic relations

With the near comprehensive U.S./EU economic siege on West Asia, economic futures in the region are being built in three main ways: self-reliance, finding some openings in the blockade, and building new economic relationships with eastern and southern blocs. The latter, while a longer-term project, offers the greatest hope, given the recalcitrance of the Western siege. While smaller nations like Palestine, Lebanon, Syria, Yemen, and Iraq are revising their own external relations, greater benefits seem likely to be transmitted through Iran's strategic partnerships with Russia and China. This is because Russia and China have moved first to the largest, most decisive West Asian nation with huge energy resources and the greatest capacity for cooperation.

Assessments of progress in restructuring must consider Iran's new strategic partnerships and the international groups led by Russia and China, notably the BRICS and the SCO. In that context we can better understand particular projects, such as regional oil and gas pipelines.

The China-Iran strategic partnership agreement, signed by the respective foreign ministers in March 2021, was the culmination of growing bilateral relations over more than four decades. China began ramping up its trade with Iran during the Iran-Iraq war, when Washington and most of the world backed Iraq (Weisskopf 1983; Hamrah and Eliasen 2021). There was always a strategic element to relations, in that both nations were struggling against U.S. hegemony. More recently, Iran's leader Sayyed Ali Khamenei concluded "the post U.S.-era has started" (Blankenship 2021).

Large Chinese investments in Iran grew steadily from 2014, when we start to see multiple projects—in several fields but particularly in oil and rail—in excess of one billion dollars (Green and Roth 2021: 20-21). The March 2021 agreement commits hundreds of billions of dollars to a very wide range of areas over 25 years. While it does not react to any particular U.S. manoeuvre—such as the 'maximum pressure sanctions' or attempts to restrict Iran's nuclear technology—there is a clear joint aim of standing up to U.S. "unilateralism" and developing a "genuine multilateralism" (Blankenship 2021). Key elements of the strategic partnership agreement are building the highest level of diplomacy, regular high-level meetings with mutual support for strategic objectives such as the 'One China' policy, and support for Iran's expanded role in its own region. Iran will support China's Belt and Road Initiative and China will invest in Iran's energy sector. There will be increased cooperation in media, defence, security, law, and culture. Cooperation in 'multipolarization' will include drawing Iran and its regional allies into the Shanghai Cooperation Organisation (Lumsden 2022).

North American analyses of this new partnership between two large nations seen as its rivals, typically carry 'exceptionalist' assumptions. For example, the agreement is often referred to as "pointedly opposed to the U.S.-led international order," including "defiance" of U.S. "sanctions" (Green and Roth 2021: 3). Of course, this refers to an order and coercive measures, which have no basis in international law.

In parallel Iran has developed strategic relations with Russia, albeit with some differences. The growing relationship between Iran and Russia was regarded at first as more of a "tactical alliance" than a strategic partnership. The goals and institutional relations were not that well developed (Kortunov 2021). However, the 2015 Russian intervention in defence of Syria and, even more so, Russia's provoked intervention in Ukraine in 2022, acted to increase levels of cooperation. The war in Ukraine helped make greater cause against U.S. coercive measures, with some Western analysts suggesting that this closer cooperation helped build a "potentially more balanced relationship wherein Russia is no longer the dominant party" (Carl, Fitzpatrick and Lawlor 2022: 1).

In any case it is plain that a fair amount of this new cooperation has been in the energy sector. In 2021 Russian gas exports (241 billion cubic metres) were fourteen times greater than those from Iran (17 billion cubic metres), but in 2022 new opportunities were opening for joint operations (Mikovic 2022). In July 2022 a US$40 billion agreement was signed by Gazprom and the National Iranian Oil Company (Iran International 2022a). This cooperation necessarily involves not only new infrastructure, including gas pipelines which sidestep U.S. blockade measures, but also military cooperation, new trade centres, passenger flights, trade in food, and financial cooperation through Russia's MIR payments system (Carl, Fitzpatrick and Lawlor 2022).

Russian energy ambitions in Iraq and Syria also draw on its partnerships with Iran. Russia's Gazprom was scheduled to help rebuild the Kirkuk (Iraq) to Baniyas (Syria) gas pipeline in 2007, but this was stalled by problems on the Iraqi side. The project was renewed in 2010 but stalled again with Washington's proxy war on Syria. Since then, Russian companies have tried to mediate between Erbil (the regional Kurdistan administration) and Baghdad. Even if Russia and Iran are competing for stakes in Syria's energy sector (Grajewski 2021: 5-6), their stronger partnership may help address these tensions (Salih 2019). In any case the wider range of Russia-Iran cooperation is steadily expanding, with energy exports as the leading edge.

A similar logic applies to the well-established cooperation between Iran and Venezuela. While Iran and Venezuela have developed a wide range of industrial partnerships, under a 20-year cooperation plan, energy ties have remained at the core. In 2020 Iran helped Venezuela restart the catalytic cracking unit at its Cardon refinery (Guanipa and Buitrago 2020) and soon after Iran opened its own El Palito refinery in Venezuela, linked to some joint petro-chemical initiatives (Al Mayadeen 2022). Iran is also engaged in important biotechnology and pharmaceutical cooperation with Cuba (ACN 2022), though its investments in Venezuela's energy and industrial sectors have greater economic weight.

The breadth and pace of restructuring can be seen in the large international groups created by China and Russia, in particular the BRICS, the Shanghai Cooperation Organization (SCO) and China's Belt and Road Initiative (BRI).

It was Russia's late 1990s suggestion of "a strategic three-way pivot between Russia, India and China" (Simha 2015) which eventually led to both the SCO and the BRICS. China's dissatisfaction with the Western dominated World Bank-IMF-WTO groups (Huang 2015) certainly helped. The SCO (with half of the world's population, a quarter of world GDP, and more than three-quarters of Eurasia's landmass) was created in 2001 (SCO 2015) and the BRICS (with over 40% of the world's population and a quarter of global GDP) in 2006 (BRICS India 2021). The SCO was, at the least, a Chinese hedge against the perceived failure of U.S.-led globalist institutions. But since the early 21st century decline of the WTO and the general pursuit of new opportunities through regional bodies, even U.S. analysts saw the SCO as part of "the rising acceptance of regionalism," especially in the emerging 'war on terror' climate promoted by Washington, with its triple focus on terrorism, ethnic separatism, and extremism (Boland 2011; Yuan 2010). Meanwhile, Washington pursued its agendas through regional blocs like the Trans-Atlantic and Trans-Pacific Partnerships (Robert 2016). China's SCO goals were also global, if not globalist. The SCO stated its broad goals as "strengthening mutual trust and neighbourliness" and building "a democratic, fair and rational new international political and economic order" (SCO 2015). Similarly, the BRICS developed distinct political/economic objectives in industry, poverty reduction and public health (BRICS Information Portal 2021).

While BRICS maintained its core five members for its first 15 years, by 2022 the group seemed on the verge of significant expansion. Seven more nations had requested access (Algeria, Argentina, Iran, Saudi Arabia, Turkey, Egypt, and Afghanistan) and, with even more likely candidates, the group may soon include more than 50% of the world (Devonshire Ellis 2022). Similarly, the $4 trillion in China's mega integration project, the Belt and Road Initiative (BRI), has attracted much interest across the world (Shira 2022). Iran President Ebrahim Raisi, for his part, before the 6th Summit of the Conference on Interaction and Confidence Building Measures in Asia (CICA), said Iran's foreign policy was "based on building relations with regional and extra-regional organizations [for] … peace, stability and security" (IRNA 2022). In September 2022 Iran began accession as a full member of the SCO (Telesur 2022) and Syria has also applied to become a member (al Jaafari 2022).

While the SCO/BRICS blocs have tremendous technological, economic and commercial potential, Washington maintains institutional dominance in finance, and this presents a key obstacle to independent development. The dominance is partly through enforcement of dollar payments in key sectors, including oil, and partly through U.S. domination of the interbank communications systems, in particular the SWIFT system. SWIFT has operated in conjunction with the U.S. systems CHIPS, FEDWIRE and BANKWIRE but in recent years has seen some competition from Russia's SPFS and China's CIPS. The Europeans have their own systems like the UK's CHAPS, but European mechanisms set up to avoid U.S. and SWIFT domination, such as INSTEX, have achieved little.

The SWIFT (Society for Worldwide Interbank Financial Telecommunication) system was created in 1973 for reliable and secure information exchange between banks. SWIFT is not a bank and does not hold funds or accounts. Though created in Brussels, Belgium, the U.S. gradually gained influence (Scott and Zachariadis 2012) and has come to dominate SWIFT through U.S. Treasury control of the dollar and threats to impose coercive measures (sanctions) on SWIFT itself. For example, in 2012 Washington threatened SWIFT with coercive measures if it failed to remove Iranian banks from the network (Eichengreen 2022: 2). In recent decades international legal protocols on surveillance and reporting on money laundering and the financing of terrorism have helped consolidate a SWIFT monopoly. The result is that SWIFT has become a vehicle for the enforcement of most of Washington's unilateral coercive measures.

Members of BRICS have considered alternatives to the SWIFT for some years, given that a new payment information system could "provide greater independence and would create a definite guarantee for countries non risks associated with arbitrary decisions … by countries that have the current payment system" (AA 2015). In 2015 the Peoples' Bank of China (PBOC, China's central bank) set up CIPS

(China International Payments System) as an independent body, supervised by the PBOC. By mid-2022 CIPS claimed 1,304 participants, about 40% in China and 60% abroad. Yet it is said that 80% of CIPS messages also go through the SWIFT system, in part because of the inconvenience of the Chinese character-based language (Eichengreen 2022: 4). Russia's version of SWIFT, called SPFS (in translation: System for Transfer of Financial Messages) has been operating for some years alongside China's CIPS. By late 2022 Russia said its SPFS system was expanding rapidly, with more foreign participants; however, the USA had managed to stop a number of participants from using Russia's MIR cards with a new round of sanctions (Marrow 2022). The combined global share of both SPFS and CIPS was said to be 10% in 2019 (Russia Briefing 2019).

At the time of writing several new mechanisms were either in play or proposed, to avoid the dollar tyranny. In Latin America Brazil and Argentina have proposed a common currency "to boost trade by getting rid of conversion costs and exchange rate uncertainty" (Glover 2023). Such an idea has been around in ALBA circles for some years. And while there has been talk of gold backed cryptocurrencies, reports began in January 2023 that Iran and Russia were about to launch a gold backed Central Bank Digital Currency (Fathi 2023). Soon after this Mohsen Karimi of the Central Bank of Iran announced that Iran's financial telecommunications system, SEPAM, has established direct informatics links with all the Russian banks "and 106 non-Russian banks in 13 countries," thus obviating the need for the SWIFT system (Tasnim 2023). This could act to reopen finance and commerce between a wide range of countries under western siege.

The BRICS logic may lead to links between the Chinese and Russian payment systems, while adding Brazil, India, South Africa and other future BRICS members. China's introduction of a Central Bank Digital Currency (CBDC), the digital Yuan (eCNY), may also supplement the autonomy of this system, with China's PBOC removing the surveillance opportunities of foreign agencies (Eichengreen 2022: 5). Notably, the e-CNY is a CBDC, not a cryptocurrency. In October 2022 the Bank for International Settlements (BIS) reported on a pilot, 'Project m-Bridge,' which assessed the use of multiple CBDCs. China's e-CNY was the largest of those. The aim was to see if they could operate efficiently, without causing harm and adding to resilience, while "assuring co-existence and interoperability with non-CBDC systems" (BIS 2022). In the context of widespread U.S./EU unilateral coercive measures, this suggests that Beijing is "seeking to speed up yuan globalization efforts amid rising geopolitical tensions." Chinese economist G. Bin Zhao commented, "This provides a historic window for China to promote yuan internationalization as the U.S. weaponizes the dollar." The e-CNY provides a "shortcut" for financial transactions (CUtoday 2022). Once strong, reliable BRICS, Russian or Chinese alternatives to SWIFT and the dollar are in place many dozens of countries wishing to escape Washington's dictates are likely to participate.

The European INSTEX (Instrument in Support of Trade Exchanges) was created in January 2019 to allow ongoing trade with Iran (E3 2019), since the Europeans did not share all U.S. coercive measures against Iran. However, the EU's first transaction with Iran did not occur until 2020, during the COVID19 Pandemic, and that transaction, in any case, may not have breached any coercive regulation (Brzozowski 2020). European attempts to chart a distinct course with Cuba have also been muted by U.S. penalties against third parties doing business with the little island (Wise 1995). In general, we can say that the Europeans have failed to break with U.S. unilateral coercive measures, even when they disagree with them. That is why Chinese, Russian, BRICS and SCO alternatives offer greater promise to countries under siege.

The sidestepping of SWIFT with a constellation of new financial mechanisms led by Russia-China-Iran and perhaps also Latin America will be reinforced by gradual displacement of the petro-dollar, that privilege afforded to U.S. purchasing power by denominating oil sales in dollars. China has already begun agreements with the Saudis and Qatar, previously dependencies of Washington, to begin using the Yuan for oil sales through China's Shanghai Petroleum and National Gas Exchange (CNA 2022). This may be another step in the "westwards extension" of the SCO (Lau 2022).

The economic future

To summarise, the siege of West Asia—and the coercive measures imposed on other independent countries and regions—has forced the pace of global restructuring. While this type of economic warfare makes it important to focus on self-reliant measures and to look for openings in the blockade, strategic participation in restructured futures must be at the centre of any independent plan. The particularly strong eastern blocs, especially the BRICS, the SCO and China's BRI initiative, offer promise not seen on the Western side. In this context the notion of an 'Iranian land bridge,' in all its senses, represents a fulcrum of strategic change. First there is the sense in which Iran, as the region's largest independent nation, forms a transport, trade and energy corridor between Russia and South Asia. Second, Iran is at the centre of the southern Eurasian land corridor between China and Europe. Third, the strategic links between Tehran and the Mediterranean Levant (Palestine, Lebanon and Syria) pose, on the one hand, a threat to the Western backed colony in Palestine and, on the other, the hope of a prosperous economic integration for West Asian peoples long divided by colonisation and war.

It is certainly the case that independent nations will pursue their own relations with the new eastern and international blocs. For example, in January 2022 Syria joined China's BRI. At the MOU signing reference was made to restoring Syria's role in the ancient Silk Road and, in particular, the role of the cities of Aleppo and Palmyra (Xinhua 2022). Similarly, it has been argued that Yemen "is an essential state" for China's BRI because its strategic location on the Gulf of Aden, the Red Sea, and the Horn of Africa can make it "the bridge between Asia and Africa, and between the Indian Ocean and the Mediterranean" (Chaziza 2021).

Nevertheless, the role of Iran in the transmission of new energy links, infrastructure for development, and integration within West Asia remains central. Real interests have dictated that Iran move ahead in its strategic partnerships with Russia, China and Venezuela and that the financing of these new ventures will help open new anti-blockade technology. The same can be said about Iran's accession to the SCO, with President Raisi observing that the group could "help thwart U.S. unilateralism" (Iran International 2022b).

Integration of West Asia could see its remarkable transformation from a divided and war-torn region to a prosperous alliance with road, rail, energy, and communication links. On the basis of joint security gains, the Iranian land bridge feared by the colonists and imperialists could include high speed rail from Tehran to Beirut and/or Tartous. That would be a large BRI style project and a major breakthrough. As part of its BRI, China is already financing similar high speed rail links in Indonesia between Jakarta and Bandung (Jibiki 2022). Such links would open many commercial and civil possibilities. The renovation of some version of the Kirkuk to Baniyas oil pipeline, stalled several times in recent decades (GEM 2022), already has interest from Russia (Salih 2019) and could well involve extensions to Iran and perhaps investment from China. Such energy integration would help stabilise the region and cast a lifeline to isolated and internally divided Lebanon. Regional integration making use of China's BRI and the SCO could open doors to wider, unobstructed exchange in science and technology, medicine, higher education, and commerce. In short, once liberated from the interventionist forces which divide the region, West Asia could benefit enormously from the independent integration provided by an Iranian land bridge, especially one that stretches all the way to China.

References

AA. "BRICS consider alternative SWIFT funds transfer system, Russian Deputy Foreign Minister says BRICS countries have led off consultations on an alternative to the global SWIFT system." June 17, 2015. https://www.aa.com.tr/en/world/brics-consider-alternative-swift-funds-transfer-system/35300#

ACN. "Cuba and Iran sign agreements on biotechnology." *Cuban News Agency.* May 18, 2022. http://www.cubanews.acn.cu/economy/17488-cuba-and-iran-sign-agreements-on-biotechnology

Adesnik, David, H.R. McMaster, and Benham Ben Taleblu. "Burning Bridge: The Iranian Land Corridor to the Mediterranean." Foundation for Defense of Democracies. June 18, 2019. https://www.fdd.org/analysis/2019/06/18/burning-bridge/

Al Jaafari, Bashar. Interview with this writer. Damascus. September 2022.

Al Mayadeen. "Iran-Venezuela relations developed despite western sanctions." November 13, 2022. https://english.almayadeen.net/news/politics/iran-venezuela-relations-developed-despite-western-sanctions

Anderson, Tim. *Axis of Resistance.* Atlanta: Clarity Press, 2019.

BIS. "Project mBridge, Connecting economies through CBDC." Bank of International Settlements. October 2022. https://www.bis.org/publ/othp59.pdf

Boland, Julie. "Ten Years of the Shanghai Cooperation Organization: A Lost Decade? A Partner for the U.S.?" Brookings. June 20, 2011. https://www.brookings.edu/wp-content/uploads/2016/06/06_shanghai_cooperation_organization_boland.pdf

Blankenship, Bradley. "China-Iran strategic partnership encapsulates China's Middle East security initiative." CGTN. March 29, 2021. https://news.cgtn.com/news/2021-03-29/China-Iran-partnership-encapsulates-China-s-security-initiative-Z1HYU6fgGI/index.html

BRICS Information Portal (2021). "13th BRICS Summit Pledges to Build on Multilateralism and Reform UN Security Council." https://infobrics.org/

BRICS India (2021). "Evolution of BRICS." https://brics2021.gov.in/about-brics

Brzezinski, Zbigniew (1997a). *The Grand Chessboard: American Primacy and Its Geostrategic Imperatives.* New York: Basic Books, 1997.

——— (1997b). "A Geostrategy for Eurasia." *Foreign Affairs.* September/October 1997. https://www.foreignaffairs.com/articles/asia/1997-09-01/geostrategy-eurasia

Brzozowski, Alexandra. "EU's INSTEX mechanism facilitates first transaction with pandemic-hit Iran." Euractiv. April 1, 2020. https://www.euractiv.com/section/global-europe/news/eus-instex-mechanism-facilitates-first-transaction-with-pandemic-hit-iran/

Carl, Nicholas, Kitaneh Fitzpatrick, and Katherine Lawlor. *Russia and Iran double down on their strategic partnership.* Institute for the Study of War. August 11, 2022. https://www.understandingwar.org/backgrounder/russia-and-iran-double-down-their-strategic-partnership

CGTN (2022). "Connecting the World." https://www.cgtn.com/how-china-works/feature/What-does-the-Belt-and-Road-Initiative-mean-to-China-and-the-world.html

Chatzky, Andrew, and James McBride. "China's Massive Belt and Road Initiative." Council on Foreign Relations. January 28, 2020. https://www.cfr.org/backgrounder/chinas-massive-belt-and-road-initiative

Chaziza, Mordechai. "The Belt and Road Initiative: New Driving Force for Sino-Yemen Relationship." *China Report* 57, no. 2 (May 26, 2021): 229–246. https://doi.org/10.1177/00094455211004231

Chen, Xiangming, and Fazilov, Fakhmiddin. "Re-centering Central Asia: China's 'New Great Game' in the old Eurasian Heartland." Palgrave Commun 4, 71 (2018). https://doi.org/10.1057/s41599-018-0125-5

Clinton, Hillary (2011). "Remarks at the New Silk Road Ministerial Meeting." U.S. Department of State. https://2009-2017.state.gov/secretary/20092013clinton/rm/2011/09/173807.htm

CNA. "China to use Shanghai exchange for yuan energy deals with Gulf nations—Xi." *Channel News Asia.* December 9, 2022. https://www.channelnewsasia.com/business/china-use-shanghai-exchange-yuan-energy-deals-gulf-nations-xi-3134551

CUtoday. "Test of China's Digital Yuan Went Well; Plans Are to Speed Up Globalization, Report Suggests." December 6, 2022. https://www.cutoday.info/THE-globe/Test-of-China-s-Digital-Yuan-Went-Well-Plans-Are-to-Speed-Up-Globalization-Report-Suggests

Devonshire-Ellis, Chris. "The New Candidate Countries for BRICS expansion." Silk Road Briefing. November 9, 2022. https://www.silkroadbriefing.com/news/2022/11/09/the-new-candidate-countries-for-brics-expansion/

E3 (2019). "Joint statement on the creation of INSTEX, the special purpose vehicle aimed at facilitating legitimate trade with Iran in the framework of the efforts to preserve the Joint Comprehensive Plan of Action (JCPOA)." Joint statement by the E3 Foreign Ministers, Jean-Yves Le Drian (France), Heiko Maas (Germany), Jeremy Hunt (United Kingdom). January 31, 2019. https://assets.publishing.service.gov.uk/government/uploads/system/uploads/attachment_data/file/775681/19_01_31_Joint_Statement_E3.pdf

Eichengreen, Barry. "Sanctions, SWIFT, and China's Cross-Border Interbank Payments System." CSIS Briefs. May 20, 2022. https://www.csis.org/analysis/sanctions-swift-and-chinas-cross-border-interbank-payments-system

Fathi, Abdelaziz. "Iran and Russia are creating gold backed stablecoin." Finance Feeds. January 16, 2023. https://financefeeds.com/iran-and-russia-are-creating-gold-backed-stablecoin/

Fu Jing. "Re-building the ancient Silk Road." *China Daily.* September 1, 2004. https://www.chinadaily.com.cn/english/doc/2004-09/01/content_370519.htm

GEM (2022) "Hafez and the failure of Kirkuk to Tartous pipeline." *Global Energy Monitor.* March 11, 2022. https://www.gem.wiki/Kirkuk-Baniyas_Oil_Pipeline

Glover, George. "Brazil and Argentina are gearing up to launch a joint currency that could become South America's euro." Markets Insider. January 23, 2023. https://markets.businessinsider.com/news/currencies/brazil-argentina-joint-currency-dollar-dominance-south-american-euro-lula-2023-1

Grajewski, Nicole. "The Evolution of Russian and Iranian Cooperation in Syria." Centre for Strategic and International Studies. November 17, 2021. https://www.csis.org/analysis/evolution-russian-and-iranian-cooperation-syria

Green, Will, and Taylore Roth. "China-Iran Relations: A Limited but Enduring Strategic Partnership." U.S.-China Economic and Security Review Commission. June 28, 2021. https://www.uscc.gov/research/china-iran-relations-limited-enduring-strategic-partnership

Guanipa, Mircely, and Deisy Buitrago. "Venezuela receives material from Iran to help restart refinery – official." Reuters. April 24, 2020. https://www.reuters.com/article/us-venezuela-oil-iran-idUSKCN2253FX

Hamrah, Satgin, and Alexander Eliasen. "The China-Iran Strategic Partnership: 40 Years in the Making." December 4, 2021. https://thediplomat.com/2021/12/the-china-iran-strategic-partnership-40-years-in-the-making/

Homayoun, Assad (1997). "Iran, the pivot of Eurasian corridor." Speech at Strategy '97 Conference Washington, D.C., September 22–24, 1997, Azadegan Foundation. https://azadeganiran.com/euroasian.asp

Iran International (2022a). "Iran, Russia Sign Energy Memorandum On Eve of Putin Trip." July 19, 2022. https://www.iranintl.com/en/202207194766

Iran International (2022b). "Iran Can Thwart US Sanctions Via Shanghai Organization." September 16, 2022. https://www.iranintl.com/en/202209162127

IRNA. "President Raisi: Iran's foreign policy based on building ties with regional, trans-regional organizations." Islamic Republic News Agency. October 12, 2022. https://en.irna.ir/news/84910798/President-Raisi-Iran-s-foreign-policy-based-on-building-ties

Jibiki, Koya. "Indonesia presents China-made high-speed train cars." *Nikkei Asia.* October 3, 2022. https://asia.nikkei.com/Business/Transportation/Indonesia-presents-China-made-high-speed-train-cars

Kortunov, Andrey. "Russia and Iran: How Far from a Strategic Partnership?" Russian Council. May 6, 2021. https://russiancouncil.ru/en/analytics-and-comments/analytics/russia-and-iran-how-far-from-a-strategic-partnership/

Kucera, Joshua. "The New Silk Road?" *The Diplomat.* November 11, 2011. https://thediplomat.com/2011/11/the-new-silk-road/

Lau, Jack. "Is Xi Jinping's trip to Saudi Arabia another step in the SCO's Mideast expansion?" *South China Morning Post.* December 5, 2022. https://www.scmp.com/news/china/diplomacy/article/3202067/xi-jinpings-trip-saudi-arabia-another-step-scos-mideast-expansion

Liliopoulou, Anastasia, Michael Roe, and Irma Pasukeviciute. "Trans Siberian Railway: From inception to transition." *European Transport\ Trasporti Europei* no. 29 (2005): 46–56.

Lin, Christina. *China's New Silk Road to the Mediterranean: The Eurasian Land Bridge and Return of Admiral Zheng He.* ISPSW Strategy Series: Focus on Defense and International Security, no. 165 (October 2011). https://www.files.ethz.ch/isn/133405/165_Lin.pdf

Lumsden, Andrew. "Media Guide: The Iran-China Strategic Partnership." American Iranian Council. March 2, 2022. http://www.us-iran.org/resources/2022/3/1/media-guide-the-iran-china-strategic-partnership

Marrow, Alexander. "Russia's SWIFT alternative expanding quickly this year, central bank says." Reuters. September 24, 2022. https://www.reuters.com/business/finance/russias-swift-alternative-expanding-quickly-this-year-says-cbank-2022-09-23/

Mikovic, Nicola. "What's driving Russia-Iran energy cooperation." *AsiaTimes.* October 7, 2022. https://asiatimes.com/2022/10/whats-driving-russia-iran-energy-cooperation/

Milburn, Franc. "Iran′s Land Bridge to the Mediterranean: Possible Routes and Ensuing Challenges." INSS. *Strategic Assessment* 20, no. 3 (October 2017). https://www.inss.org.il/publication/irans-land-bridge-mediterranean-possible-routes-ensuing-challenges/

Roberts, Paul Craig. "Trans-Atlantic & Trans-Pacific 'Partnerships' Complete Corporate World Takeover." *Foreign Policy Journal.* April 15, 2016. https://www.foreignpolicyjournal.com/2016/04/15/trans-atlantic-trans-pacific-partnerships-complete-corporate-world-takeover/

Rousseau, Richard. "The New Iron Silk Road." *The Diplomatic Courier.* June 4, 2011. https://www.diplomaticourier.com/posts/the-new-iron-silk-road

Russia Briefing. "Russian & Chinese Alternatives For SWIFT Global Banking Network Coming." June 17, 2019. https://www.russia-briefing.com/news/russian-chinese-alternatives-swift-global-banking-network-coming-online.html/

Ruta, Michele. "Belt and Road Initiative." World Bank. March 29, 2018. https://www.worldbank.org/en/topic/regional-integration/brief/belt-and-road-initiative

Salih, Diyari (2019) Russia and the Geopolitics of the Kirkuk-Baniyas Pipeline, TGP. September 29, 2019. online: https://thegeopolitics.com/russia-and-the-geopolitics-of-the-kirkuk-baniyas-pipeline/

Sciolino, Elaine (2001) 'Persian Mirrors: The Elusive Face of Iran,' New York Times, 31 January 31, 2001. https://archive.nytimes.com/www.nytimes.com/books/first/s/sciolino-persian2.html

SCO (2015) 'The Shanghai Cooperation Organisation,' online: http://eng.sectsco.org/about_sco/

Scott, Susan V., and Zachariadis, Markos. "Origins and development of SWIFT, 1973–2009." *Business History* 54, no. 3 (2012): 462–82.

Shira, Dezan (2022). "The Belt and Road Initiative." Silk Road Briefing. https://www.silkroadbriefing.com/the-belt-and-road-initiative.html

Simha, Rakesh Krishnan. "Primakov: The man who created multipolarity." Russia Beyond. June 27, 2015. https://www.rbth.com/blogs/2015/06/27/primakov_the_man_who_created_multipolarity_43919

Stratfor. "The Geopolitics of Iran: Holding the Center of a Mountain Fortress." *WorldView.* December 16, 2011. https://worldview.stratfor.com/article/geopolitics-iran-holding-center-mountain-fortress

Tasnim. "Iranian Banks Don't Need SWIFT Anymore: Official." February 2, 2023. https://www.tasnimnews.com/en/news/2023/02/02/2847224/iranian-banks-don-t-need-swift-anymore-official

Telesur. "Iran to Become Full Member of Shanghai Cooperation Organization." September 15, 2022. https://www.telesurenglish.net/news/Iran-to-Become-Full-Member-of-Shanghai-Cooperation-Organization-20220915-0004.html

Vaid, Manish. "India and China: Time to Hit a Right Note on the New Silk Road." *Liberal Studies* 1, no. 2 (July-December 2016). https://sls.pdpu.ac.in/downloads/A3MV.pdf

Weisskopf, Michael. "China Plays Both Sides In Persian Gulf War." *Washington Post.* January 13, 1983. https://www.washingtonpost.com/archive/politics/1983/01/13/china-plays-both-sides-in-persian-gulf-war/e5f921aa-5797-467c-9d6d-293eed9911dc/

Wise, Elizabeth. "Europe chances clash with US over Cuba talks." *Politico.* October 4, 1995. https://www.politico.eu/article/europe-chances-clash-with-us-over-cuba-talks/

Xinhua. "Syria Joins China's Belt and Road Initiative." January 13, 2022. https://english.news.cn/20220113/819fc4163f384be6b8fdf2f4d9956a1c/c.html

Yuan, Jing-Dong. "China's Role in Establishing and Building the Shanghai Cooperation Organization (SCO)." *Journal of Contemporary China* 19, no. 67 (2010): 855–69. https://doi.org/10.1080/10670564.2010.508587

Zhang, Pepe. "Belt and Road in Latin America: A regional game changer?" Atlantic Council. Issue Brief, October 8, 2019. https://www.atlanticcouncil.org/in-depth-research-reports/issue-brief/belt-and-road-in-latin-america-a-regional-game-changer/

Zhang, Xu, and Hans-Joachim Schramm (2020). "Assessing the market niche of Eurasian rail freight in the belt and road era." *The International Journal of Logistics Management* 31, no. 4 (2020): 729–51.

15. Iran's Resistance Economy and Regional Integration

Tehran, Iran's capital

Iran's 'resistance economy' is sometimes presented as merely defensive, even as a cost to the people. Despite Washington's New Middle East wars and the rapid evaporation of expected benefits from the long JCPOA (nuclear deal) process, some illusions remain within Iran that a general 'normalisation' with the outside powers might still bring economic benefits to the country. Nevertheless, it remains true that, while Iran is a large country, pure self-sufficiency would impose undesirable physical limits. So where are the better economic opportunities for the nation?

This chapter argues that the answer lies in a resistance economy which builds an economically integrated regional bloc. It begins by demonstrating the false promises of global economic liberalism, then locates Iran's resistance economy ideas in context of the 'new regionalism' debates. That forms a basis for discussing the economic potential of West Asian integration. This is an interpretive study, testing the economic liberal project with evidence, then comparing it with some contemporary regional initiatives.

Neoliberalism and economic warfare

Neoliberal globalism's ideology of compulsory corporate globalisation (Hoogvelt 1997) sought nonetheless to suggested that complete openness to foreign capital would bring benefits similar to those theorised for so-called free trade. Yet the systems to deliver this openness embodied rigged rules and delivered asymmetric benefits.

This Anglo-American neoliberal project drew selectively on economic liberal ideas of 'comparative advantage' (Ricardo 1817), which encourage specialization and trade, and the 'open market' ideas of the European neoclassical economists of the 1870s, supplemented by mid-twentieth-century ideas of macroeconomic management (Keynes 1936). Ideas of universal liberalisation aimed at generalised economic growth have been promoted by international financial institutions such as the World Bank (2009). Some need for diversification (and so 'broad based growth') was accepted but not planned industrial upgrades. The developmental prospects of 'comparative advantage' were always limited, as the idea was based on comparative statics and only addressed short-term opportunities. Economic liberals spoke of a minimal economic role for the state, opposing public investment that might crowd out (or compete with) private investment (Spencer and Yohe 1970). In this view of the world, the state should minimize its commitments and introduce 'user pays' and privatized services to encourage consumer participation and market formation. The liberal idea of a minimalist state always faced a double standards contradiction highlighted by what was said to be (in the North American exceptionalist tradition) the need for a powerful 'benevolent hegemon' to stabilise the world system.

There have been many criticisms of open market ideas, in particular because market theories do not correspond to the reality of industrial production dominated by giant corporations, including monopolistic finance corporations. However, the most telling criticism is that liberal models do not describe the actual historical development path of the wealthy countries. Open market strategies were not the principal means for the industrialization of Europe, North America, or Japan. Liberal attempts to suggest the contrary (e.g. Rostow 1960) have little historical substance.

Development in much of Europe was enabled by a substantial economic surplus from the colonies and slave-based economies (e.g. Williams 1944) absorbed into commerce and industry. European, North American, and Japanese capitalist development grew both their human resources and technologies with state sponsorship, financial assistance, and public-private monopolies (Ettlinger 1991). After World War II, the USA suggested that Japan should pursue its 'comparative advantage' as a provider of cheap labour in basic industry. The Japanese, to the contrary, in a war-devastated, resource-poor country, decided instead to invest in human resources and upgrade their productive capacities (Johnson 1982).

Nevertheless, the USA and the Europeans were keen to open export markets for their industrial products, in the post-World War II period. That was the chief motive behind the General Agreement on Tariffs and Trade, from 1947 onwards, and for its successor, the World Trade Organization (WTO), established in 1995. However, the fine sounding principles of equal opportunity and non-discrimination in trade did not match Western practice. The details of the agreements and a manipulated 'consensus' decision-making processes dominated by the big powers saw to that. Agriculture was included for the first time in the final Uruguay Round of GATT (1986-1994), so as to draw in a group of agricultural exporters, looking for new trade opportunities. Yet when the WTO talks ground to a halt, in the early 21st century, the failure of promises over agriculture exports was a leading reason. The agricultural subsidy rules were said to have been 'rigged' in favour of the Europe and the USA, who "weren't willing to give up their agricultural subsidies" (Amadeo 2019). Jawara and Kwa (2003) studied the process and found a toxic negotiating environment which was "entirely at odds with the official picture of a rules-based consensus." They found "closed doors rather than open access," decisions made without full approval of the developing countries and, "illegitimate pressures and inducements … including threats ... and hints that aid to countries refusing to kow-tow may be withheld." The failure of the WTO process and the subsequent boom in regional agreements has been widely discussed. Hussain (2004) puts the failure down to the “uneven playing field” facing developing countries, increased unilateralism, and farm protection in the wealthy countries.

In parallel there had been tremendous reaction amongst developing countries to ‘structural adjustment programs’ (SAPs) created by the World Bank and the IMF in the early 1980s. These policy prescriptions (balanced budgets, openings to foreign capital, privatizations, the removal of tariffs, and reduction in social controls on investors) were attached to debt relief packages, for the public debt crisis which followed the lifting of controls on bank interest rates. The SAPs were widely associated with austerity budgets and the sale of public assets to foreign companies. In 1999 SAPs were re-named Poverty Reduction Strategy Papers and the word ‘privatization’ disappeared from the World Bank-IMF lexicon, to be replaced by a variety of ‘partnerships.’ Analysts pointed to serious compromises made in those countries under structural adjustment, in particular political repression and a weakening of the ‘buffer’ role of the state to protect populations from external shocks (Cheru 1999). Others found that the SAPs acted to “worsen government respect for physical integrity rights,’ such as torture, political imprisonment and extra-judicial killings (Abouharb and Cingranelli 2006).

By the late 20th century there was internal revolt against the neoliberal program. Former World Bank chief economist and later Nobel Prize winner Joseph Stiglitz (2002) decried the IMF-World Bank liberalisation program as dysfunctional because, in the absence of a proper institutional framework, hasty capital ‘liberalization’ (as in Russia and some eastern European countries) could simply aggravate a country’s economic problems. Some years later Stiglitz pronounced the neoliberal project “dead in both developing and developed countries” (Martin 2016).

Iran missed many of these experiences, as it was never a member of the GATT or the WTO. The Islamic Republic did apply to join the WTO in 1996 (Yousefvand 2016) but was blocked by the USA. Tehran is reported as saying that accession is no longer a priority (Jalili 2017). Nor are Iraq, Syria, Lebanon, or Palestine members of the WTO. Amongst West Asian countries only Yemen was admitted (in 2014) to enjoy the dubious benefits of WTO ‘most favoured nation’ status (WTO 2019b).

It is hardly a coincidence that today Iran, Iraq, Syria, Lebanon, and Yemen are all subject to siege or sanction from the USA and its allies on various pretexts, including virtually all the Palestinian Resistance groups (U.S. Dept. of Treasury 2019). Would WTO membership prevent discrimination in trade? No, as the case of besieged Yemen illustrates. Such is also the case with Cuba, a WTO member subject to U.S. economic sanctions (which the Cubans call a 'blockade') since 1962.

There is little doubt that much in these unilateral sanctions goes against international law, which prohibits the exercise of economic coercion by the principle of non-intervention and through an implied ban in the UN Charter. This is supplemented by customary and treaty law in areas such as trade, shipping, and telecommunications. The illegality is more obvious when there is an 'unlawful intent,' such as political coercion or damaging a national economy (Shneyer and Barta 1981: 468, 471-475). Also illegal are measures which damage the rights of third parties. Unlawful aims, aggressive intent, and damage to third parties can be seen throughout much of Washington's sanctions regimes, including those against the Islamic Republic of Iran. The false promises of neoliberal regimes have paralleled consistent economic and physical aggression against Iran and most of the independent countries of the region, as outlined in Table 1 below.

Table 1: The false promises of neoliberalism

Globalism	Economic liberal ideology of integration with universal benefits, but 'rigged rules' and contrived outcomes
Structural adjustment	1980s-90s conditional loans, created a strong reaction and rejection, especially of privileges for foreign capital
GATT-WTO	'Rules based system', rejected in the 21st century mainly over (a) agriculture (b) IPRs and (c) investment privileges
Unilateral sanctions	Widespread economic war, aggravated by 'rigged rules', as a declining US economy demanded monopoly rents
West Asia	Invasions, economic and proxy wars drove systematic exclusion for the independent peoples of West Asia.

Source: the author

Washington has tried to pressure the Cuban people and "to control actions of third party states" (Shneyer and Barta 1981: 452). The tightening of the blockade on Cuba in the 1990s has been described as a policy of imposing 'deliberate harm' (White 2018: 166). In the early

1960s, senior U.S. official Lester Mallory argued for damaging economic attacks on the entire population as a means of undermining what they acknowledged was a popular Cuban government: "every possible means should be undertaken promptly to weaken the economic life of Cuba …to bring about hunger, desperation and overthrow of government" (Mallory 1960). Similarly, in the early 1970s, U.S. President Nixon expressed the hope of forcing political upheaval and change in Chile by measures "to make the economy scream" (Kornbluh 2017). Nixon intended direct damage to public health, food security, well-being, and safety. These actions against Cuba and Chile—as also today against Iran, Venezuela and Syria—are economic warfare and arguably crimes against humanity (Selby-Green 2019).

So before we come to the direct aggression against the independent countries of West Asia (the ethnic cleansing in Palestine, the destruction of states in Afghanistan, Iraq and Libya, the invasions and occupation of Syria, the aggression against Yemen and the terrorist proxy wars conducted against much of the region) we can identify a systematic economic exclusion and aggression against those same nations, going back some decades. All this forms a critical background, essential for considerations of economic strategy.

Strategic concerns of the Resistance Economy

Calls for a 'resistance economy' came after years of aggression and emerged in context of Iran's '20-year national vision' announced in 2005. Principles at that time included calls for Iran to become a developed country "founded on ethical principles and Islamic, national and revolutionary values," which will take a lead in "advanced knowledge … economy, science and technology" (Khamenei 2005). The national vision goals suggested that Iran should be "a fully advanced country, rising to the number-one rank in economic, scientific and technological progress among 28 nations in the Middle East and Southeast Asia." That would mean (a) achievement of fast-paced and sustainable economic growth; (b) creation of durable employment opportunities; (c) enhancement of factor productivity; (d) active presence in regional and international markets; (e) development of a diverse, knowledge-based economy free of inflation and blessed by food security; and (f) establishment of a market environment conducive to domestic and international business entrepreneurship" (Amuzegar 2006). However, a new wave of economic aggression (sanctions) was joined to U.S. and Israeli attempts to block Iran's nuclear program.

In that context Iran's leader, Ayatollah Ali Khamenei, elaborated his idea of an "economy of resistance" in 2012, noting that "the enemy's goal was to focus on our economy, work against our national growth, undermine efforts to create employment opportunities, disrupt and jeopardize our national welfare, create problems for the people, make the people disappointed and isolate them from the Islamic Republic" (Khamenei 2012). In response to this the leader suggested

> an economy of resistance … [which means] putting the people in charge of the economy … minimizing our dependence on oil … managing consumption—that is to say, moderate consumption and avoidance of extravagance … making the best of the available time, resources and facilities ... moving forward on the basis of plans … reliance on domestic talents, on the domestic capacities of the country, on these youth, on their creativeness, on the tasks that they follow, on the knowledge that they acquire, and on the knowledge that they turn into technology (Khamenei 2012 & 2016).

The idea can be summed up as a process to achieve growth and prosperity under pressure. Iran would support local industries to turn threats into opportunities (Sharara 2019).

Based on this idea we can observe several articulated strategic concerns, beginning with a concerted effort to boost domestic production. How could the threats be turned into opportunities? Sanctions during the administrations of President Khatami and President Ahmadinejad had already "stimulated Iran's industrial development, insofar as they kept foreign competition at bay. Iran was in fact able to become something of an industrial powerhouse" (Sharara 2019). The resistance economy emphasised national production, with roles for government, cooperatives, and workers, but including elites and their technologies. Increasing national production implied stabilising the economy, boosting innovative national production, and reducing dependence on oil revenues (Piran and Dorche 2015: 648-651).

The country's industrial development, whilst targeted with sanctions, included eliminating imports of steel and fuel. Indeed, the U.S.-based International Trade Administration recognised that, between 2015 and 2018, Iran had moved from a net importer of steel into one of the world's top 20 steel exporters (ITA 2018). Steel production averaged more than 2 million tonnes per month from October 2018 to June 2019 (Trading Economics 2019) or 25 million tonnes per year (Rahmani 2019). Iran no longer exports crude oil and imports fuel because its expanded refinery capacity has ensured national fuel self-sufficiency (Paraskova 2019). The country's mobile telephony and computer hardware sector is well advanced (PBC 2019). Motor vehicle production, including export production, has grown strongly and will grow more since U.S. third party sanctions forced French automakers (Renault, Peugeot, and Citroen) to withdraw (Khatinoglu 2018). A foreign industry analyst termed Iran's motor vehicle market (2019-2024) a "consolidated market with strong growth prospects" (MI 2019). Meanwhile Iran has been reverse engineering foreign built tunnelling machines and pharmaceuticals. Barakat pharmaceutical town (Alborz province), opened in 2018, employs 7,000 and indirectly another 30,000 (Sharara 2019). In some of these cases an export potential has been built.

Outside commentators sometimes speak of a 'securitization' of the Iranian economy, indicating that security forces have come to play an important economic role. So Toumaj (2014) observes that the resistance economy implies 'securitization,' where the security forces, including the IRGC, play an important role in managing both economic policy and strategic enterprise. The Intelligence Ministry has also become involved, as economic concerns are linked to Iran's strategic position in the region, with Iran looking to a multipolar world and greater linkages with Asia (Toumaj 2014: 7-8). Sometimes the term 'securitization' is used disparagingly, suggesting either inefficient management or something that somehow reflects adversely on the government. In fact, security forces involvement in strategic enterprise is a rather natural adaptation to decades of aggression. In Cuba, for example, the military is involved in tourist operations at the outer edges of the main island, where surveillance and defence also have a priority (Frank 2017). In north Korea (the DPRK) securitization has become a systemic matter, termed 'Songun,' where there is security force involvement in virtually all major infrastructure and strategic industry (Park 2007).

As well as strategic economic ventures Iran has made substantial progress in military industry. The contextual history is that almost all the major powers helped Saddam Hussein wage his war against Iran in the 1980; and many of those same powers (including Russia and China) in more recent years helped subject Iran to great pressure to place its nuclear industry under outside controls and surveillance. One result of this pressure is that, as at 2019, Iran says it is very close to manufacturing all the jet and helicopter engines that it needs (Tasnim 2019). The country has also produced a wide range of missiles, the Kosar fighter jet (Sharara 2019), and its own anti-missile defence system, the Bavar-373, an upgraded counterpart of Russia's S-300 (IFP 2019).

The idea of greater participation in a resistance economy has been linked to Article 44 of the constitution which requires the state, cooperative and private sectors to contribute to development under a planned system. As regards 'resistance' there have been calls for further empowering the private sector, decreasing the country's dependence on oil, while promoting more efficient resource management and stable planning (Farhi 2012).

Internal management and planning challenges are linked to participation; that is, the Iranian state has to foment this participation while overcoming its own problems. In 2012 the Speaker or President of the Parliament, Ali Larijani, was quoted as saying that sanctions only accounted for 20% of Iran's economic problems of inflation, foreign exchange and production, and that domestic mismanagement was a bigger problem (Farhi 2012). Such problems are made more complex by internal divisions over policy, between the liberal faction and what are called the 'principalists' inside the country and 'hardliners' outside. For example, President's Rouhani's 'mismanagement' of exchange rates in early 2018 was blamed for production problems, because it was said to have "favoured consumption over production" at a time of crisis (Sharara 2019). Recriminations over the 2015 JCPOA nuclear deal, over which the liberals were so enthusiastic, also illustrate the internal divide.

Internal division of opinion is also seen in the relative importance given to developing reliable strategic partners, as compared to greater

Table 2: Strategic concerns	
Leader's idea	Provide for 'growth and prosperity ... even under pressure'; turn vulnerabilities into opportunities
Boost domestic production	Substitute local production for imports; build local and export industries (e.g. steel)
Securitization	A military role in the organisation of production and exchange
Greater participation & improved management	Participation at elite, technology, cooperative and popular levels. Proper state planning, address corruption, stabilise currency
Strategic partners and Iran's regional role	Choose secure partners, especially for major investments; the state to engage in regional stabilisation
Source: the author	

attention to the demands of the Western powers. Yet the resistance economy idea strongly favours the search for new economic opportunities with strategic partners, not least with those in the region (Piran and Dorche 2015: 648-651). U.S. analysts are keenly aware of a 'consensus' of Iran's factions around strategic policy while noting differences over the desired strength of economic ties with the Europeans and the USA (Toumaj 2014: 2). Yet there are important strategic partners outside the region, such as Russia, China, and Venezuela. Further, despite the vicious U.S. sanctions, Iran's non-oil trade with Vietnam, Indonesia, South Africa, Turkey, and Argentina (the VISTA group with a population of more than 540 million) grew very strongly in the first months of 2019 (FT 2019). Nevertheless, Iran's regional relations remain central.

New Regionalism: lessons for West Asia

'New regionalism' is a way of talking about different approaches taken in the wake of the failure of multilateral talks at the WTO and in the wake of the failure of U.S.-led globalism. In some discussions it refers simply to the search for new trade opportunities; often it implies the development of competitive blocs (e.g. NAFTA following the EU), sometimes involving new hegemonic strategies, and in others there is a developmental or counter-hegemonic impetus. For example, Linares (2011) speaks of the 'new socio-cultural strategy' of the Latin American ALBA group founded by Cuba and Venezuela; while Porter, Osei-Hwedie and Bertha (2015) speak of new regionalism as a way of promoting regional development; and Grugel (2004) stresses

Table 3a: New regionalism	
New regionalism	Reaction to the collapse of US-driven globalism: for new trade opportunities, competition between blocs and/or counter-hegemony
Trade opportunities	Most new trade opportunities in the 21st century have been within regional agreements, as WTO talks failed
Strategic bloc concerns	EU, NAFTA, SCO, BRICS, ALBA, CEFTA, etc - all have competitive and /or counter-hegemonic aims
West Asian context	Fragmented and sabotaged region, facing systematic exclusion, hybrid wars, local failures in political will and lack of critical infrastructure

differences in the 'new regionalism' of the EU and the USA towards Latin America. The term is quite flexible (see Table 3a below).

In any case, regional agreements are certainly the new game. According to the WTO, as at June 2019 there were at least 294 RTAs in force and another 170 notified, compared to less than 30 in 1992 (WTO 2019a). Most of these agreements were registered after the multilateral talks began to collapse from 2003 onwards. That means that most new trade opportunities in the last two decades have come through regional and bilateral 'preferential' trade agreements. In the mix have been several failed attempts by the USA to create 'mega-regional trade agreements' (MRTAs), such as the Transatlantic Trade and Investment Partnership (TTIP), the Trans-Pacific Partnership (TPP) (Mevel 2016) and the Free Trade Area of the Americas (FTAA), which was scuttled by a coalition of independent Latin American states in 2005 (Amadeo 2018). Those proposals carried elements rejected in the WTO Doha round, such as stronger intellectual property rights and investor access claims, which can be seen as new attempts to drive European and North American corporate privilege.

Earlier, in the '50s and '60s, plans for regional integration among developing countries stressed (as does Iran's resistance economy) making use of "import substitution on a regional scale," while facing problems of inefficiencies in production, especially if not confronted with competition (Balassa and Stoutjesdijk 1975). Iran today does not face the same developmental challenges as many of those developing countries, which have far less development in human capital, technology, and industrialisation. Yet it is worth briefly reviewing the developmental arguments by way of addressing the liberal arguments against regionalism, and in the context of economic aggression. Table 3b below shows key points and suggested aims outlined by Lanhammer

Table 3b: Regional integration and development: potential benefits	
'Training ground'	Industrial development builds skills and technology
Expand domestic market	Expanded market helps economies of scale
Improve resource allocation	Regional division of labour helps efficiencies
Enhance industrialisation	The multiple benefits of industrialisation compensate for possibly cheaper imports
Joint production of public goods	Cooperation in (e.g.) infrastructure and services
Protection against global shocks	Reduce vulnerability to sudden outside changes
Collective bargaining power	Bulk shared purchases can leverage prices
Build security consensus	Joint practice can help identify common aims
Source: Langhammer and Hiemenz 1990	

and Hiemenz (1990). These aims closely parallel those set out for the resistance economy, albeit with a regional focus: expanding the domestic market, improving resource allocation, enhancing industrialisation, protection against outside shocks, and building a security consensus.

The Bolivarian Alliance for our America (ALBA), Latin America's counter-hegemonic regional bloc, offers some additional lessons, from a parallel experience. Founded by Venezuela and Cuba, then Bolivia and several other countries, this progressive bloc grew in direct reaction to Washington's hegemonic plan for the Americas, the failed Free Trade Area of the Americas (FTAA). That project was seen as an extension of an annexationist, exclusionary and subjugating practice which stretched back to the 19th century.

The late Hugo Chavez stressed the need for integration to be a participatory process: "necessary integration, liberating integration, not neocolonial integration … the social movements of Latin America, the workers, the students, the small farmers, the organised women have a key role," in a struggle against neoliberalism and imperialism (Chavez 2004). This group would build an integration which did not include the chief imperial power, the United States of America (nor, said the ALBA, the oligarchs of the region); the need for integration would go well beyond trade, 'free trade' or economic issues, into a deep and inclusive social and political integration based on solidarity, complementarity and cooperation (Martinez 2005).

Chavez spoke of "constructing a Great Country (*Patria Grande*) in Latin America" (Lopez Blanch 2009: 2). Venezuela and Cuba enunciated several founding principles: "just and sustainable development"; "special and differential treatment" for unequal partners; guaranteed access to benefits for those who participate (as opposed to a competitive system where the big players win); "cooperation and solidarity," particularly as expressed by strong regional social programs; special funds and measures for the environment and for emergencies; energy integration (a theme pushed by Venezuela); less dependence of foreign investment and inter-member preferences for public and joint venture capital; protection of Latin American and Caribbean cultures and the establishment of Telesur, a public television channel to present "our realities." There would also be shared positions on democratic struggles (ALBA-TCP 2004). A Cuban economist said the project had two ideas: to create "a regional integration scheme that promotes social justice together with economic development," and to create "a space of anti-hegemonic power projection to neutralise the U.S. domination of the Western Hemisphere" (Alzugaray Treto 2011).

Practical complementarity can be seen in the first Cuba-Venezuela exchanges, which were large-scale barter swaps, most prominently Cuba's provision of medical and educational services and training in exchange for Venezuela's assistance in rebuilding Cuba's energy sector and the provision of discount oil. For the five years from 2004 and 2008 (when the U.S. financial crisis hit) Cuba's average per capita economic growth rate was 8% while Venezuela's was 8.6%, compared to a Latin American average of 4% (ECLAC 2012). Within a few years the ALBA group had grown to 11 nation states.

The most powerful expressions of ALBA in its first years were the social programs—literacy, primary health care, educational and health programs—typically financed by and with logistic support from Venezuela and staffed by Cuban professionals. Through these programs, Venezuela, Bolivia, and Nicaragua all reduced their adult illiteracy to minimal levels in just a few years (Nehru 2011). By 2011 achievements of the new grouping were said to include: lifting 11 million people out of poverty; making 3.5 million more people literate, thus raising overall literacy from 84% to 96%; increased school and college enrolments; massive joint health programs reducing infant mortality by 32%; and assisting 900,000 handicapped people in 2010 alone (ERBV 2011).

ALBA-type agreements were formed with non-member countries. For example, in early 2005 Venezuela signed nine agreements with Argentina, which included: a commitment to Telesur; technical cooperation between state oil agencies; supply of Argentine ship-building facilities to Venezuela in exchange for agreements on concessional oil supply; cooperation on health, hospitals, health science and social sciences (ALBA-TCP 2008); and agreement to develop the project of a continental gas pipeline. Other countries expressed their interest in participating in some of the ALBA's social programs, such as the disabilities mission. Further, ALBA articulated the call for a 'new regional financial architecture,' which included a new regional currency and a Bank of ALBA, to finance large joint venture projects (ALBA-TCP Secretariat 2010).

Some of the 'Great Nation' projects and enterprises went into new territory. ALBAMED, for example, listed 475 essential medicines which would be made available to the member countries under a new regulatory system. ALBATEL was constructing a new system of communications, including by use of its own satellite (Sanz 2012). Cooperation in pharmaceuticals would mean greater efficiency in producing necessary medicines and, if necessary, greater bargaining power in making purchases outside the bloc (Cuba Standard 2013; RTV 2014).

Although the ALBA bloc is still young and has faced some setbacks, there seem some lessons here for Iran and her neighbours. First, a regional counter-hegemonic bloc with diverse political systems but a shared social solidarity can produce rapid benefits. Second, such a bloc can consolidate real interests to lessen the threat of outside hegemonic powers. Third, the principles established by such a bloc can have a wider influence. Existing West Asian bilateral agreements might usefully be reshaped into more formal regional cooperation mechanisms.

4. Iran and West Asian integration

Iran is again under pressure and the government must have as its priority the security and stabilisation of the livelihoods of its citizens. But that cannot mean disengagement from the region, as its enemies demand. The 'resistance economy' has wider implications for both Iran and the region. It implies active engagement in, and the construction of, new political economic realities, rather than attaching hope to the false promises of neoliberalism. There is little doubt that the Islamic Republic of Iran, with its principled stability and great capacity, is best placed to lead a West Asian economic alliance, as well as an independent security bloc. Such integration would benefit Iran, as well as the region. The often stated imperial and zionist fear of such an alliance simply reinforces this view. This final section outlines the key relevant elements of Iran's capacity and some of the benefits and practical implications of regional integration.

Propaganda never sleeps. On the 40th anniversary of the revolution U.S. President Donald Trump published a series of propaganda graphics suggesting Iran had experienced '40 years of failure' (AFP 2019). No one can take claims from a dedicated enemy at face value. In fact, independent evidence from the United Nations Development Programme shows us that, despite the constant aggression, Iran made outstanding progress. Between 1990 and 2017 the country's Human Development Index grew on average 1.21% per year, second only to China (UNDP 2018b: Table 2). Iran's progress was due to exceptional and sustained improvements in life expectancy, mainly due to health care improvements and child survival and improvements in education (UNDP 1999; UNDP 2018a). Between 1980 and 2017, average life expectancy in Iran rose from 54.1 to 76.2 years, and average years of schooling rose from 2.2 to 9.8, a more than fourfold increase, almost at gender equity (UNDP 2016; UNDP 2018a). Inequality and poverty fell substantially (UNDP 1999; World Bank 2019). Iran moved ahead while its enemies waged dreadful and futile wars.

In the region Iran's role was critical in its support of the people of Palestine, of Lebanon, of Syria, of Iraq and of Yemen. That real solidarity with independent and suffering people under attack is what attracts aggression from the zionist regime and from Washington. They rightly fear that Iran is most likely to lead an alliance of independent peoples in rejecting imperial intervention. That 'threat' rests in Iran's principles, its stability, its political will, and its human and natural capacity.

For example, former U.S. official Larry Wilkerson acknowledged that, in face of the U.S. plan "to sweep the Middle East" and to "destabilise the entire region," Washington was confronted by Iran as "one of the most stable countries in the region" (Wilkerson 2018). Cheap polemics against Iran these days are refuted by independent sources.

According to the World Bank (2019b), Iran reduced its inequality (as measured by the Gini index) from 47.40 in 1986 to 38.80 in 2014. Inequality in the U.S. remains significantly higher at 41.5 (Gini). Despite its rhetoric of 'freedom,' the U.S. imprisonment rate (the highest on earth at 698 per 100,000 population) was more than double that of Iran (at 287); and far more Iranians trust their national government (71%) than is the case in the USA (39%) (UNDP 2018b: Tables 3, 12 & 14). That progress and that trust are at the root of Iran's current stability.

With that stability and capacity, what role could Iran play in regional integration? Zionists and their allies fear Iran's role in forming a united front facing occupied Palestine and dread the emergence of an Iranian land bridge from Tehran to Beirut (Ibish 2017). In fact, such infrastructure corridors would represent a great economic and social advance for the peoples of the sabotaged and divided region. The positive spill-over effects of major infrastructure, properly managed, can work at the regional level as it does at the national level (Najkar, Kohansal and Ghorbani 2018). Something similar could be said about the Russia-Iran joint rail project, linking to Asia and Europe (SRB 2017). The resurrection of energy projects such as the Kirkuk-Baniyas oil pipeline (Boev 2017) fall in the same category. Such cross-national projects can break the attempted siege of West Asian countries and open up new possibilities to benefit the peoples of the region. But they require cooperation, joint investment, and close security cooperation. That raises the question of enforcing security guarantees from outside investors who might wish to join in the likely boom from West Asian development. Shouldn't strategic partners be required to contribute to the protection of large projects from repeated attempts at destabilisation?

Land-based connectivity is proving important both for trade and for avoiding oceanic interventions by outside powers—despite the fact that rail links, while often faster, can be more expensive than sea transport (Ruta 2018). That land connectivity remains an important factor in China's Belt and Road Initiative (BRI) as also for Iran in building its regional and extra-regional networks. The great promise for Ankara and Tehran in Russia-China relations has been stressed (Duarte 2014), as also the importance of Central and West Asia to India's pipelines and transport corridors (Mubarik 2017), and a

China-Pakistan corridor as a mechanism for "regional integration and peace" (Khan and Marwat 2016).

An integrated trade zone with preferential terms clearly opens up an expanded market. Maybe some of that market already exists, for example with Iran's automobile industry. However, systematic trade preferences deepen such advantages. If we take just a simple four nation model as shown in Table 4a, we can see that a preferential trade bloc could more than double Iran's market—but it could expand the market of the smaller partners to a much greater extent. Initial concessional allocations can boost peripheral production. For example, if there were a particularly efficient industry in Yemen (assuming the country were unified and stable), an integration agreement and initial concession could expand its national market of 29 million to a regional market of 171 million. This is what happened with Cuba's Ernesto Guevara Electronic Components Complex under the ALBA. A small rural factory that supplied rural schools with solar panels suddenly became a much bigger enterprise after it gained preferential access to several other countries. That factory was then able to diversify into other electronic components (Prensa Latina 2014).

Table 4a: Four country model of market integration		
4 countries	National population/market	Regional population/market
Iran	83m	171m
Yemen	29m	171m
Iraq	39m	171m
Syria	20m	171m

However, integration is not simply a matter of expanded markets. Inchoate regional growth may generate "powerful centrifugal forces within regions," and so not necessarily strengthen coherent capacity (Garzón 2017). Further, effective leadership with shared values is necessary for an economic bloc to have leverage in agreements struck with other blocs and powerful states. Leverage, or weight, is needed for advantageous terms on specific and broad issues, both with more neutral countries and with adversaries. That principle also applies to the West Asian place in China's Belt and Road infrastructure initiative (Lehr 2018). An Indian analyst has pointed out the challenge to Washington's ambitions posed by Iran-China relations (Bhat 2012); such a challenge would have greater substance with an Iran-led West-Asian bloc linked to China.

There is the important question of strengthening shared values and the character of a West Asian Alliance, which can build internal strength while maintaining a degree of openness to trusted neighbours and other partners. This also applies to industrial development. Two decades ago, UNCTAD pointed out that the criteria for successful industrial clusters went further than competition and exports. Successful industrial clusters were characterised by high levels of innovation, trust, cooperation, learning and skill development (UNCTAD 1998). Cultivation of these qualities requires more than just markets.

Both Iran and the region stand to gain from a counter-hegemonic regional alliance. Naturally, such an alliance pre-supposes a security alliance, but strategic concerns have always been central to the idea of a resistance economy. So much is recognised by one Washington-based academic who, while suggesting that U.S. influence in the region is a constant, also recognises that Iran's geopolitical role and its expanded trade are closely linked (Peyrouse 2014). Some necessary implications of the economic integration of a region subject to repeated aggression are that (i) some form of participation in security guarantees would most likely be an appropriate requirement for those seeking to benefit from investment in large infrastructure, energy, and other strategic joint venture projects; (ii) strategic partners (whether countries or corporations) might best be rated on levels of trust for the purpose of investment partnerships and fiscal concessions.

This discussion of the region has focussed mostly on Iran and its independent Arab neighbours. However, also important are relations with the Persian-speaking neighbours of Tajikistan and with Afghanistan (Muzalevsky 2010). Relations with Turkey, select Persian Gulf countries and of course the Asian continent need not be prejudiced by the formation of a West Asian alliance. Regional integration, like industrialisation, can develop spread effects.

As the largest and leading independent country of the region, Iran is well able to chair a coalition of proven and experienced regional

Table 4b: Foundations of and potential benefits to Iran and regional partners from West Asian integration	
1	Resistance alliance council to determine joint security, strategy and regional infrastructure priorities
2	Joint development of trusted strategic partnerships and agreements with other blocs and powerful states
3	Systematically expanded markets and joint planning of economic concessions
4	Coordinated development of education, culture, science, industry, commerce and social programs
5	Coordinated development of the values and character of the resistance alliance

resistance leaders, so as to determine joint security, strategic partnerships and regional infrastructure. That group could also coordinate cooperation in education, science, culture, social programs, industry, and commerce. Such a coalition would build existing cooperation, making it more systematic and resilient.

This chapter outlined the failed promises of neoliberalism, which moved from a partisan construction of liberal markets with rigged rules to a fairly comprehensive rollout of siege warfare against the independent countries and peoples of West Asia. The Europeans, for the most part, have proven themselves either complicit or unable to break from the aggression driven by Washington, whose hybrid wars have aimed at keeping the entire region fragmented and weak.

In these circumstances a decisive and distinct economic path is necessary for the future of the people of Iran and of the region. Resistance economy ideas, in particular the call to transform pressures into opportunities and to develop strategic partnerships, have become even more relevant. A wider, counter-hegemonic 'new regionalism' is essential, and might draw some lessons from the parallel experiences of Latin America,; notwithstanding the distinct conditions of West Asia. Iran's promotion of a counter-hegemonic bloc, with diverse political systems but shared institutions, could produce rapid benefits, consolidating real interests to lessen outside threats and building distinctive forms of cooperation. This is not simply altruism. Iran would economically benefit from an integrated and expanded market, as would the smaller countries even more. A West Asian economic bloc could upgrade human and industrial capacity, reinforcing security and stability while entrenching decent human values.

References

AFP (2019) "US slams Iranian revolution for 40 years of failure as Rouhani threatens military expansion." Arab News, 11 February, online: http://www.arabnews.com/node/1450261/middle-east

Abouharb, M. Rodwan, and David L. Cingranelli. "The Human Rights Effects of World Bank Structural Adjustment, 1981–2000." *International Studies Quarterly* 50, no. 2 (June 2006): 233–62.

ALBA-TCP (2004). "Agreement for the ALBA Application." December 14, 2004. http://www.alba-tcp.org/en/contenido/agreement-alba-application

——— (2008). "Acuerdos entre Argentina y Venezuela." July 3, 2008. http://www.alianzabolivariana.org/modules.php?name=Content&pa=showpage&pid=1765

ALBA-TCP Secretariat (2010). "SUCRE: Respuesta del ALBA a la Crisis Financiera." Caracas: Alianza Bolivariana para los Pueblos de Nuestra América-Tratado de Comercio de los Pueblos (July 2010): 1–3.

Alzugaray Treto, Carlos. "The future of ALBA and regional integration: an introduction." *International Journal of Cuban Studies* 3, no. 2/3, Special Issue: A new dawn? ALBA and the future of Caribbean and Latin American Integration (Summer/Autumn 2011): 95–97.

Amadeo, Kimberly (2018). "FTAA Agreement, Its Members, With Its Pros and Cons." The Balance. December 21, 2018. https://www.thebalance.com/ftaa-agreement-member-countries-pros-and-cons-3305577

——— (2019). "Doha Round of Trade Talks: The Real Reason Why It Failed." The Balance. June 25, 2019. https://www.thebalance.com/what-is-the-doha-round-of-trade-talks-3306365

Amuzegar, Jahangir (2006). "Iran's 20-Year Economic Perspective: Promises and Pitfalls." *Middle East Policy* XVI, no. 3. https://www.mepc.org/journal/irans-20-year-economic-perspective-promises-and-pitfalls

Balassa, Bela, and Ardy Stoutjesdijk. "Economic integration among developing countries." *Journal of Common Market Studies* 14, no. 1 (September 1975): 37–55. https://doi.org/10.1111/j.1468-5965.1975.tb00736.x

Bhat, Mukhtar Ahmad (2012) "Iran-China Relations: A challenge for U.S. hegemony." *Quarterly Journal of Chinese Studies* 3, no. 2 (2012): 113–25.

Boev, Borislav. "Kirkuk-Baniyas: The forgotten pipeline." South Front. August 1, 2017. https://southfront.org/kirkuk-baniyas-forgotten-pipeline/

Chávez, Hugo (2004). "Inventamos la Nueva América LatinoCaribeña" – speech from meeting on December 6, 2004. In *Cuadernos para la Emancipación,* no. 27. Caracas: Fundación Emancipación por la Unidad de América Latina y el Caribe, 2005.

Cheru, Fantu. "Effects of structural adjustment policies on the full enjoyment of human rights." UN Commission on Human Rights, 55th session, review by independent expert. February 24, 1999. https://www.ohchr.org/EN/Issues/Development/IEDebt/Pages/Resolutions.aspx

Cuba Standard (2013). "Cuba stands to gain as ALBA creates common medical market." https://www.cubastandard.com/cuba-stands-to-gain-as-alba-creates-common-medical-market/

Duarte, Paulo Afonso Brardo. "Ankara and Tehran in Russia's 'Near Abroad': The Way to Central Asia." *Turkish Journal of Politics* 5, no. 2 (Winter 2014).

ECLAC (2012). Statistical Yearbook, Latin America and the Caribbean: Annual growth rates of per capita Gross Domestic Product, 2.1.1.2. http://websie.cepal.org/anuario_estadistico/anuario_2012/en/contents_en.asp, 2.1.1.2

ERBV. "ALBA logra mas avances en Metas del Milenio que otros paises." Embajada de la Republica Bolivariana de Venezuela en Washington. February 15, 2011. http://venezuela-us.org/es/2011/02/15/alba-logra-mas-avances-en-metas-del-milenio-que-otros-paises/

Ettlinger, Nancy. "The Roots of Competitive Advantage in California and Japan." *Annals of the Association of American Geographers* 81, no. 3 (September 1991): 391–407.

Farhi, Farideh. "Sanctions and the shaping of Iran's 'resistance economy.'" Lobe Log. July 27, 2012. https://lobelog.com/sanctions-and-the-shaping-of-iran's-"resistance-economy"/

Frank, Marc. "Cuban military's tentacles reach deep into economy." Reuters. June 16, 2017. https://www.reuters.com/article/us-usa-cuba-military/cuban-militarys-tentacles-reach-deep-into-economy-idUSKBN1962VK

FT. "42% Rise in Iran's Non-Oil Trade With VISTA." *Financial Tribune*. August 16, 2019. online: https://financialtribune.com/articles/domestic-economy/99444/42-rise-in-irans-non-oil-trade-with-vista

Garzón, Jorge F. "Multipolarity and the future of economic regionalism." *International Theory* 9, no. 1 (March 2017): 101–135. https://doi.org/10.1017/S1752971916000191

Grugel, Jean B. "New Regionalism and Modes of Governance – Comparing US and EU Strategies in Latin America." *European Journal of International Relations* 10, no. 4, (December 2004): 603–628.

Hoogvelt, Ankie. *Globalization and the Postcolonial World: The New Political Economy of Development*. Baltimore: The Johns Hopkins University Press, 1997.

Hussain, Imtiaz. "After Cancún: G21, WTO, and Multilateralism." *Journal of International and Area Studies* 11, no. 2 (December 2004): 1-16

Ibish, Hussein. "Iran's long-cherished Tehran to Beirut 'land-bridge' moves closer to reality." November 11, 2017. https://www.thenational.ae/opinion/iran-s-long-cherished-tehran-to-beirut-land-bridge-moves-closer-to-reality-1.674875

IFP. "Iran Unveils Homegrown 'Bavar-373' Missile Defence System." *Iran Front Page*. August 22, 2019. https://ifpnews.com/iran-unveils-homegrown-bavar-373-missile-defence-system

ITA. *Steel Exports Report: Iran*. Washington: International Trade Administration, September 2018. https://www.trade.gov/steel/countries/pdfs/2018/q2/exports-iran.pdf

Jalili, Saeed. "Iran Says WTO Accession No More a Priority." *Financial Tribune*. August 16, 2017. https://financialtribune.com/articles/economy-business-and-markets/70521/iran-says-wto-accession-no-more-a-priority

Jawara, Fatoumata, and Aileen Kwa. *Behind the Scenes at the WTO: The Real World of International Trade Negotiations/Lessons of Cancun*. London: Zed Books, 2003.

Johnson, Chalmers A. *MITI and the Japanese Miracle*. Stanford, CA: Stanford University Press, 1982.

Keynes, John Maynard. *The General Theory of Employment, Interest and Money*. London: Palgrave MacMillan, 1936.

Khamenei, Ali (2005). "20 Year National Vision." Iran Data Portal. http://irandataportal.syr.edu/20-year-national-vision

——— (2012). "Leader's Speech to Government Officials." *Khamenei.IR*. July 24, 2012. http://english.khamenei.ir/news/1655/Leader-s-Speech-to-Government-Officials

——— (2016). "Our problems with America are not solved by negotiations: Ayatollah Khamenei." *Khamenei.IR,* August 1, 2016. http://english.khamenei.ir/news/4052/Our-problems-with-America-are-not-solved-by-negotiations-Ayatollah

Khan, Shabir, and Zahid Ali Khan Marwat. "CPEC: Role in regional integration and peace." *South Asian Studies* 31, no. 2 (July-December 2016): 103–112.

Khatinoglu, Dalga. "French Automakers Suffer As They Lose Iran Market." *Radio FARDA*. October 24, 2018. https://en.radiofarda.com/a/french-automakers-suffer-as-they-lose-iran-market-/29561854.html

Kornbluh, Peter (2017). "Chile and the United States: Declassified Documents Relating to the Military Coup, September 11, 1973." National Security Archive Electronic Briefing Book No. 8. https://nsarchive2.gwu.edu/NSAEBB/NSAEBB8/nsaebb8i.htm

Langhammer, Rolf, and Ulrich Hiemenz. *Regional Integration among developing countries: opportunities, obstacles and options*. Kieler Studien, no. 232 [ISBN 3161456246], Tübingen: Mohr, 1990.

Lehr, Deborah. "How China is winning over the Middle East." *The Diplomat.* July 21, 2018. https://thediplomat.com/2018/07/how-china-is-winning-over-the-middle-east/

Linares, Rosalba (2011) "The ALBA alliance and the construction of a new Latin American regionalism." Special issue: A New Dawn? ALBA and the Future of… *The International Journal of Cuban Studies* 3, no. 2/3 (Summer 2011): 145–56, 263.

Lopez Blanch, Hedelberto. "La integración política del ALBA." Rebelión. December 15, 2009. http://www.rebelion.org/noticia.php?id=97037

Mallory, Lester (1960) "499. Memorandum From the Deputy Assistant Secretary of State for Inter-American Affairs (Mallory) to the Assistant Secretary of State for Inter-American Affairs (Rubottom)." *Foreign Relations of the United States, 1958–1960, Cuba,* Vol. VI. U.S. Department of State, Office of the Historian. Washington, April 6, 1960. https://history.state.gov/historicaldocuments/frus1958-60v06/d499

Martin, Will. "Nobel prize-winning economist Stiglitz tells us why 'neoliberalism is dead." *Business Insider.* August 19, 2016. https://www.businessinsider.com.au/joseph-stiglitz-says-neoliberalism-is-dead-2016-8?r=US&IR=T

Martínez, Osvaldo (2005) "ALBA y ALCA: El Dilema de la Integración o la Anexión." Rebelión. September 9, 2005. https://rebelion.org/alba-y-alca-el-dilema-de-la-integracion-o-la-anexion/

Mevel, Simon. "Mega-regional trade agreements: Threat or opportunity for the future of African trade?" International Centre for Trade and Sustainable Development. April 18, 2016. https://www.ictsd.org/bridges-news/bridges-africa/news/mega-regional-trade-agreements-threat-or-opportunity-for-the-future

MI (2019). "Iran Vehicle Market – Growth, Trends, and Forecast (2019–2024)." Mordor Intelligence. https://www.mordorintelligence.com/industry-reports/iran-vehicles-market

Mubarik, Mudasir. 'Connectivity and Geopolitics: Factoring Iran in India-Central Asia Relations." *The IUP Journal of International Relations* XI, no. 2 (2017).

Muzalevsky, Roman. "The 'Persian Alliance' and Geopolitical Reconfiguration in6 Central Asia." *Eurasia Daily Monitor* 7, no. 161 (September 9, 2010). https://jamestown.org/program/the-persian-alliance-and-geopolitical-reconfiguration-in-central-asia/

Najkar, Nastaran, Mohammad Kohansal, and Mohammad Ghorbani. "Estimating Spatial Effects of Transport Infrastructure on Agricultural Output of Iran." *Agris on-line Papers in Economics and Informatics* 10, no. 2 (2018): 61–71.

Nehru, Meesha. "Latin America's alternative alliance." *Times Higher Education.* April 3, 2011. http://www.timeshighereducation.co.uk/story.asp?storycode=415693

Paraskova, Tsvetana. "Iran Says It's Now Self-Sufficient In Gasoline." Oil Price. February 18, 2019. https://oilprice.com/Latest-Energy-News/World-News/Iran-Says-Its-Now-Self-Sufficient-In-Gasoline.html

Park, Han S. (2007). "Military-First Politics (Songun): Understanding Kim Jong-il's North Korea." Korea Economic Institute of America. http://keia.org/publication/military-first-politics-songun-understanding-kim-jong-ils-north-korea

PBC (2019). "Iran – Telecoms, Mobile and Broadband – Statistics and Analyses." Paul Budde Communication. February 2019. https://www.marketresearch.com/Paul-Budde-Communication-Pty-Ltd-v1533/Iran-Telecoms-Mobile-Broadband-Statistics-12264972/

Peyrouse, Sebastian. "Iran's Growing Role in Central Asia? Geopolitical, Economic and Political Profit and Loss Account." *Al Jazeera.* April 6, 2014. http://studies.aljazeera.net/en/dossiers/2014/04/2014416940377354.html

Piran, Shamseddin Jalili, and Mohammad Soleymani Dorche. "Resistance Economy in International Law." *International Journal of Humanities and Cultural Studies* Special Issue, December 2015. https://text2fa.ir/wp-content/uploads/Text2fa.ir-Resistance-Economy-in-International.pdf

Porter, Jesse K., and Bertha Z. Osei-Hwedie. "Regionalism as a tool for promoting economic and regional development: A case study of the economic community of West African states (ECOWAS)." *Economic and Social Development: Book of Proceedings.* Varazdin Development and Entrepreneurship Agency (VADEA) (September 25, 2015): 31–38.

Prensa Latina (2014). "Cuban Electronic Components Factory Widens Production." Caribbean Energy Information System. Jan. 15, 2014. http://www.ceis-caribenergy.org/cuban-electronic-components-factory-widens-production/

Rahmani, Reza. "Iran enjoys appropriate self-reliance in steel sector: industry min." The Iran Project. June 26, 2019. https://theiranproject.com/blog/2019/06/26/iran-enjoys-appropriate-self-reliance-in-steel-sector-industry-min/

Ricardo, David. *On the Principles of Political Economy and Taxation.* London: John Murray, 1817.

Rostow, Walt. *The Stages of Economic Growth: A Non-Communist Manifesto.* Cambridge: Cambridge University Press, 1960.

RTV. "Cuba vende medicamentos a más de 50 países." Martinoticias.com. November 25, 2014. https://www.radiotelevisionmarti.com/a/cuba-vende-medicamentos-a-mas-de-cincuenta-paises/80917.html

Ruta, Michele. "Three Opportunities and Three Rusks of the Belt and Road Initiative." The Trade Post. May 4, 2018. https://blogs.worldbank.org/trade/three-opportunities-and-three-risks-belt-and-road-initiative

Sanz, Rodolfo (2012) "Rodolfo Sanz: No me imagino a una América Latina con un ALCA y sin un ALBA." *Telesur.* December 13, 2012. http://www.telesurtv.net/articulos/2012/12/13/rodolfo-sanz-no-me-imagino-a-una-america-latina-con-un-alca-y-sin-un-alba-4701.html

Selby-Green, Michael. "Venezuela crisis: Former UN rapporteur says US sanctions are killing citizens." *The Independent.* January 26, 2019. https://www.independent.co.uk/news/world/americas/venezuela-us-sanctions-united-nations-oil-pdvsa-a8748201.html

Sharara, Karim. "How 'Maximum Pressure' Can Yield Economic Prosperity For Iran." Lobe Log. August 2, 2019. https://lobelog.com/how-maximum-pressure-can-yield-economic-prosperity-for-iran/

Shneyer, Paul A., and Virginia Barta. "The legality of the U.S. Economic Blockade of Cuba under International Law." *Case Western Reserve Journal of International Law* 13, no. 3 (1981): 450–82.

Spencer, Roger W., and William P. Yohe. "The 'Crowding Out' of Private Expenditures by Fiscal Policy Actions." *Federal Reserve Bank of St. Louis Review* (October 1970): 12–24.

SRB. "Iran-Russia Rail Corridor Direct to Europe." Silk Road Briefing. September 12, 2017. https://www.silkroadbriefing.com/news/2017/09/12/iran-russia-rail-corridor-direct-europe/

Stiglitz, Joseph. *Globalization and It Discontents.* New York: Norton, 2002.

Tasnim. "Top General: Iran on Verge of Self-Sufficiency in Making Aircraft Engines." *Tasnim News.* August 17, 2019. https://www.tasnimnews.com/en/news/2019/08/17/2077268/top-general-iran-on-verge-of-self-sufficiency-in-making-aircraft-engines

Toumaj, Amir. *Iran's Economy of Resistance: Implications for Future Sanctions.* A Report by the Critical Threats Project of the American Enterprise Institute. November 2014. https://www.criticalthreats.org/wp-content/uploads/2016/07/imce-imagesToumajA_Irans-Resistance-Economy-Implications_november2014-1.pdf

Trading Economics (2019). "Iran Steel Production." https://tradingeconomics.com/iran/steel-production

UNCTAD (1998) *Promoting and Sustaining SMEs Clusters and Networks for Development.* Issues Paper, TD/B/COM.3/EM.5/2. United Nations Conference on Trade and Development, June 26, 1998. https://unctad.org/en/docs/c3em5d2.pdf

UNDP (1999). "Human Development Report of the Islamic Republic of Iran, 1999." United Nations Development Programme, Tehran. http://hdr.undp.org/sites/default/files/iran_1999_en.pdf

——— (2016). Human Development Report, Table 2, "Human Development Index Trends, 1990–2015." United Nations Development Programme. http://hdr.undp.org/sites/default/files/2016_human_development_report.pdf

——— (2018a). "Briefing note for countries on the 2018 Statistical Update, Iran (Islamic Republic of)." United Nations Development Programme. http://hdr.undp.org/sites/all/themes/hdr_theme/country-notes/IRN.pdf

——— (2018b). "Human Development Indices and Indicators, 2018 Statistical Update." United Nations Development Programme. http://

hdr.undp.org/sites/default/files/2018_human_development_statistical_update.pdf

US Dept. of Treasury. “Active Sanctions Programs.” March 2019. https://www.treasury.gov/resource-center/sanctions/programs/pages/programs.aspx

White, Nigel. “Ending the US Embargo of Cuba: International Law in Dispute.” *Journal of Latin American Studies* 51, no. 1 (2018): 163–186. https://doi.org/10.1017/S0022216X18000718

Wilkerson, Larry (2018). “Wilkerson: On Iran, Trump follows the Iraq war playbook.” The Real News. February 6, 2018. https://therealnews.com/stories/wilkerson-on-iran-trump-follows-the-iraq-war-playbook

Williams, Eric. *Capitalism and Slavery.* Chapel Hill, NC: University of North Carolina, 1944.

World Bank (2009). “What Is Inclusive Growth?” http://siteresources.worldbank.org/INTDEBTDEPT/Resources/468980-1218567884549/WhatIsInclusiveGrowth20081230.pdf

——— (2019a). “Poverty & Equity Data Portal: Islamic Republic of Iran.” http://povertydata.worldbank.org/poverty/country/IRN

——— (2019b). “GINI index (World Bank estimate), Iran, Islamic Rep.” https://data.worldbank.org/indicator/SI.POV.GINI?locations=IR

WTO (2019a). “Regional Trade Agreements.” https://www.wto.org/english/tratop_e/region_e/region_e.htm#facts

——— (2019b). “Yemen and the WTO.” https://www.wto.org/english/thewto_e/countries_e/yemen_e.htm

Yousefvand, Saman. “The Islamic Republic of Iran: Accession to the WTO.” May 2016. https://www.wto.org/english/thewto_e/acc_e/iran_sesssion1_e.pdf

16. The Challenge of Multipolarity

There is a long queue of countries ready to join the BRICS group, one of the key institutions in the move away from a unipolar world. Source: www.gstimes.in

The end of a period of global dominance by Washington is being marked by the failure of multiple wars in West Asia. The USA, in relative economic decline for several decades, accelerated the collapse of its influence by launching a series of disastrous 21st century New Middle East (NME) wars—notably those against Afghanistan, Iraq, Libya, Syria and Yemen. At the heart of all these has been the steadily expanding Israeli colonisation of Palestine and conversion of that colony into an apartheid state (Falk and Tilley 2017).

Those NME wars—designed to dominate the West Asian region by removing independent political will—have, by their failure, produced entirely the opposite effect. A new regional power bloc is emerging, led by Iran, and the regional role of both Russia and China has expanded.

All empires are obsessed by potential rivals and, in this case, Washington has long feared the rise of multiple independent power blocs, per se. The U.S. even feared the rise of an independent European Union, creating NAFTA in response. Seeing the dilemmas of U.S.

decline in the late 20th century, Zbigniew Brzezinski argued, in *The Grand Chessboard,* for a "new type" of hegemony, drawing on old 'Hegemonic Stability' ideas (Keohane 1984; Schmidt 1998; Grunberg 2009). The Pentagon addressed this challenge in 2000 with its *Full Spectrum Dominance* doctrine (U.S. Department of Defense 2000). However, those ambitions are fading; it is already quite clear that there will be no 'New American Century.'

None of this had anything to do with the agreed upon norms of the post-colonial era. Each new invasion, proxy war or other intervention—including attempts to act as the world's policeman and to punish miscreants through unilateral coercive measures, wrongly termed 'sanctions'—breached both the United Nations Charter and the established principle of the right of peoples to self-determination (OHCHR 2021: Article 1). A widespread rejection of what was effectively a new form of imperialism, including rejection by rising powers, has already destroyed its future possibilities.

So, the question arises: what might be the shape of a post Washington world? I say, 'post-Washington' instead of 'post-American,' out of deference to the 600 million people and 33 American states in the Americas which are not part the USA. Even though the people of the USA call themselves 'Americans,' the distinction is important; it was discussed eloquently by Cuban independence hero Jose Marti in his 1891 article, "Our America" (Marti 1891).

A second reason to prefer 'post-Washington' is that the regime in Washington is a very long way from democratically representing its own peoples in the United States. No imperial power, without any mandate from subjugated peoples, nor any state that spends trillions on wars of conquest yet fails to provide even basic public health guarantees for its own population (Reich 2020), can be considered a real democracy.

In any case, no single power is ready, willing, or able to replace Washington. Despite constant accusations from U.S. sources (e.g. CFR 2012) and the concerns of some of its neighbours (Bello 2019), China explicitly rejects the idea of unilateralism (Xinhua 2020). The transition mostly commonly cited by critical thinkers is that we are moving from a unipolar world (with a single hegemon) to a multipolar world (Graebner 1988). But what sort of multipolarity will it be, and what is the likely viability of such a new order?

From that consideration this chapter poses two questions: is the need for multipolarity well recognised among counter-hegemonic forces? And can effective cooperation be built on multipolar values?

Is the need for multipolarity well recognised?

While multipolarity is often discussed in global terms (Graebner 1988; Schwenninger 2003), it does not really form the basis for local or regional independence struggles in the post-colonial world. Rather we see doctrines based on regional, cultural, and religious values. So, to what extent can these doctrines talk to each other and jointly recognise the project of replacing unipolarity with multipolarity?

Successive Anglo-American empires did build a common mythology, often referred to these days as neoliberalism. That project borrowed economic liberal ideas but applied them selectively. Free market ideas were used to break open new frontiers, but then monopoly cartels were used to dominate the newly conquered territories, resources and peoples. And the idea of weak, 'non-interventionist' states was for others, not for the great and benevolent 'hegemon' (Kindleberger 1981; Keohane 1984).

Yet free market ideas also sometimes suited the interests of rising powers, not least the People's Republic of China (PRC) which, to Washington's chagrin, has become the world's new powerhouse of industry and trade. The PRC uses its economic weight to its own advantage but in most cases, and unlike Washington, mostly works within international norms. It does not wage multiple wars of conquest and does not possess hundreds of military bases in dozens of countries across the world, as does the U.S. (Slater 2018). But how well recognised is the principle of multipolarity amongst the forces of this emerging world?

The notion of multipolarity was popularised in Russia in the late 20th century, as that nation recovered from the collapse of its predecessor, the Soviet Union, and from a subsequent devastating economic depression. According to Kratochvil, "in the second half of the 1990s, multipolarity became a mantra of Russian diplomats," who emphasised its importance in building domestic consensus within Russia and offering a rationale to oppose U.S. hegemony. Prime Minister Yevgeny

Primakov was a key advocate of the term, which was said to create a "tool" to advance relations with other power blocs (Kratochvil 2002).

The term was picked up in the early 21st century by Venezuela's Hugo Chávez, who said "neoliberalism is the road that leads to hell," proclaiming that Venezuela would "raise the flag of sovereignty and join in the call for a multipolar world" (Comas 2002). Chávez followed this up by moving beyond his Latin Americanism to build relations with Russia, Iran, and the Arab world.

Even Western financial groups like Morgan Stanley acknowledge the emerging multipolarity, saying that while "the U.S. and China aren't decoupling [they] are disassociating in key economic areas." The group says that U.S.-China tensions are likely to persist and that other economic powers would seek a 'balancing act.' Multilateralism (in the form of U.S.-led globalism, as at the WTO) was "in retreat," alternate models were on offer, and health security concerns—given the great failure of Washington to manage its own COVID-19 crisis (Reich 2020)—would encourage moves away from U.S.-centrism (Morgan Stanley 2020).

Yet among regional movements opposed to Washington's hegemonic ambitions, resistance ideologies have been defined mostly in regional and cultural terms.

In the Middle East, Pan Arabism was put into practice by Michel Aflaq, Gamal Abdel Nasser, Hafez al Assad and others. According to Nasser it was Arab solidarity "which constituted the firm basis upon which Arab nationalism could be built." Arab solidarity would make "the Arab states stronger through their cooperation in the economic, military and cultural fields, and in the sphere of foreign policy" (Dawisha 2002: Ch 1). Aflaq spelt out the Ba'athist Arab creed as a mission to resurrect the Arab people in a cultural 'Renaissance,' to revive the humanity and creativity which has been suppressed through political divisions. He called for unity, bringing "artificial and counterfeit countries and statelets" into a single Arab nation which would allow recovery of their "upstanding spirit, clear ideas and upright morality" (Dawisha 2002: Ch 1).

Similarly, the Pan Africanism of Jomo Kenyatta, Kwame Nkrumah and others, was said to have had two initial primary goals: to unite people of African descent, reminding them of their common culture and history, and to end European colonization (Davis 2018).

In Latin America, long standing ideas of regional integration, based on common history and culture, were linked to historic independence leaders, like Simón Bolívar, José Martí and Túpac Katari. This Latin Americanism was used to create 21st century regional groups such as the ALBA (the Bolivarian Alliance for the Peoples of the Americas, formed in 2004), UNASUR (Union of South American Nations, created in 2008) and the CELAC (The Community of Latin American and Caribbean States, from 2011) (Anderson 2013).

The immediate catalyst for the ALBA—which began as an 'alternative' until it was rebadged an 'alliance'—was to build a radical bloc to derail Washington's hegemonic FTAA (Free Trade Area of the Americas) proposal (ALBAInfo 2014). Crossing several different Latin American traditions, the ALBA did not attempt to impose one model but rather spelt out common values of radical transformation—originality, popular solidarity, egalitarianism, independence—which were, for the most part, socialist (PortalALBA 2021).

The broader CELAC group recognised a common history in culture and anti-colonialism, but allowed for a wider range of political economies, stressing social inclusion, equitable growth, sustainable development and integration (CELAC 2011).

In West Asia the long-standing idea of a great Islamic Nation (Ummah Islamiya) has been promoted by Iran and some of its allies but was undermined by the sectarian Islamist collaborators with the NATO powers, such as Saudi Arabia's Wahhabis and the Muslim Brotherhood (Anderson 2014). Allies like Syria, Palestine, Cuba and Venezuela are more committed to pluralist resistance.

Nevertheless many of the goals of "an Islamic society" have been defined by Iran's leader, Ayatollah Ali Khamenei, in fairly secular terms, as "a society in which there is justice ... freedom ... in which the people play a role in running their country ... [with] national dignity and wealth ... [without] poverty and hunger ... with comprehensive advances in scientific, economic and political areas ... a society that makes constant progress" (Khamenei 2018). When expressed in such a way, these are values which can be recognised by non-Muslims.

The notion of an 'Asian Century,' a regional concept and a counterpoint to the notion of an 'American Century,' signifies a shift in the weight of productive and technological forces (Neville 2021). It has not yet suggested the rise of a Chinese or Asian equivalent to the imperial regime in Washington.

So there is a paradox with these regional, cultural and religious emancipatory groupings: they can be tremendously powerful as sources of inspiration and cohesion, but do not translate well across communities and regions. None of them, in isolation, can create a common international ideology or mythology with which to confront the hegemonic neoliberal project.

This is the case even at some local levels. For example, while Hezbollah is by far the most cohesive and capable party in Lebanon, because it is defined in minority religious terms it can never become the ruling party of that culturally diverse small nation.

All this means, I suggest, that we should differentiate between the inspiration and adaptations of counter-hegemonic groups; and that the language of broader multipolar cooperation must be more broadly humanistic, rather than culturally specific.

That would mean a relatively flexible definition of common values, both for and against, something along these lines:

- Not neoliberal globalism but for the defence of sovereignty and culture;
- Not privileged corporate liberalism but for mutuality and social cooperation;
- Not individualistic privilege but for social participation, social benefits, and social progress.

Can effective cooperation be built on multipolar values?

Can effective cooperation be built in a multipolar network, escaping the domination of a single strong state and beyond culturally specific ideologies? We already see a number of 21st century initiatives, but to what extent can they thrive and cohere?

There is no doubt that counter-hegemonic groupings are still a long way from mobilising the capabilities of the Washington-led bloc, which enjoys near monopoly control over international finance and maintains well networked media monopolies. All this is despite the substantial diversification in global production, technological development, and trade.

Yet we have seen some important initiatives, especially since the turn of the century. Dissatisfaction with U.S.-dominated multilateral institutions—NATO, the World Bank-IMF, the G7, the OECD and the WTO—grew in the late 20th century to the point where those institutions began to decline in importance. And as World Trade Organization talks ground to a halt, in the early 2000s, new Washington-led regional blocs have been confronted by a counterweight in overlapping coalitions of emerging powers and their partners.

China's longstanding dissatisfaction with the World Bank-IMF group (Huang 2015) helped it initiate the Shanghai Cooperation Organization (SCO) and the BRICS bloc. Created in 2001, the SCO is a huge contiguous bloc representing half of the world's population, a quarter of world GDP, and more than three-quarters of Eurasia's landmass (SCO 2015). The states of the cross-continental BRICS group, formed in 2006, represent over 40% of the world's population and a quarter of global GDP (BRICS India 2021).

The SCO has the broad goals of 'strengthening mutual trust and neighbourliness' and building "a democratic, fair and rational new international political and economic order" (SCO 2015). The BRICS has developed political and economic objectives in areas such as industry, poverty reduction and public health—objectives quite distinct from those of the neoliberal order (BRICS Information Portal 2021).

In Latin America the ALBA bloc of ten nations (Telesur 2021) boasts of its substantial social achievements, especially in heath, literacy and regional solidarity (Minrex 2019) across its 17 year history. The wider 33 member CELAC, with its greater economic weight, almost immediately formed partnerships with China and the European Union, with action plans for trade and a wide range of more specific areas of cooperation (EU-CELAC 2015; COPOLAD 2021), including the EU-CELAC Platform for cooperation in research and innovation (EU-CELAC 2021).

More recently China has begun strategic cooperation programs with Iran (Xinhua 2021) and Venezuela (Today 2021). Russia is following suit, with infrastructure and defence initiatives in Syria, Iran and Venezuela. Cuban pharmaceuticals are being sold to Vietnam and mass produced in Iran (Frank 2021). These are quite novel moves which will certainly undermine the economic siege imposed on an array of independent West Asian and Latin American nations (Escalonilla 2021). The China-Iran deal is widely recognised as a potential game changer for the region (Saikal 2021).

In the financial sphere the Belgium-based but Washington-controlled SWIFT system, has maintained the U.S. dollar (despite recent 'diversification') as the central exchange currency (Reuters 2020), a key element in Washington's global influence. The role of the dollar has been weakened recently by large bilateral swaps, but the European INSTEX mechanism, designed to avoid U.S. unilateral coercive measures ('sanctions') on targeted states like Cuba and Iran, has not yet had much impact (*Tehran Times* 2021). China's Central Bank controlled digital Yuan might have greater capacity to provide a real alternative to the SWIFT system and the dollar (Deutsche Bank 2021).

So while diversification in the centres of production, technology and trade are underway, substantial initiatives in strategic cooperation, finance and media are needed to provide substance to practical multipolarity. Escaping the SWIFT system monopoly has become an economic necessity, in view of Washington's increased use of unilateral coercive measures against dozens of independent countries; and better organised independent media networks are needed to confront the propaganda offensives of an empire in decline.

Is the need for multipolarity in a post-Washington world well recognised, and can effective cooperation be built on shared multipolar values? Washington's strategic and relative decline is evident, and seems to be accelerated by its anxious over-extension, which led it to pursue a series of failing wars in West Asia, to punish its allies for opening relations with independent states, and to make a series of unprovoked threats against China.

The natural entropy of this process, well underway, suggests ongoing diminution of Washington's power and the rise of distinct regional blocs, if only for reasons of self-preservation. Important counter hegemonic groupings have been formed in Asia and in Latin America. Counterweights in production and trade are already widespread. However, the coherence and definitive independence of these independent groupings still requires greater clarity in shared aims, strategic cooperation, new financial architecture, and strong media networks.

References

ALBAInfo (2014). "What is the ALBA?" https://albainfo.org/what-is-the-alba/

Anderson, Tim (2013). "Chávez and Regional Integration." In Luis Fernando Angosto-Ferrandez (Editor). *Democracy, Revolution and Geopolitics in Latin America.* New York: Routledge, 2013. Available at: https://counter-hegemonic-studies.site/wp-content/uploads/2020/12/5-anderson-chavez-2013.pdf

——— (2014). "Wahhabis, the Brotherhood and the Empire: Syria and the Limits of Political Islam." Excerpts available at In Gaza: https://ingaza.wordpress.com/2014/08/29/excerpts-from-a-detailed-2-part-article-wahhabis-the-brotherhood-and-the-empire-syria-and-the-limits-of-political-islam/

Bello, Walden. "China: An Imperial Power in the Image of the West?" Focus Web. October 2, 2019. https://focusweb.org/publications/china-an-imperial-power-in-the-image-of-the-west/

BRICS Information Portal (2021). "13th BRICS Summit Pledges to Build on Multilateralism and Reform UN Security Council." https://infobrics.org/

BRICS India (2021). "Evolution of BRICS." https://brics2021.gov.in/about-brics

CELAC (2011). "Caracas Declaration." Summit of the Community of Latin American and Caribbean States (CELAC). http://www.pnuma.org/forodeministros/19-reunion%20intersesional/documentos/CARACAS%20DECLARATION.pdf

CFR (2021). "China's Approach to Global Governance." https://www.cfr.org/china-global-governance/

Comas, José (2002) "Hugo Chávez: 'El neoliberalismo es el camino que conduce al infierno.'" *El Pais.* May 17, 2002. https://elpais.com/diario/2002/05/17/internacional/1021586404_850215.html

COPOLAD (2021). "Thematic Areas." http://copolad.eu/en/areastematicas

Dawisha, Adeed. "Defining Arab Nationalism." In *Arab Nationalism in the Twentieth Century: From Triumph to Despair.* Princeton, NJ: Princeton University Press, 2002. http://assets.press.princeton.edu/chapters/s7549.pdf

Davis, Ben. "What was the first goal of the Pan-African Movement?" MVOrganizing. November 11, 2018. https://www.mvorganizing.org/what-was-the-first-goal-of-the-pan-african-movement/

Deutsche Bank. "Digital Yuan: What is it and how does it work?" July 14, 2021. https://www.db.com/news/detail/20210714-digital-yuan-what-is-it-and-how-does-it-work

Engdahl, F. William. *Full Spectrum Dominance: Totalitarian Democracy in the New World Order.* Boxborough, MA: Third Millennium Press, 2009.

Escalonilla, Alvaro. "Syria and Iran strengthen economic cooperation to counter 'oppressive sanctions imposed by enemies.'" Atalayar. August 30, 2021. https://atalayar.com/en/content/syria-and-iran-strengthen-economic-cooperation-counter-oppressive-sanctions-imposed-enemies

EU-CELAC (2015). *EU-CELAC Action Plan.* Summit 2015 Brussels. http://alcuenet.eu/assets/25.%20Action%20Plan%20Brussels%20EU-CELAC%202015.pdf

——— (2021). "About Us." https://www.eucelac-platform.eu/

Falk, Richard, and Virginia Tilley. "Israeli Practices towards the Palestinian People and the Question of Apartheid." *Middle East Policy* XXIV, no. 2 (Summer 2017). https://mepc.org/journal/israeli-practices-towards-palestinian-people-and-question-apartheid

Frank, Marc. "Cuba kicks off COVID-19 vaccine exports with shipment to Vietnam." Reuters. September 25, 2021. https://www.reuters.com/business/healthcare-pharmaceuticals/cuba-kicks-off-covid-19-vaccine-exports-with-shipment-vietnam-2021-09-25/

Graebner, Norman A. "Multipolarity In World Politics: the Challenge." *VQR.* Summer 1988. https://www.vqronline.org/essay/multipolarity-world-politics-challenge

Grunberg, Isabelle. "Exploring the 'myth' of hegemonic stability." *International Organization* 44, no. 4 (Autumn 1990): 431–477. https://doi.org/10.1017/S0020818300035372

Huang, Cary. "China frustrated by delayed reforms to increase its say at IMF." SCMP. April 20, 2015. https://www.scmp.com/news/china/economy/article/1771630/china-frustrated-delayed-reforms-increase-its-say-imf

Keohane, Robert, O. *After Hegemony: Cooperation and Discord in the World Political Economy.* Princeton, NJ: Princeton University Press, 1984.

Khamenei, Ali. "What does 'Islamic society' mean? Imam Khamenei explains." *Khamenei.IR*. February 21, 2018. https://english.khamenei.ir/news/5484/What-does-Islamic-society-mean-Imam-Khamenei-explains

Kindleberger, Charles, P. "Dominance and Leadership in the International Economy: Exploitation, Public Goods, and Free Rides." *International Studies Quarterly* 25 (June 1981).

Kratochvil, Petr. *Multipolarity, American theory and Russian practice.* Moscow: CEEISA, 2002. https://www.files.ethz.ch/isn/31431/2002-00-Multipolarity.pdf

Marti, José (1891). *Our America.* Available at: https://writing.upenn.edu/library/Marti_Jose_Our-America.html

Minrex. "Declaration of the XVII Summit of Heads of State and Government of ALBA-TCP: 15 years in defense of unity, peace and integration." December 15, 2019. http://misiones.minrex.gob.cu/en/articulo/declaration-xvii-summit-heads-state-and-government-alba-tcp-15-years-defense-unity-peace-0

Morgan Stanley. "Five reasons for the trend towards Multipolarity." July 17, 2020. https://www.morganstanley.com.au/ideas/five-reasons-for-the-trend-towards-multipolarity

Neville, Laurence. "The Asian Century." *GFMag.* March 5, 2021. https://www.gfmag.com/magazine/march-2021/asian-century

OHCHR (2021). "International Covenant on Civil and Political Rights." https://www.ohchr.org/EN/ProfessionalInterest/Pages/CCPR.aspx

PortalALBA (2021). "¿Qué es el Alba?" https://portalalba.org/que-es-el-alba/

Reich, Robert. "America has no real public health system – coronavirus has a clear run." *The Guardian.* March 15, 2020. https://www.theguardian.com/commentisfree/2020/mar/15/america-public-health-system-coronavirus-trump

Reuters. "Chinese banks urged to switch away from SWIFT as U.S. sanctions loom." July 29, 2020. https://www.reuters.com/article/us-china-banks-usa-sanctions-idUSKCN24U0SN

Saikal, Amin. "Iran–China strategic agreement could be a game-changer." The Strategist. March 29, 2021. https://www.aspistrategist.org.au/iran-china-strategic-agreement-could-be-a-game-changer/

Schmidt, Helmut (1998). "The Grand Chessboard: American Primacy and Its Geostrategic Imperatives." Review of Zbigniew Brzezinski, *The Grand Chessboard* (1997). https://ciaotest.cc.columbia.edu/olj/fp/schmidt.html

Schwenninger, Sherle. "The Multipolar World Vs. The Superpower." The Globalist. December 5, 2003. https://www.theglobalist.com/the-multipolar-world-vs-the-superpower/

SCO (2015). "The Shanghai Cooperation Organisation." http://eng.sectsco.org/about_sco/

Slater, Alice. "The US Has Military Bases in 80 Countries. All of Them Must Close." *The Nation.* January 24, 2018. https://www.thenation.com/article/archive/the-us-has-military-bases-in-172-countries-all-of-them-must-close/

Tehran Times. "Iran blames EU on INSTEX ineffectiveness." January 18, 2021. https://www.tehrantimes.com/news/457059/Iran-blames-EU-on-INSTEX-ineffectiveness

Telesur. "ALBA-TCP Holds XIX Summit of Heads of State in Venezuela." June 24, 2021. https://www.telesurenglish.net/news/ALBA-TCP-Holds-XIX-Summit-of-Heads-of-State-in-Venezuela-20210624-0024.html

Today. "Venezuela and China agree to deepen their comprehensive strategic partnership." *Today.* September 27, 2021. https://today.in-24.com/News/389978.html

U.S. Department of Defense (2000). *Joint Vision 2020.* Available at Matt Cegelske, "Joint Vision 2020: America's Military—Preparing for Tomorrow [Strategy]." A Cyber Fellow. May 21, 2012. https://mattcegelske.com/joint-vision-2020-americas-military-preparing-for-tomorrow-strategy/

Xinhua (2020). "Xi's UN speech shows 'clearly focused vision,' says renowned expert." September 23, 2020. http://www.xinhuanet.com/english/2020-09/23/c_139390200.htm

——— (2021). "China, Iran sign agreement to map out comprehensive cooperation." March 28, 2021. http://www.xinhuanet.com/english/2021-03/28/c_139841044.htm

17. Why West Asia after Washington?

The peoples of West Asia have suffered intervention, re-colonisation, division, and destabilisation over the past century, with a new wave of invasions, proxy wars and economic siege taking place this century. That is a great contrast with what the late Anis Naqqash called a relative 'state of imperial unity' in the Levant during the centuries of Ottoman rule. The 'Sykes-Picot-Balfour triangle' changed all that (Naqqash 2021), with the British and French application of divide and rule. Subsequently, Washington's 21st century New Middle East wars sought to deepen those divisions.

Now that the U.S. plan is failing, we can observe two dialectical processes. First, there are those peoples who organised to resist the incursions (as in Iran, Syria, the revolutionary government in Yemen and well organised resistance groups in Lebanon and Iraq) which have faced massive attacks yet also developed tremendous political will and cohesion—the sort of will that is necessary for the construction of independent social structures and states. Second, there is Washington's reckless prosecution of a despised hegemonic agenda which has helped accelerate the formation of countervailing networks, particularly in Latin America and in East and West Asia. Its repeated provocations of Iran, Russia and China have helped drive the creation of new trade, investment, media and, more recently, financial networks.

Human beings are social creatures who enjoy the benefits of cooperation based on responsible local social structures. Extreme individualism cannot help a species which spends many years turning children into adults. We respond to external (and necessarily irresponsible and unaccountable) attacks by mobilising and rebuilding. Such functionality exists in all societies, before it is overlaid by dysfunction. When societies are under external attack, functional social development cannot proceed until the threats are removed. But after that, responsible development can draw on the cohesive matrix of local culture and values.

West Asia has lacked that necessary space for rebuilding over the past century. Imposed divisions, wars and interventions have blocked the construction of shared networks that privileged peoples take for granted. Ethnic, cultural, and religious barriers have been hammered into the region by the NATO states which, for their part, cement and draw on their combined strength through federations, customs unions and warlike 'coalitions of the willing.'

Indigenous development—rather than externally imposed structures—presupposes a period of consolidation after the defeat and repulsion of invasions and interventions. The networks and structures built to defeat the enemies may well form the basis for civil construction. In any case, new alliances and unions are necessary to protect against new attacks and to defend social and political gains. That is a lesson often repeated in colonial and post-colonial Latin American history from Bolívar to Martí to Chavez. In the late 19th century Jose Martí stressed the need to protect the new republics of the Americas from European or North American predation. "The trees must form ranks to block the seven-league giant!" Martí (1891: 119) declared in his famous essay, "Our America." A century later, before being elected president of Venezuela, Hugo Chavez told an audience at Havana University, "It is not adventurism to think of a political project, an association of Latin American states. Why don't we think of that? Why continue fragmented?" (Anderson 2018: 14 min). For the rest of his life Chavez remained focussed on that project, playing a major role in the creation of regional groups the ALBA, UNASUR and the CELAC (Anderson 2013).

That lesson of union in the face of great power has not been lost on the peoples of West Asia, but there is much ground to be regained. Resilient social structures at all levels are needed to consolidate the defeat of the New Middle East scheme with its sectarian, divisive aims. But how and on which values can such a union be built? There will not be agreement on this across the region and it is likely that the inspiration for mobilisation and union will differ. Naqqash (2021) says no single nation, no matter how powerful, can unite the region. Neither Arab nationalism nor ideas of a greater Islamic community have so far succeeded in uniting and socialising the region and liberating Palestine. In those circumstances he called for a Levantine Confederation without the hegemony of any one sect, The must mean identifying common human values inspired by but not tied to distinct cultures.

In many respects that is happening, informally. While the Islamic Republic of Iran maintains its focus on Islamic civilisation, it is plain that its cooperation with key allies (like China, Russia and Venezuela) relies on shared values across distinct cultures. On the other hand, most of the Persian Gulf monarchies, nominally Islamic, have at one time or another allied themselves with Washington, directly opposed Iran, and even sponsored the slaughter of Shia Muslims by sectarian armed groups. Even within the Levant it has been obvious for decades that the strongest of alliances persist between Shia Islamic Iran, secular or pluralist Syria and Lebanon and the nationalist, socialist and Sunni Palestinian resistance groups. What this alliance might be based on and called is precisely a matter for the peoples of West Asia.

As Washington drags much of the world into its vortex of paranoid war, it is important to remember that resistance, alliance and cooperation open up new possibilities. The progressive defeat of wars of hegemonic decline and the retreat of this monster allow us to anticipate and plan for the dismantling of the Israeli colony, the construction of an Iranian land bridge and consideration of new possibilities in a Levantine Confederation and a multipolar world. New inclusive and resilient social and regional structures are absolutely necessary to capitalise on such opportunities. Not least of these is a regional bloc which will provide a platform to negotiate the terms of engagement with the emerging multipolarity.

References

Anderson, Tim (2013). "Chavez and American Integration." In Luis Fernando Angosto-Ferrandez (Editor). *Democracy, Revolution and Geopolitics in Latin America.* New York: Routledge, 2013. https://www.taylorfrancis.com/chapters/edit/10.4324/9781315890111-2/chávez-american-integration-tim-anderson

——— (2018). "ALBA Part One Cuba and Venezuela, when Chavez met Fidel" October 24, 2018. Video, 19:08. https://www.youtube.com/watch?v=p7_kj9v73C8

Martí, Jose (1891). "Our America." In *Jose Marti Reader: Writings on the Americas.* Melbourne: Ocean Press, 1999.

Naqqash, Anis. "Anis Naqqash: proposal for a Levantine Confederation" [translation of speech]. Centre for Counter Hegemonic Studies. March 8, 2021. https://counter-hegemonic-studies.site/naqqash-1/

Index

C

D

T

Y

Z